THAT FIELD OF GLORY

THE STORY OF CLONTARF
FROM BATTLEGROUND TO GARDEN SUBURB

That field of glory

The story of Clontarf
from battleground to garden suburb

Colm Lennon

Wordwell

First published 2014
Wordwell Ltd
Unit 9
78 Furze Road
Sandyford Industrial Estate
Dublin 18

ISBN: 978 1 905569 81 6

British Library Cataloguing-in-Publication Data.
A catalogue record for this book is available from the British Library.

Typeset by Alicia McAuley Publishing Services, Belfast.
Copy-editor: Emer Condit.
Book design: Alicia McAuley.
Cover design: Nick Maxwell.

Cover image: James Ward, 'Brian Boru and the battle of Clontarf': mural at City
Hall, Dublin, 1919 (© Dublin City Council, courtesy of Dublin City Library and
Archive).

Printed by Graficas Castuera, Pamplona.

For my family, nuclear and extended,
denizens of old Clontarf.

Contents

List of illustrations

Preface

CLONTARF HAS BEEN famous since the eleventh century because of the battle fought there or thereabouts in 1014. This celebrity status has tended to overshadow its existence as one of Dublin's villages and later townships. The two aspects of historic site and living district have come together since the Victorian period, when, under the influence of rapid suburban and seaside development, new and older residents forged a local identity to which the ancient heritage was integral. But in all phases of its growth since the Middle Ages, Clontarf has been more than a stage for great events in national political struggles: it has also mirrored in its own topography, society and economy the changes that were occurring in the wider world.

The purpose of the book is to tell the story of Clontarf, beginning with the events of 1014 and the subsequent passage into legend of the Irish king Brian Boru, who died at the battle. The succeeding ages have seen the growth of Clontarf as a manor and fishing port under the ownership of a number of proprietors, ranging from crusading knights to gentry landlords. In order to understand the character of the district in the present day, with its distinctive atmosphere and architecture, for example, it is necessary to trace its evolution through these various stages from medieval manor through early modern estate to modern suburb, these latter two phases being largely under the auspices of the Vernon family, whose tenure as lords of Clontarf lasted 300 years.

This book is the product of many years of research into the locality in which I have lived for most of my life. It began while I was teaching in Kostka College, a small secondary on the site of Merchamps on Seafield Road. I am grateful to the pupils there who enthusiastically walked the historical trails and completed projects on the locality. During my career at the university at Maynooth I continued to collect information drawn from a wide variety of sources upon which I worked for other purposes. It is only in recent years that I have homed in on the records as part of a dedicated history of Clontarf, set in its national context. I hope that the result will be of interest not just to people who are curious about the local history of Clontarf but also to those who seek a local perspective on national developments.

During the long gestation of this project I have received great help and encouragement from many people. The foundation of the Clontarf Historical Society by Dennis McIntyre and other local historians gave a major fillip to local historical studies. I am fortunate to have had a number of opportunities to present papers on my work in progress to knowledgeable residents at meetings of the Society, and to have heard in turn most informative talks from other local researchers and visiting lecturers. Among those who have been very helpful to me are Douglas Appleyard, Claire Gogarty, Joan Ussher Sharkey and Bernardine Ruddy, as well as Kay and Joe Lonergan, Collette Gill and David Evans.

Living among Clontarf people has been a source of inspiration over the years, and many of them have kept up an interest in my work on the area. In particular, I would like to thank the Clancy family, Kevin and Fiona Williams and family, Gerry McNamara, Fergal Tobin, Ian Murphy and his extended family, James O'Dea, John Blennerhassett and Helen Forrest. My late parents, Marie and Kevin Lennon, inculcated a love of the area in my siblings and myself, and I should like to pay tribute to them, and to thank Cathy, Paddy and Peter and their families for the love and support first fostered in No. 2 Clontarf Road.

My colleagues in NUI Maynooth have offered collegial and congenial conditions for all my researches over the years, and I am especially grateful to Professor Raymond Gillespie, Professor Jackie Hill and Dr Jacinta Prunty for their pioneering work in the field of Dublin studies, within which, I hope, this book fits, and for their friendly advice to me at all times. Many talented researchers and scholars have passed through the local studies programmes at NUI Maynooth, and I am very grateful to all of them, particularly Maighréad Ní Mhurchadha for her sharing of her insights into Clontarf and Fingal, and also to Séamus Ó Maitiú and Joseph Byrne. Máire Ní Chearbhaill very generously read the text and commented insightfully on it. Robin Kavanagh offered valuable advice on illustrative material.

For assistance in acquiring images and reproduction rights, I wish to acknowledge the kindness of Mary Clarke, Dublin City Archivist, Glenn Dunne and Berni Metcalfe of the National Library of Ireland, Dr Paul Ferguson of the Glucksman Map Library, Trinity College, Dublin, Sarah Gearty of the Irish Historic Towns Atlas in the Royal Irish Academy, Peter Holder of Irish Historical Images, Adelle Hughes of Whyte's, the Isaacs Art Centre, Hawaii, Louise Morgan of the National Gallery of Ireland, Jasmine Rogers of the Science and Society Picture

Library, Petra Schnabel and Amy Hughes of the Library, Royal Irish Academy, Andrew Smith of St Patrick's Cathedral, Dublin, the Library of the National University of Ireland, Maynooth, the British Library Board and the National Maritime Museum, Greenwich. I am very appreciative of Nick Maxwell's interest in publishing the book under the distinguished Wordwell imprint.

Above all, for my family, who have lived with the 'Clontarf book' for so long, I am pleased to bring the work to fruition. Margaret has been abidingly supportive and a font of wise counsel, while Róisín (who kindly helped with the documents), Deirdre and Caoimhe have dutifully sat through many talks and impromptu lectures, raising apposite questions about their neighbourhood and its past. I hope that they, and the next generation, now represented by Cian Sherlock, will be as proud of the locality of Clontarf as I have been.

Introduction

Clontarf: a famous name

H UNDREDS OF TROOPS and police swarmed over the shoreline at Clontarf on
Sunday 8 October 1843. From early morning their movements had created a
stir among the inhabitants of the north side of Dublin. A foot regiment was drawn
up on the North Strand, while fusiliers, dragoons and other infantry wandered
about the coastal spit opposite the Sheds at Vernon Avenue. Out to sea, the
warships *Rhadamanthus* and *Dee* rode at anchor, and the guns mounted on the
Pigeonhouse were trained on the northern shore of Dublin Bay. Nothing more
threatening than cockle-gathering soldiers at the beach presented themselves
to the gunners, while the military pickets resorted frequently to Mooney's tavern
at the strand below the Sheds. The bored policemen lined up along the road
between the hinterland of the Green Lanes and the shore were fortified with
pints of porter and biscuits provided by residents. Visiting dignitaries such as
the commander-in-chief, Sir Edward Blakeney, and the splendidly attired earl
of Cardigan surveyed the scene with satisfaction. For them, a non-event was a
success. Those on duty that day were conscious of the ludicrousness of such a
massive security operation at a quiet seaside place on an autumn Sunday just
outside Dublin, but good humour characterised the demeanour of all. Hundreds
of trippers were attracted by the prospect of seeing the military array, and the
hostelries between the city and Clontarf did a roaring trade. By 5.30pm the
operation had been called off and all of the troops marched away, leaving the
village to its bewildered denizens.[1] [0.1]

It should all have been so different. Five hundred thousand people from all
over Ireland and from Britain had been expected to congregate at the hillock
called 'Conquer Hill' to the east of the Sheds at Clontarf that Sunday, where there
was to take place the most imposing assembly yet in support of Daniel O'Connell's

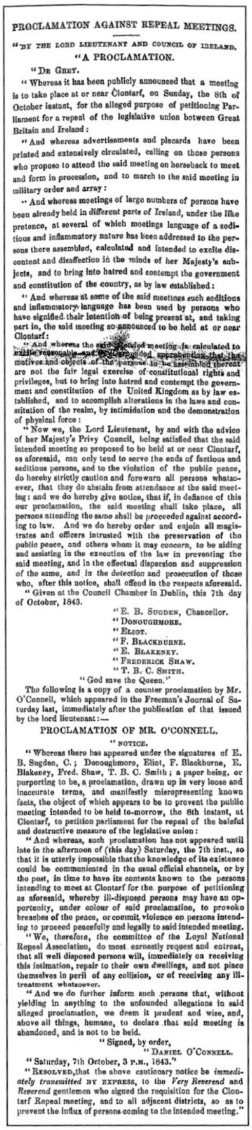

PROCLAMATION AGAINST REPEAL MEETINGS.

"BY THE LORD LIEUTENANT AND COUNCIL OF IRELAND.

"A PROCLAMATION.

"DE GREY.

" Whereas it has been publicly announced that a meeting is to take place at or near Clontarf, on Sunday, the 8th of October instant, for the alleged purpose of petitioning Parliament for a repeal of the legislative union between Great Britain and Ireland :

" And whereas advertisements and placards have been printed and extensively circulated, calling on those persons who propose to attend the said meeting on horseback to meet and form in procession, and to march to the said meeting in military order and array :

" And whereas meetings of large numbers of persons have been already held in different parts of Ireland, under the like pretence, at several of which meetings language of a seditious and inflammatory nature has been addressed to the persons there assembled, calculated and intended to excite discontent and disaffection in the minds of her Majesty's subjects, and to bring into hatred and contempt the government and constitution of the country, as by law established :

" And whereas at some of the said meetings such seditious and inflammatory language has been used by persons who have signified their intention of being present at, and taking part in, the said meeting so announced to be held at or near Clontarf :

" And whereas the said intended meeting is calculated to excite reasonable and well-grounded apprehension that the the motives and objects of the persons to be assembled thereat are not the fair legal exercise of constitutional rights and privileges, but to bring into hatred and contempt the government and constitution of the United Kingdom as by law established, and to accomplish alterations in the laws and constitution of the realm, by intimidation and the demonstration of physical force :

" Now we, the Lord Lieutenant, by and with the advice of her Majesty's Privy Council, being satisfied that the said intended meeting so proposed to be held at or near Clontarf, as aforesaid, can only tend to serve the ends of factious and seditious persons, and to the violation of the public peace, do hereby strictly caution and forewarn all persons whatsoever, that they do abstain from attendance at the said meeting : and we do hereby give notice, that if, in defiance of this our proclamation, the said meeting shall take place, all persons attending the same shall be proceeded against according to law. And we do hereby order and enjoin all magistrates and officers intrusted with the preservation of the public peace, and others whom it may concern, to be aiding and assisting in the execution of the law in preventing the said meeting, and in the effectual dispersion and suppression of the same, and in the detection and prosecution of those who, after this notice, shall offend in the respects aforesaid.

" Given at the Council Chamber in Dublin, this 7th day of October, 1843.

"E. B. SUGDEN, Chancellor.
" DONOUGHMORE.
" ELIOT.
" F. BLACKBURNE.
" E. BLAKENEY.
" FREDERICK SHAW.
" T. B. C. SMITH.

" God save the Queen."

The following is a copy of a counter proclamation by Mr. O'Connell, which appeared in the Freeman's Journal of Saturday last, immediately after the publication of that issued by the lord lieutenant :—

PROCLAMATION OF MR. O'CONNELL.

" NOTICE.

" Whereas there has appeared under the signatures of E. B. Sugden, C. ; Donoughmore, Eliot, F. Blackburne, E. Blakeney, Fred. Shaw, T. B. C. Smith ; a paper being, or purporting to be, a proclamation, drawn up in very loose and inaccurate terms, and manifestly misrepresenting known facts, the object of which appears to be to prevent the public meeting intended to be held to-morrow, the 8th instant, at Clontarf, to petition parliament for the repeal of the baleful and destructive measure of the legislative union :

" And whereas, such proclamation has not appeared until late in the afternoon of (this day) Saturday, the 7th inst., so that it is utterly impossible that the knowledge of its existence could be communicated in the usual official channels, or by the post, in time to have its contents known to the persons intending to meet at Clontarf for the purpose of petitioning as aforesaid, whereby ill-disposed persons may have an opportunity, under colour of said proclamation, to provoke breaches of the peace, or commit violence on persons intending to proceed peacefully and legally to said intended meeting.

" We, therefore, the committee of the Loyal National Repeal Association, do most earnestly request and entreat, that all well disposed persons will, immediately on receiving this intimation, repair to their own dwellings, and not place themselves in peril of any collision, or of receiving any ill-treatment whatsoever.

" And we do further inform such persons that, without yielding in anything to the unfounded allegations in said alleged proclamation, we deem it prudent and wise, and, above all things, humane, not to declare that said meeting is abandoned, and is not to be held.

" Signed, by order,

" DANIEL O'CONNELL.

" Saturday, 7th October, 3 P.M., 1843."

" RESOLVED, that the above cautionary notice be immediately transmitted BY EXPRESS, to the Very Reverend and Reverend gentlemen who signed the requisition for the Clontarf Repeal meeting, and to all adjacent districts, so as to prevent the influx of persons coming to the intended meeting."

Fig. 0.1—The government proclamation of Saturday 7 October 1843, banning the proposed Repeal meeting, as well as Daniel O'Connell's acquiescence.

campaign for repeal of the Union. The culmination of a series of carefully stage-managed events, as much carnival as political rally, the meeting was to have had as its central moment the public appearance by O'Connell, popularly called 'the Liberator', accompanied by dramatic effects, including music and *tableaux vivants*. The committee of the Clontarf demonstration had planned the occasion meticulously, though in a late change to the programme the previous Friday the time of the assembly had been switched out of deference to the sensibilities of the Church of Ireland community. Originally a huge cavalcade of mounted repealers was to have converged on Clontarf from their assembly points west, south and north of the city. The horsemen from the west and south were to have ridden from their meeting-place at Harcourt Street fields through Grafton Street to the Crescent at Marino. There they were to join with contingents from the northern parts and proceed to the rally at 2pm. The changed arrangement was for the procession to begin at Marino Crescent so as not to interfere with Protestant worship.

What had prevented the great meeting from taking place? The government had decided to ban the assembly on Saturday 7 October, even as the demonstrators from remoter parts of Ireland were already making their way to Clontarf. A proclamation was issued from Dublin Castle formally prohibiting the Clontarf meeting. The reason was the potential of the speeches to 'excite disaffection' and to arouse 'hatred and contempt for the government and constitution of the United Kingdom'. Previous meetings had become 'seditious and inflammatory' through the use of 'intimidation and the demonstration of physical force'. All

---

Advertisement the day after the Clontarf meeting was due to take place, 1843

The Privy Council
The Proclamation

Whereas, in consequence of the Clontarf Meeting having been prohibited, the Five Hundred Thousand PENNY BUNS – that were prepared at the celebrated FANCY BAKERY AND CONFECTIONARY ESTABLISHMENT, PARLIAMENT HOUSE, PARLIAMENT STREET, to feed the multitude on that ever-memorable occasion – will be Sold off this day, without the least reserve, at Half Price – being One Halfpenny each, Government having promised to make up the difference in consideration of the short notice interdicting the meeting.

N.B. – Should there be any Teetotal Tea Parties this evening, to discuss the policy of the Proclamation, those buns are of the nature of the good old Irish Barnbrack, and consequently the very thing for Tea and Coffee.

Freeman's Journal, 9 October 1843

Fig. 0.2—'A standing army stranded at Clontarf': a satirical view of the abortive Repeal meeting at Clontarf in 1843 (courtesy of the National Library of Ireland).

were warned to abstain from attendance. To carry the message throughout the city and beyond, thousands of bills and placards were printed and posted at places along the approaches to Dublin. Daniel O'Connell backed down from his plan to assemble a huge throng at Clontarf for fear of the possibility of violence and bloodshed. His Repeal Association cooperated fully in the suppression of the Clontarf meeting by requesting all would-be attendees to repair to their dwellings. In spite of the lateness of the proclamation, the massive campaign for cancellation was successful, as comparatively few people turned up at Clontarf on Sunday in the expectation of hearing O'Connell speak.[2] [0.2]

Daniel O'Connell's campaign for the repeal of the Act of Union of 1800 was supposed to reach a crescendo in 1844, designated the 'year of Repeal'. Of all the strategies adopted to bring this about through popular and parliamentary agitation, the most successful appeared to be the series of 'monster' meetings held at sites of historic importance throughout the country in 1843. In readiness for these rallies in support of repeal, a campaign of historical consciousness-raising preceded the events in popular and literary journals. Previous meetings at Tara and Mullaghmast had been used to evoke remembrance of Ireland's sovereignty and subjection. The latter location had been the scene of a frightful massacre of members of the O'More clan in 1578 when the Tudor administration was attempting to conquer the country; the former was the ancient seat of political power in Ireland. Combining rhetoric and ritual, the meetings were preparing the huge audiences for the next step: the formal restoration of native rule. And now Clontarf was chosen to be the place of the climactic meeting of the series, before the final parliamentary push for repeal took place in early 1844.

Close proximity to Dublin with its radiating system of roads recommended it for this important role, as did the openness of its fields for hosting a massive gathering. Services such as transport and catering were to hand, and the dramatic sweep of the sea and mountains across the bay would provide a glorious backdrop for the speeches, culminating in O'Connell's. Most importantly, though, Clontarf picked itself as an assembly-place because of its historic significance. In the advance publicity for the meeting, the place dubbed 'the Marathon of Ireland' was carefully presented as the site for the ultimate excitation to freedom from the Union. Clontarf, or *Cluain Tarbh*, had long been an evocative place-name, owing principally to the great battle fought in its vicinity. The events of Good Friday 1014 passed into legend, ensuring the abiding fame of the battle of Clontarf and the assassinated victor, Brian Boru. In the popular mind, it now represented the liberation of Ireland from the chains of foreign enslavement. No other battlefield in Ireland could match 'Clontarf's plain' as a place of triumph for an Irish army, Brian Boru's victory over the Viking enemy being presented as having established an earlier form of national self-determination. O'Connell's campaign hoped that these resonances would echo in the nationalist cause, and the task was furthered by the Young Ireland movement and its newspaper, *The Nation*, through a series of articles and poems. [0.3]

The name 'Clontarf' was given by patriotic Irish emigrants to several of the places where they settled overseas. One of these was an Australian suburban village called Clontarf, near Sydney in New South Wales. It was here on 12 March 1868 that an assassination attempt was made on Prince Alfred, the duke of Edinburgh and son of Queen Victoria, who was making the first British royal visit to the country. The assailant was Henry James O'Farrell, a Fenian sympathiser, who carefully chose Clontarf as the place of ambush because of the historical associations of the place-name, and within days these resonances were being conveyed in the Australian and international press. The extended drama of the prince's recovery from his shooting, and the trial and execution of O'Farrell on 21 April 1868, gave rise to an intensive and agonised debate in Australia about colonial political and religious identities, one effect being the emergence of a strong Orange movement among the Irish Protestant community there. Thus, translocated because of its patriotic meaning for Irish exiles, the toponym 'Clontarf' now reverberated with added significance as an assertion of nationality within an imperial setting.[3]

Report on attempted assassination at Clontarf, New South Wales, 1868

It is with the deepest sorrow that we have to chronicle a most determined attempt to assassinate his Royal Highness the Duke of Edinburgh, at the Sailors' Home Picnic on the 12th of March. Shortly after the arrival of the Prince upon our shores, the committee of the Sailors' Home conceived the idea of having a large picnic under the patronage of his Royal Highness, with a view to raising sufficient funds to complete the institution ... The locality fixed upon for the fete was the picturesque spot known as Clontarf, on the north shore of the Middle Harbour; a spot on this occasion to be rendered ever memorable by a deed of blood that will convulse popular feeling throughout the world ... The Prince and Sir William then resumed their walk and conversation, and the latter gentleman called the attention of his Royal Highness to a large number of aboriginal blacks, who had been brought down from Sydney by direction of the committee, and landed at Cabbage Tree Bay, adjoining Clontarf ... While they were thus engaged in conversation a treacherous assailant, who had just left the crowd of persons congregated under the shade of the trees, stole up behind his Royal Highness, and when he had approached to within three or four feet pulled out a revolver, took deliberate aim, and fired. The shot took effect about the middle of the back of his Royal Highness. He fell forward on his hands and knees, exclaiming, "Good God, my back is broken." A number of people ... ran to his assistance, lifted him from the ground and proceeded to carry him towards the Royal pavilion. It was evident from the demeanour of his Royal Highness that he was suffering great pain, and he asked his bearers to carry him more gently. This wish was complied with as far as possible, and thus he was borne into his tent ... The dress of his Royal Highness was removed, and upon examination of the wound, it was found that the bullet had penetrated the back, about half an inch to the right of the vertebral column on a level with the ninth rib, and traversing the course of the ribs round by the right had lodged in the flesh, not far below the surface within two inches of the breast bone. No vital organ, fortunately, appeared to be injured, the course of the bullet being, to all appearance, quite superficial.

Sydney Morning Herald, 27 March 1868

Fig 0.3—A view of Conquer Hill at the time of the proposed Repeal meeting in 1843, with the new bridge to the Bull Wall in the background (Illustrated London News*).*

A beautiful place of settlement

'The villages of Clontarf and Dollymount are pleasant little bathing-places, much frequented in the summer months. Behind Clontarf, the country, thickly-planted, is intersected by sequestered roads, called "The Green Lanes". The appearance from the bay of the long, low, woody shore, studded by detached clusters of white cottages and handsome villas, is remarkably beautiful. The views, both coastwise and inland, as we sweep round the north side of the bay, are singularly attractive'

—W.H. Bartlett, *Scenery and antiquities of Ireland* (1841), ii, 158.

These sanguinary associations are at odds with Clontarf's status as, until comparatively recently, a small and sleepy maritime village. Habitation has been attracted to Clontarf through the ages not just because of its proximity to Dublin but also because of the natural features of the terrain and coastline. Nestling in the low-lying floodplain of the Liffey and the Tolka on the north side of Dublin Bay, between the latter river to the west and the escarpment of the Sutton/Howth peninsula to the east, Clontarf has a Carboniferous limestone base covered with a fertile soil in its inland areas.[4] Fields suitable for successful arable and pastoral farming had been reclaimed well before the late Middle Ages. At least until the late seventeenth century, part of the landscape was fairly thickly wooded with an outgrowth of the large woods at Santry and Coolock.[5] Along the coastal stretch from the Tolka to Sutton there was a tract of tidal mud-flats and slob land, much of which was not finally reclaimed until the twentieth century. The tidal channels were suitable for the fishing of salmon and other species, and the farming of shellfish, including oysters. Off the shore, the waters of the bay were affected by estuarine deposits that clogged the passages of the Liffey, preventing navigation to the city by all but small and shallow-bottomed boats. Two maritime features assisted Clontarf in exploiting the difficulties of Dublin port and in becoming a thriving fishing and trading post: the small sliver of land off the western end of the shoreline, which came to be called Clontarf Island, and a comparatively deep anchorage known as Clontarf Pool. Together, they provided protection for larger vessels calling in at Dublin from the fourteenth century. Just under 200 years ago, the building of the sea wall from the Clontarf shore promoted the birth of Bull Island, which came to play such an important part in the growth of the Clontarf–Dollymount area as a seaside resort for tourists and day-trippers.[6]

Fig. 0.4 — Watercolour of one of two Bronze Age burial mounds at Clontarf, this one located near the site of the old railway station, Howth Road (courtesy of the Royal Irish Academy).

A small number of archaeological finds point to some settlement at Clontarf in prehistoric times. The earliest evidence includes a flint flake and two axeheads of Bronze Age date.[7] At least two burial mounds, one to the west of the district near the old railway station and the other to the east at Conquer Hill, were noted as possibly substantiating Bronze Age activity.[8] [0.4] A slightly later find, known only from documentary sources, is a Roman brooch dating from the first century AD.[9] In the early medieval period Clontarf may have come under the sway of a ruler from one of the branches of the kingdom of Brega, centred on Meath, possibly the Uí Cumain. In ecclesiastical terms, the bishop of Finglas exerted authority over much of the north of the Dublin region, including Clontarf and other maritime communities, before the eleventh century.[10] A tradition persists that a monastery was founded there by St Comgall in AD 550, but no near-contemporary documentary or physical evidence of such a foundation survives. Any settlement

The beauty of Clontarf and its surroundings, 1822

Clontarf ... is distinguished by its neatness, cleanliness and regularity. The church, castle, and many of the houses, being embosomed in trees, have a pleasing and romantic appearance. [It] is intersected by roads, appropriately denominated the 'Green Lanes', on account of their verdant and umbrageous foliage, and also thickly studded with cottages and villas. The prospect is everywhere beautiful and extensive. The eye reposes with pleasure on highly cultivated fields, or roves delighted over a magnificent expanse of aquatic and mountain scenery. On one side it surveys a long sweep of level coast, the romantic little island of Ireland's Eye, and the bold promontory of Howth; and on the other, Dalkey isle, the Rochestown Hills, covered with obelisk and telegraph, and the pyramidal mountains of Wicklow. These objects form the outline of a circle, which comprehends much to gratify a taste for natural beauty. A capacious bay, girdled by a shore adorned with hamlets and groves to the water's edge; the lighthouse, rising fair and majestic from the azure surface of the deep; the pigeon-house, with its piers and fortifications, almost insulated by the tide; the vessels spreading their sails to the wind, and the city of Dublin in the distance, with its spires and domes illumined by the rising sun; all together form a picture whose richness and variety being seldom equalled, may well excuse the enthusiastic admiration which it is frequently known to elicit.

William Hamilton Drummond, *Clontarf: a poem* (Dublin, 1822), preface, pp v–vii

Fig. 0.5 — William Ashford (1746-1824), 'View of Dublin from Clontarf', Irish, eighteenth century, c. 1795-8. Oil on canvas, 114cm x 183cm. Photo © National Gallery of Ireland NGI 4137 (courtesy of the National Gallery of Ireland).

in the district would have been on the road from Dublin to Howth and thus vulnerable to early Viking raids on the east coast, which included an assault on the peninsula and the carrying off of 'a great prey of women' in 819. The only definite evidence of settlement in the hinterland before the battle is the presence of a weir near the estuary of the Tolka, mentioned in a chronicle account of 1014.[11]

Visitors to Clontarf since early modern times have rhapsodised about the beauty of the location in their writings. A combination of the natural verdure of the immediate environment, perspectives of the nearby city and views of the more distant mountains across the bay have enchanted commentators. The picturesque rusticity of the district has attracted painters such as William Ashford, the famous academician of the late eighteenth century, who painted the landscape surrounding Clontarf on at least two occasions, incorporating the marine, coastal and rural elements. His 'View of Dublin' from Lord Charlemont's demesne is a romanticised picture of Clontarf, and his depiction of the coast with the Charter School in the foreground emphasises the maritime character of the district. Attention is directed both to the broader environment of Clontarf and to its intrinsic qualities as a village. [0.5] Contemporary paintings of the castle and its demesne by Thomas Snagg and J.M.W. Turner also indicate the innate charm of features of the district for leading artists.

Besides the Green Lanes, the sylvan landscape of Clontarf is suggested in picturesque street- and place-names such as Woodside, Hollybrook, the Black Quarry, the Prior's Wood, Furry Park (from Furze Park) and Blackheath. Names of features in the district reflect also its historical and cultural heritage. In the denomination of some roads and residences there is a reminder of Clontarf's role as a stage for epoch-making events, as in the Kincora estate, which conjures up Brian Boru's stronghold on the Shannon. The king himself is commemorated in Brian Boru Avenue and Street, and in the names of lodges called Boroimhe and Kinkora nearby, while a number of residences and districts have 'Viking' or 'Dane' in their appellation. Several roads in the district have come to bear the name of the Vernon family, who took over and shaped the estate of Clontarf after 1660. Their place of origin in England is recalled in Haddon Road, and their successor-proprietors in Oulton Road. In the suburban expansion of the nineteenth century, new roads were called after Queen Victoria (who presided over the era and in fact visited Clontarf in 1900) and her consort, who gave his name to Albert Terrace. English place-names and surnames occur in the seafront terraces, Walpole, Whitehall and Brighton, the latter called after the main English exemplar for Clontarf as a seaside suburb. [0.6]

Fig. 0.6—'Green Lanes, Clontarf', c. 1900, specifically the lane off Seafield Road, between the rectory and St John the Baptist Church (courtesy of the National Library of Ireland).

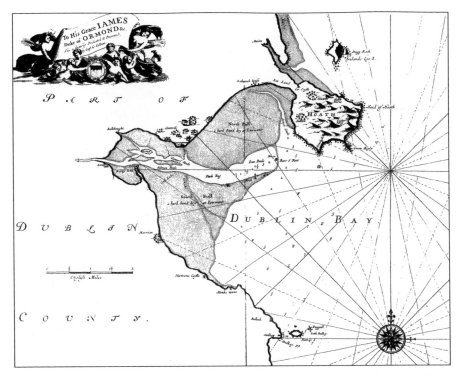

Fig. 0.7—One of the earliest maps of Dublin Bay, showing the maritime features off the coast of Clontarf (Greenville Collins, Great Britain's coasting-pilot *(London, 1693)).*

The long history of Clontarf as a fishing and seafaring harbour is also suggested in the toponymy of the area. In accounts of the battle in 1014, the fishing-weir at Clontarf (*corad Chluana Tarb*, located at the site of the later Ballybough bridge) was referred to as being at the heart of the conflict. The significance of Clontarf as a fishing community is evident on maps of the seventeenth and eighteenth centuries, which show the coastal village as a satellite of a larger nucleation around Clontarf Castle. At the entrance to the Liffey channel, opposite Clontarf, was a deeper sea expanse called the Salmon Pool. Also shown on these early maps are places named Crab Lough (or Crablake Water, to the west of Clontarf Head), Cockle Point (a promontory opposite Haddon Road), the Oyster Beds (in the sea off Castle Avenue) and the Herring Sheds at the meeting of Vernon Avenue and the shoreline. On some maps, indeed, the fishing village of Clontarf is called Herringtown. The marine location also influenced the naming of landward features of the district, such as Seafield Road, and more recently laid-out roads and avenues, including Seaview, Seapark, Seacourt, Seabank and Seapoint. Marino, a neighbouring district, also bespeaks a coastal perspective. [0.7]

Dublin's outlier

The symbiotic relationship between city and village (and later suburb) has shaped the topography, patterns of settlement and economic activity of Clontarf through the ages. King Henry II recognised the strategic value of the village, with its openness to the sea, when granting it to his trusted retainers, the Knights Templar, after the arrival of the Normans in 1170. As a maritime district containing fruitful lands, with easy access to urban markets, Clontarf attracted farming and fishing folk to inhabit the twin manorial and harbour villages in the late medieval period. Ownership of the manor passed from religious to secular lords in the sixteenth century, ushering in a period of 200 years of legal contention between rival proprietors for the prized estate. The quarries of Clontarf were exploited for their stones for the refurbishment of Christ Church Cathedral during the Tudor period, and the local port benefited from the success of its fishing fleet in supplying the city markets. In the eighteenth century the landscape was shaped by the estate management of its Vernon lords. As the coastal morphology was transformed by the great engineering works carried out by the Ballast Office in Dublin Bay to deepen the channel of the Liffey, rivalry between the Vernons and the municipality for control of the Clontarf shoreline persisted down to the twentieth century. During the flight of thousands of Dublin residents from the insanitary conditions in the city in the Victorian period, Clontarf became a convenient seaside refuge for new suburbanites, aided by excellent transport facilities by road and rail. Since the absorption of Clontarf within the municipality of Dublin in 1900, tension has continued to arise from time to time between the wider interests represented by the civic corporation and port of Dublin and the proponents of what might be seen as its traditional village identity, in respect of issues such as reclamation in the bay and flood defences.

At various times throughout the last millennium Clontarf has experienced or been threatened with violent events, most of which are related directly or indirectly to its closeness to Dublin. Lying barely two and a half miles to the north-east of the heart of the old city, Clontarf has always been significant in the affairs of the urban hinterland. The events of 1014, for example, represented a struggle for control of the strategic Viking kingdom of Dublin, the battle being fought at a vital fording-point on the north-eastern approaches to the town. As an accessible harbour in the sand-barred bay of Dublin in medieval and early modern times, Clontarf was linked to the traffic of the main port. In 1534 Archbishop John Alen of Dublin was brutally murdered in the neighbourhood, as the boat in which he was fleeing his enemies fetched up on the sands off Clontarf. Later that year, the followers of the rebellious Thomas Fitzgerald encountered a royal force marching from Howth to Dublin to break the siege of the city, leaving several dead. Just over a century later, in late 1641, the village of Clontarf was burned and largely destroyed in retaliation for an uprising against the parliamentary government in Dublin. Daniel O'Connell was acutely aware of the impact that a major rally would have had so close to the metropolis in 1843, with a parade through the city beforehand, and a banquet and speeches in the Rotunda afterwards. The district also witnessed a skirmish in 1914 between the military and the supporters of the Irish Volunteers, who were marching to the city with a consignment of guns imported at Howth. This was a prelude to a more serious confrontation at Bachelor's Walk later that resulted in three people being shot and many injured. And the fighting in Easter Week 1916 directly affected the residents of the neighbourhood. Soldiers at Clontarf guarding the bridge and embankment carrying the main railway line into Dublin used their vantage point to fire on rebels in Marino.

This account of Clontarf interweaves its history as a famous name, as an attractive place of settlement and as an outlying village of Dublin. While local history in general aspires to be a focal point of the extraneous, in the case of Clontarf this is particularly piquant in view of the national associations of the place. The following chapters address this tension between the local and the national, the suburban and the urban, in describing not only the impress of big events upon Clontarf but also the slow adaptation of the community to longer-term social, economic and cultural developments over the course of a millennium. The starting-point is the battle of Clontarf and the mythologising of Brian Boru in the medieval historiography subsequent to 1014. In examining the uses to which successive generations of writers put the story of the battle, the second chapter establishes how evocative Clontarf became as a place-name in Irish history. The third and fourth chapters show how a distinctive settlement emerged at Clontarf in the form of two villages, one agricultural and the other fishing, under the successive headship of the Norman knightly orders, the Templars and the Hospitallers. The Tudor and earlier Stuart period, from the dissolution of the monastic house of Clontarf to 1660, when Vernon ownership was permanently established, is covered in the fifth chapter, which raises questions about the complexity of local manifestations of colonisation and Reformation. Out of the imbroglio of rebellion and land confiscations there emerged the proprietorship of the Vernons, who came as planters but stayed to become the real shapers of modern Clontarf in the 'long eighteenth century' from 1660 to 1837. This story of

Fig. 0.8—Crest of the Vernon family on a gatelodge near Clontarf Castle, 1885, with the inscribed motto Vernon semper viret *('Vernon always flourishes').*

estate-building and consolidation against the backdrop of major topographical changes in Dublin Bay is treated in Chapters Six and Seven. In the Victorian period at Clontarf, the subject of Chapter Eight, the growth of suburbanisation and a culture of leisure in the district is seen to have redefined the relationship between the district and the nearby municipality, and the continuation of this trend is evident in the discussion of the development of twentieth-century Clontarf in Chapter Nine. A final longitudinal study addresses the question of how community bonds were formed in Clontarf through an examination of local social, cultural and religious institutions and associations. [0.8]

1 *Freeman's Journal* [hereafter *FJ*], 9 October 1843.

2 *Preston Chronicle*, 14 October 1843.

3 *Sydney Morning Herald*, 27 March 1868.

4 Margaret Murphy and Michael Potterton (eds), *The Dublin region in the Middle Ages: settlement, land-use and economy* (Dublin, 2010), 34.

5 John Dunton, 'Letter No. 5', in Edward MacLysaght, *Irish life in the seventeenth century* (2nd edn, Cork, 1950), 366.

6 Murphy and Potterton (eds), *Dublin region in the Middle Ages*, 37; Donal Flood, 'The birth of the Bull Island', *Dublin Historical Record* [hereafter *DHR*] **28** (1975), 142–53.

7 Charles Mount, 'The collection of early and middle Bronze Age material culture in south-east Ireland', *Proceedings of the Royal Irish Academy* [hereafter *PRIA*] **101**C (2001), 14.

8 Thomas O'Gorman, 'On the site of the battle of Clontarf', *Journal of the Royal Historical and Archaeological Society of Ireland* (4th ser.) **5** (1879), 169–70.

9 J.D. Bateson, 'Roman material from Ireland: a re-consideration', *PRIA* **73**C (1973), 67.

10 For an overview see Howard B. Clarke, 'Conversion, church and cathedral: the diocese of Dublin to 1152', in James Kelly and Dáire Keogh (eds), *History of the Catholic diocese of Dublin* (Dublin, 2000), 19–50; Brian Mac Ghiolla Phádraig, 'The Irish form of "Clontarf"', *DHR* **11** (1950), 127–8.

11 Patricia Fagan and Anngret Simms, 'Villages in County Dublin: their origin and inheritance', in F.H.A. Aalen and K. Whelan (eds), *Dublin city and county: from prehistory to the present. Studies in honour of J.H. Andrews* (Dublin, 1992), 86; James H. Todd (ed.), *Cogadh Gáedhel re Gallaibh: the war of the Gaedhil with the Gaill, or the invasions of Ireland by the Danes and other Norsemen* (Dublin, 1867), 193.

CHAPTER ONE

Brian Boru's battle, 1014

What really happened at Clontarf in 1014?

L ET US LOOK first at the facts of the battle story insofar as we can know them,
without the encrustations of a millennium of myth and legend. On a spring
day in 1014, in the northern hinterland of Dublin, two opposing armies engaged
in an intensive military struggle. One was led by the would-be ruler of Ireland,
Brian, son of Cennétig, and consisted of troops from his native Munster as well
as Connacht, and probably Vikings from Limerick and Waterford and some Scots.
Brian was in alliance with Máel Sechnaill mac Domnaill, the most powerful king in
the northern half of Ireland, though the latter's actual role on the battlefield that
day is uncertain. On the other side, the Vikings of Dublin were joined by Máel
Mórda mac Murchada, king of Leinster, and some Scandinavian allies, including
Sigurd, earl of Orkney, and Brodar, a naval leader from the Isle of Man. After a fierce
contest, which witnessed many casualties on both sides, including Brian, his son,
Murchad, and his grandson, Tairdelbach, the balance of advantage appeared to
lie with Brian's army. The battle was not unusual in the context of contemporary
regional struggles for supremacy, in either its motley line-up of antagonists or its
bloodiness. What was untypical, however, was the way in which an important but
not exceptional encounter came to be charged with huge significance both for
its time and for the ensuing history of Ireland.

Let us also accept the association of the place that we know today as Clontarf
with the battlefield of 1014, despite the topographical changes that have occurred
in the district in the meantime. Unlike most other details of the battle, the
meagre place-name evidence has remained free from manipulation by partisan
commentators. Although there has been much debate about the geographical
extent of the fighting on the day, modern experts agree that it climaxed on the
north side of the bay of Dublin. Early sources call it the battle of Mag nElta, which

was the plain between Dublin and Howth on which Clontarf stood. Coupled with the reference to the death of Tairdelbach at 'the weir of Clontarf' (*corad Chluana Tarb*), on one of the stakes of which he was impaled, this situating of the battle indicates that the zenith of the fighting was reached to the north-east of the Tolka River. It is quite likely that much of the combat during the battle ranged along the elevated ridge between the Liffey and the Tolka, from modern-day Cabra through Glasnevin and Drumcondra, down to the shore. The locating of the weir of Clontarf at the late medieval Ballybough bridge near the mouth of the Tolka by modern commentators is speculative, as are the various suggestions for the situation of Tomar's Wood (near which Brian was killed). It has been argued that had most of the strife been south-west of the Tolka the battle might have borne the designation of one of the early established place-names there, such as Clonliffe or Crinan. Although early modern maps of Dublin Bay remind us of how much of the present-day coastline has been reclaimed from the sea since the early eighteenth century, the tidal phenomena and shoreline events, which are such an impressive and integral part of the battle narrative, surely relate to what was called the north strand, stretching to Clontarf. Thus the earliest names for the battle, *cath corad Cluana Tarb* ('the battle of the weir of Clontarf') and *cath torach Tarbchluana* ('the battle of the hosts of Clontarf'), seem to be firmly based on the geographical realities.[1.1]

There is no real controversy about 1014 as the date of the conflict at Clontarf. Good Friday, 23 April, has been accepted by many modern scholars as the day on which the battle was fought. Scientific analysis of evidence of the times of the tides

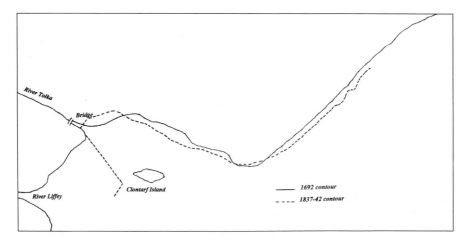

Fig. 1.1—Contour of the pre-modern Clontarf shoreline, contrasted with that on a map of 1837–43.

along the shore of Dublin Bay in the morning and the evening of that Friday, which was found to chime with the details given in early sources, has been adduced in support of that dating. In a recent study of Brian Boru, Máire Ní Mhaonaigh accepts a spring day in 1014 as the most probable and sees the association with Good Friday by early chroniclers as in keeping with the presentation of the king as a martyr figure.[2] Some of the episodes in the Irish and Norse traditions associated with the battle hinge on the especially solemn and portentous time of Holy Week. Even if these are later accretions and if the symbolic nature of Good Friday has been used for mythologising the battle and Brian's holy death, the relation to the liturgical season, and possibly the day, cannot be ruled out. The most recent historian of the battle, Darren McGettigan, sees no reason to doubt that the battle was fought on Good Friday, 23 April 1014, both because the date became ingrained very quickly in the historical memory and owing to its likely choice by the Munster army as powerfully symbolic of ultimate victory.[3]

Apart from these scant details, everything else about the history of the battle of Clontarf seems to have been subject to magnification and myth-making. But while all historical events are subject to reinterpretation by historians, relatively few become legendary in the way that Clontarf has done. This is mainly due to the extraordinary profusion and nature of the sources for the battle. The earliest were chronicle accounts in the form of annals written in Ireland and elsewhere, which became more and more elaborate in their treatment of the battle in the century or so after 1014. Depending on their geographical origin, they tended to favour the side of Brian or that of his opponents. Eventually, under the influence of his descendants, who now styled themselves Uí Briain in his honour, literary works of prose and poetry appeared in which the imagination was given full play. The purpose of the most important of them, *Cogadh Gáedhel re Gallaibh*, written around the centenary of the battle, was to further the career of Brian's great-grandson, Muirchertach, through the memory of the glories of his ancestor. Essentially a fictionalised biography of Brian, the *Cogadh* was to shape the way in which the battle of Clontarf was perceived for subsequent generations. Another important literary strand was woven by the Norse sagas, particularly the saga of Burnt Njall, which depicted the events of 1014 from a Scandinavian perspective. Thus by the late Middle Ages there were in circulation highly embroidered accounts of the causes of the battle, the number of participants, the toll of casualties, the style of combat and weaponry, its outcome and consequences, the portentousness of the occasion and even the day of the year. In raising the question as to why the Clontarf battle assumed such importance, we are led inexorably to the figure of its hero, Brian.[4]

The inflation of Brian's reputation

The first draft of the legend of the son of Cennétig and successor to his brother, Mathgamain, as king of Cashel in 976 belongs to Brian's own lifetime. This is because he himself was very conscious of the need to project an image of power and glory, thereby giving a lead to his later encomiasts in their epic narratives and poems. His own dynasty, who were new arrivals to the ruling of Munster, were in the process of creating a royal pedigree for themselves as the Dál Cais (the seed of Cas, brother of Éogan, from whom their Munster rivals, the Éoganachta, claimed descent). By patronising many churches and monasteries in Munster and elsewhere during his rise to power, Brian (the Boru sobriquet, from Béal Bórama, near his Killaloe heartland, was applied after his death) carefully cultivated the learned churchmen who, among their scholarly activities, compiled the annals of

Fig. 1.2—Illustration of Brian Boru as emperor of the Irish as the frontispiece of The general history of Ireland ... *by Dermo'd O'Connor (London, 1723), the first printed version (in English translation) of Geoffrey Keating's* Foras feasa ar Éirinn.

events for posterity. In his aspirations to the kingship of Ireland, as well as seeking to control Tara, the secular centre of royal authority, Brian forged close links with Armagh, the seat of ecclesiastical primacy, as a guarantor of his rule. Apart from settling disputes involving the church of Armagh, he is said to have donated twenty ounces of gold to the altar there in 1005 and to have had his confessor inscribe his visit in the hallowed Book of Armagh under the title 'Emperor of the Irish' (*Imperator Scotorum*). Perhaps the greatest publicity triumph lay in his assassination at Clontarf, which ensured not only that Brian would enjoy phenomenal posthumous fame and popularity but also that the importance of Clontarf would, by association, be aggrandised, becoming known even in the Norse sagas as 'Brian's battle'.[5] [1.2]

That this identification of king and battle is justified can be seen in the pattern of events leading to Clontarf, which revolved around Brian's ambitions for ruling Ireland. Having emerged in 976 as head of his north Munster (Thomond) dynasty at Cenn Corad (Kincora) in his mid-thirties, Brian went on to become king of the province within a few years through defeating his southern rivals, the Éoghanachta, and the Norse of Limerick. Other provincial rulers took heed of this newly ascendant Munster king, especially when he extended his campaigns to southern Connacht and Leinster in the early 980s. By allying himself with Vikings and Irish, using land and waterborne onslaughts, fortifying his base and securing church support, Brian was in a position to claim rulership of the traditional Leth Moga, or southern half of Ireland, by 996. His main antagonist to that point had been Máel Sechnaill mac Domhnaill, the Uí Néill high-king of Ireland, but the latter was forced to agree in 997 to rule Leth Cuinn (the northern half of the country) alone, relinquishing the rest to Brian's rule. The two kings continued to act in concert in the years around the turn of the millennium, especially in a revolt of the Norse rulers of Dublin and their allies of Leinster against Brian, which resulted in a major victory for him at the battle at Glenn Máma (near Newcastle Lyons, Co. Dublin) in 999. Brian marched on Dublin, banished its Viking ruler, Sitric Silkenbeard, and announced his aspirations to control the trade and wealth of the great economic hub of the Irish Sea. Thereafter Brian moved to take over the high-kingship of Ireland in a series of campaigns to force the Ulster rulers into submission. Although he succeeded in forging quasi-national sovereignty in 1002, recurring revolts in Ulster and among the Dublin Vikings and their Leinster allies forced the septuagenarian Brian to mount an indecisive campaign in late 1013, followed by the major expedition in the spring of 1014.

Similar to Brian's centrality in the causes of the battle, it is his absence through death in its aftermath that has influenced modern interpretations of Clontarf. Whether they take the view that the battle ended in stalemate or in a pyrrhic victory for the army led by the Dál Cais, recent historians agree that Viking power was not totally eclipsed in Ireland thereafter but rather somewhat checked in its commercial and political scope. More important in the interpretation of the outcome were the implications for the wielding of authority in the interprovincial struggles of the eleventh century and afterwards, especially in respect of the position of the descendants of Brian Boru. With the demise of leading members of three generations of the ruling family at Clontarf, the power of the surviving family of Uí Briain was seriously diminished in Munster and Ireland for the best part of a century. Without the dominating presence of Brian, there was no-one to restrain the ambitions of other provincial rulers such as the Uí Néill and the Leinstermen, as they fought for regional or national hegemony. It was not until the emergence of Brian's grandson, Tairdelbach, son of Tadc, as king of Munster in the late 1060s that a southern ruler emulated the great predecessor in successfully challenging the control of northern rulers. During the reign of Tairdelbach's son, Muirchertach Uí Briain, the enduring legends of Brian Boru and the battle of Clontarf began to be constructed as part of the claims of the great-grandson of the hero to the kingship of Ireland.

It is now time to investigate how and why these facts about Brian Boru, his battle and its aftermath were massaged by a variety of different writers over several centuries to fashion a fictionalised version. The basic records of what happened are to be found in the annals, which are chronological listings of the events, written nearly contemporaneously. Even these bald accounts, however, contain a bias in that they were produced by monastic scribes in the different provinces who were loyal to their local kingly patrons. The Annals of Innisfallen, for example, were compiled in Munster during and shortly after the lifetime of Brian Boru and reflect very favourably the achievements of the Dál Cais ruler. By contrast, the annals associated with Clonmacnoise in the Irish midlands show a predilection for Máel Sechnaill mac Domhnaill, Brian's rival for the high-kingship, and a downgrading of the contribution of the Munster king. Although originating in the north, the Annals of Ulster present a very positive account of Brian's rise to power and climactic battle, as do the Annals of Loch Cé, which have a Connacht provenance. Not only did Irish annals register the events of 1014 in the light of their own prejudices but chroniclers writing abroad also took note of the battle. It was mentioned in a Welsh chronicle, 'The chronicle of princes', possibly of the early eleventh century, and also by the Frenchman Adémar de Chabannes in his history written about 1025. An Irish monk in exile in Germany, Marianus, refers in his chronicle, compiled before 1083, to the death of Brian as he prayed to God.[6]

Spare account of the battle of Clontarf from the *Annals of Innisfallen*

Great warfare between Brian and the foreigners of Áth Cliath, and Brian then brought a great muster of the men of Ireland to Áth Cliath. After that the foreigners of Áth Cliath gave battle to Brian, son of Cennétig, and he was slain, with his son Murchad, royal heir of Ireland, and Murchad's son, namely, Tairdelbach, as also the princes of Mumu round Conaing, son of Donn Cúán, and round Domnall son of Diarmait, king of Corcu Bascinn, and round Mac Bethad son of Muiredach, king of Ciarraige Luachra, and also Tadc Ua Cellaig, king of Uí Maine, and many others. There were also slain in that battle Mael Mórda son of Murchad, king of Laigin, together with the princes of the Laigin round him, and the foreigners of the western world were slaughtered in the same battle.

Annals of Innisfallen, s.a. 1014

The revising by the annalists of the narrative of events on the eve and day of the battle was their response to the growing perception that Clontarf was a confrontation that was out of the ordinary. In the Annals of Innisfallen, the Munster-based chronicler gave a summary of what probably are the core facts: Brian, supported by his son, grandson and nephew, Conaing, as well as by the rulers of Corcu Baiscinn and Ciarraige Luachra in Munster and Uí Maine in Connacht, battled against the Vikings of Dublin, abetted by Máel Mórda mac Murchada, king of Leinster, and 'the Vikings of the western world'. As the significance of the battle of Clontarf was magnified by succeeding generations, however, the numbers of participants expanded, at least as listed among the fallen in some other annals. No less than patriots after the 1916 Rising, it became important for clan rulers to be able to answer positively the question, 'Where were your ancestors on Good Friday, 1014?' Thus, according to the annals of Ulster, Loch Cé and the Clonmacnoise group, Brian's forces included many other Munster warriors and the rulers of the Éoghanachta septs of south-west and south Munster, the Déssi and Fir Maige and Uí Fhiachrach Aidne of Connacht, as well as a Scottish ally, Domnall mac Eimín, *mormaer* ('sea steward') of Mar in Moray. To the opposing side were added the leaders of the territories of Leinster, Forthuatha and Uí Fáilghe, and the names of at least ten Scandinavian warriors, including Earl Sigurd of the Orkneys and Brodar, a leader of the Vikings in the Isle of Man, who are well known and others whose identity is very shadowy. Numbers cited also became inflated, the figure of 1,000 overseas fighters said to have swollen the ranks of Brian's antagonists, who lost 3,000 in total, according to the Annals of Clonmacnoise, or 6,000, as estimated by the Annals of Ulster. By contrast, modern historians have put the total number of troops involved on both sides at 5,000.[7] [1.3]

Slightly expanded account from the *Annals of Ulster*

Brian son of Ceinnétig son of Lorcán, king of Ireland, and Mael Sechnaill son of Domnall, king of Temair, led an army to Áth Cliath. All the Laigin were assembled to meet him, and the foreigners of Áth Cliath, and a like number of the foreigners of Scandinavia, i.e. *to the number of* 1,000 breastplates. A valiant battle was fought between them, the like of which was never *before* encountered. Then the foreigners and the Laigin first broke in defeat, and they were completely wiped out. There fell on the side of the foreign troop in this battle Mael Mórda son of Murchad, king of Laigin, and Domnall son of Fergal, king of the Forthuatha, and of the foreigners there fell Dubgall son of Amlaíb, Siucraid son of Lodur, jarl of Innsi Orc, and Gilla Ciaráin son of Glún Iairn, heir designate of the foreigners, and Oittir Dub and Suartgair and Donnchad grandson of Erulb and Griséne and Luimne and Amlaíb son of Lagmann and Brotor who slew Brian i.e. chief of the Scandinavian fleet, and six thousand who were killed or drowned. Of the Irish moreover there fell in the counter-shock Brian son of Ceinnétig, over-king of the Irish of Ireland, and of the foreigners and of the Britons, the Augustus of the whole of north-west Europe, and his son Murchad, and the latter's son, i.e. Tairdelbach son of Murchad, and Conaing son of Donn Cuan son of Cennéitig, heir designate of Mumu, and Mothla son of Domnall son of Faelán, king of the Déisi Muman; Eochu son of Dúnadach and Niall ua Cuinn and Ceinnéitig's son, — Brian's three companions; two kings of Uí Maine, Ua Cellaig . . . ., and Mael Ruanaid ua hEidin, king of Aidne, and Géibennach ua Dubagáin, king of Fernmag, and Mac Bethad son of Muiredach Claen, king of Ciarraige Luachra and Domnall son of Diarmait, king of Corcu Baiscinn, and Scannlán son of Cathal, king of Eóganacht of Loch Léin, and Domnall son of Eimen son of Cainnech, earl of Marr in Scotland, and many other nobles. Mael Muire son of Eochaid, successor of Patrick, with his venerable clerics and relics, came moreover to Sord Coluim Chille, and brought away the body of Brian, king of Ireland, and the body of his son Murchad, and the head of Conaing and the head of Mothla, and buried them in Ard Macha in a new tomb. For twelve nights the community of Patrick waked the bodies in honour of the dead king.

Annals of Ulster, s.a. 1014

Fig. 1.3 — This Bronze Age burial site at Conquer Hill, the second of two located in the Clontarf district, was associated for a time in the popular mind with the interment of the fallen at the battle of Clontarf (courtesy of the Royal Irish Academy).

It is clear, then, that ever more elaborate accounts of the battle of Clontarf were being transmitted orally and in written form in Ireland and abroad in the decades after the fighting. Before the twelfth century there had been adumbrated three elements of the enduring mythology: the struggle as one between Vikings and Irish, the triumph of Christianity in the person of Brian, the holy emperor, and the doom-laden portents surrounding the day of battle. That the information travelled overseas is evident from Adémar of Chabanne's depiction of the battle as essentially being between Irish Christians and Viking pagans. In Marianus's *Chronicon*, Brian is shown to have been killed while at prayer during the Easter triduum. The Annals of Loch Cé, which contain a listing of casualties almost identical to that of the Ulster annals, differ from the other collections in that two supernatural episodes are seen to have prefigured the day of battle. In one, the appearance of St Senan to a servant of Brian, calling on the king to honour a debt due to the saint's sanctuary before the morrow, did not augur well for his chances of survival beyond that. And in a vision of Óebinn from the otherworldly mound of Craig Léith, Brian learned that he would die the following day and that his successor would be the son upon whom he laid eyes first. Despite his calling for the favoured Murchad, it was Donnchad who first appeared before the king. In thus summoning up an atmosphere of foreboding and danger, the annalist was presenting the battle to come as no ordinary fight but as an event filled with portentousness.[8]

Imaginative history in Ireland and Iceland

All of these annalistic excrescences were to be infused into the greatest of the literary accounts of Brian and the battle, *Cogadh Gáedhel re Gaillaibh* ('the war of the Irish with the foreigners'). Composed in or around 1114 (possibly to mark the centenary of Clontarf), the *Cogadh* was to be hugely influential in the transmission of the romanticised version of the life and death of Brian. The primary purpose of this hagiography was to boost the standing of Muirchertach, the great-grandson of Brian and ruler of the Uí Briain, under whose patronage the *Cogadh* was produced. By associating himself with the glorious deeds of his ancestor, Muirchertach wished to be seen as emulating him as a powerful and cultured ruler both in his own Ua Briain territory and on a wider political stage. Thus the highly inflated biography of Brian with all its triumphs over the Vikings and others, which was written principally as propaganda for the Ua Briain family, established the foundations for the eventual apotheosis of the hero of Clontarf. In this biased work of historical fiction, it was a requirement that the hero, a Christian leader, be confronted by barbarian heathens, who were supported by villainous allies in Ireland and from abroad.[9]

The era of Brian's reign is presented as a golden age, and the victory in 1014 as the climax of a prodigiously successful career. We have seen already that the seeds of this spinning, in current parlance, of Brian's triumphs were sown in his own time, and the bountiful harvest is manifest in *Cogadh Gáedhel re Gallaibh*. Quite apart from his exceptional martial prowess, the ruler of the Dál Cais is shown to have fostered the arts of peace. Brian is presented as having imposed the rule of law in the secular sphere in the decades before Clontarf, and as having offered ecclesiastical patronage through the protection of sanctuaries and the building of new churches and bell-towers. In this respect, his beneficence towards the religious paid dividends, as the eulogistic works, including the *Cogadh*, emanated from a monastic milieu. As a patron of learning, Brian cherished the activity of professors and teachers, and he sent agents overseas to purchase books in order to replace those destroyed by the Scandinavian invaders. In the civil sphere, he was also shown to be a builder and restorer, not just of castles and forts but also of bridges and roads. As a symbol of the benign and effective kingship of Brian in

Ireland, the author of the *Cogadh* adduces the tale of a lone woman who travelled the length of Ireland from north to south, carrying prominently a golden ring, without being molested or interfered with in any way.[10]

Portrait of Brian from *Cogadh Gáedhel re Gallaibh*

After Erinn was reduced to a state of peace, a lone woman came from Torach, in the north of Erinn, to Cliodhna, in the south of Erinn, carrying a ring of gold on a horse-rod, and she was neither robbed nor insulted; whereupon the poet sang –

> From Torach to pleasant Cliodhna,
> And carrying with her a ring of gold,
> In the time of Brian, of the bright side, fearless,
> A lone woman made the circuit of Erinn.

By him were erected also noble churches in Erinn and their sanctuaries. He sent professors and masters to teach wisdom and knowledge; and to buy books beyond the sea, and the great ocean; because their writings and their books in every church and every sanctuary where they were, were burned and thrown into water by the plunderers, from the beginning to the end; and Brian, himself, gave the price of learning and the price of books to every one separately who went on this service. Many works, also, and repairs were made by him. By him were erected the church of Cell Dálua, and the church of Inis Cealtra, and the bell tower of Tuam Greine, and many other works in like manner. By him were made bridges and causeways, and high roads. By him were strengthened, also, the duns, and fastnesses, and islands, and celebrated royal forts of Mumhain. He built, also, the fortification of Caisel of the kings, and of Cenn Abrat, the island of Loch Cend, and the island of Loch Gair, and Dún Eochair Maige, Dún Cliath, and Dún Crot, and the island of Loch Saiglend, and Inis an Ghaill Duibh, and Rossach, and Cend Conradh, and Borumha, and the royal forts of Munster in like manner. He continued in this way prosperously, peaceful, giving banquets, hospitable, just-judging; wealthily, venerated; chastely, and with devotion, and with law and with rules among the clergy; with prowess and with valour; with honour and with renown among the laity; and fruitful, powerful, firm, secure; for fifteen years in the chief sovereignty of Erinn.

Cogadh Gáedhel re Gallaibh, ed. J.H. Todd, pp 139, 141

For the author of the *Cogadh*, the significance of the era of Brian's peace is underscored by its being contrasted with the preceding decades and centuries of warfare between the Irish and the Vikings. In this juxtaposition of war and peace, it was necessary for the Scandinavians to be portrayed as evil oppressors and for the Irish to be presented as righteous victors, personified most notably in the heroic figure of Brian Boru. From the very first sentence, in which the Danes are presented as 'fierce' and 'hard-hearted', through to the climactic description of the battle of Clontarf, dozens of pejorative adjectives are applied to the Vikings or *Gaill*, including the oft-used 'murderous', 'cruel', 'barbarous', 'fearful', 'villainous' and 'ferocious'. There is no doubt that the black legend of the Scandinavians in Ireland received a massive fillip from this hostile depiction. By contrast, the sympathetic representation of the Irish or *Gáedhel* culminates in the valorous story of the Dál Cais, especially under the rule of Mathgamain and his brother, Brian Boru. Epithets such as 'heroic', 'honourable', 'noble' and 'righteous' cluster around the deeds of these leaders, who led the turning of the tide against Viking tyranny. Two signal Irish victories were won in the half-century before Clontarf, the first at Sulcóit in 967 and the second at Glenn Máma in 999, both of which were followed up by the capture and spoiling of Viking ports, at Limerick and Dublin respectively. In the *Cogadh*, Brian is presented as the joint leader of the army at Sulcóit (although in reality the victor was Mathgamain) and as the sole victor at Glenn Máma (even though Máel Sechnaill mac Domhnaill is mentioned in some chronicles as co-commander). The latter encounter, which took place south of Dublin, was shown to be a highly significant one: according to a poetic paean, reproduced in the *Cogadh*, 4,000 of the foreigners and their Irish allies were slain, the battle being described as even more important than that of Mag nEalta, a reference possibly to Clontarf.[11]

That history came to judge Glenn Máma to be no more than a rehearsal for 1014, however, is largely due to the lurid and sensationalist account of the later battle given in the *Cogadh*. How does the author of that work explain its causes? Besides the crux of opposition to Brian's assertion of national suzerainty during the first decade of the new millennium, elements of a family feud are identified as having exacerbated the protagonists' grievances. The constant campaigning of Brian out of Munster into the other provinces was necessary to enforce the giving of hostages by the regional kings, as symbolic of their submission to his high-kingship. Included among these journeys was what the *Cogadh* terms his 'royal visitation' of 1005, during which he took hostages 'of all the men of Erinn' and thereafter declared 'the peace of Erinn'. Gradually, opposition to Brian came once again to focus on Máel Mórda mac Murchada, king of Leinster, who had been

Portrait of the Vikings from *Cogadh Gáedhel re Gallaibh*

Now on the one side of that battle were the shouting, hateful, powerful, wrestling, valiant, active, fierce-moving, dangerous, nimble, violent, furious, unscrupulous, untameable, inexorable, unsteady, cruel, barbarous, frightful, sharp, ready, huge, prepared, cunning, warlike, poisonous, murderous, hostile Danars; bold, hard-hearted Danmarkians, surly, piratical foreigners, blue-green, pagan; without reverence, without veneration, without honour, without mercy, for God or for man.

Cogadh Gáedhel re Gallaibh, ed. J.H. Todd, p. 159

defeated with the Vikings of Dublin at Glenn Máma in 999. Now Máel Mórda was to build an alliance—containing the Viking ruler of Dublin, Sitric Silkenbeard, and Irish from Leinster and Ulster—that seriously challenged the Tara king, Máel Sechnaill mac Domhnaill, Brian's erstwhile partner in ruling Ireland and nominal ally.[12]

All of these personalities were intertwined through familial ties, which, according to the *Cogadh*, piqued the strong emotions on both sides on the eve of and during the battle. A colourful episode at Kincora is said to have galvanised Máel Mórda into the rebellion which preceded the Clontarf encounter. When he came to present Brian with timber for ships' masts, his sister, Gormlaith, who was the Dál Cais ruler's second wife, was in the palace. Gormlaith taunted her brother with the evidence of his submissiveness to Brian Boru, saying that their father and grandfather would never have submitted. A further incitement to action on Máel Mórda's part was the insulting behaviour during a chess match of Murchad, Brian's favoured son (by a previous marriage), which prompted the Leinster king to leave in high dudgeon and to murder a mediating messenger sent after him by Brian. Before she married Brian, Gormlaith is said to have been wedded to Máel Sechnaill mac Domhnaill, and also to Amlaíb Cuarán, the Viking king of Dublin. By the latter she was mother to Sitric Silkenbeard, also king of Dublin and Máel Mórda's ally, who nevertheless remained aloof from the battle of Clontarf, according to the *Cogadh*. While he watched the murderous fighting from the walls of the city, Sitric had to contend with the scornful comments of his own wife, Sláine, about the rout of his allies, which angered him to the point of striking her. She was the daughter of Brian Boru and thus married to the son of her stepmother.[13]

It is in its very density and turbidity that the account of the battle in *Cogadh Gáedhel re Gallaibh* has captured the imagination over the centuries. The number of participants, particularly on the side opposing Brian, is inflated with dozens of names, some of which at least are fictitious. Swelling the ranks of the Dublin Vikings were Saxon, Cornish and French warriors, as well as fighters from places in the Irish and North Sea archipelago, including the isles of Orkney, Shetland, Man, Skye, Lewis and Kintyre. Among these there were massive casualties on the battlefield. Notable by their absence from the opposing sides in the fray, according to the *Cogadh*, were Sitric Silkenbeard, who stayed behind his Dublin ramparts, and Máel Sechnaill, who remained aloof on the periphery of the field of battle. The lethal nature of the weaponry used, especially by the Vikings, is graphically conveyed, their warriors wielding bows with poisoned arrows, spears

Fig. 1.4—C.F. Sargent, 'Brian Boru at the battle of Clontarf', 1845 (courtesy of the National Library of Ireland).

and swords. While reference is made to battalions in the battle order, the sense of the fighting conveyed is of fragmentation into separate duels of small companies or individuals. Among the most stirring encounters were those involving Domhnall, son of Eimín, with Plat or Plait, Dúnlaing Ua hArtacáin with both Cornabliteoc and Máel Mórda, king of Leinster, and Murchad, son of Brian, with both Sigurd of Orkney and Ebric. Symbolic of victory or defeat in the sanguinary struggle were the carrying or falling of banners and standards. Overall, the impression is of disorder, mayhem and murderous clustering on the shores of Dublin Bay.[14] [1.4]

Perhaps the most notable absentee from the actual fighting, although not from the extended battlefield, was Brian himself. In the *Cogadh*, the 73-year-old king is shown as kneeling in prayer throughout the battle's duration in the vicinity of a wood, within sight of the conflict. As he recited the psalms and paternosters, Brian received updates throughout the day on the progress of the fight from his attendant, Latean. When, towards evening, he heard of the fall of Murchad's standard, Brian refused to flee, addressing himself instead to the details of his own demise and funeral arrangements. He expressed his wish to be buried in Armagh through the agency of the monks of Swords and the community of the

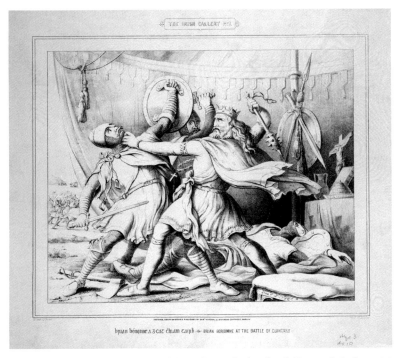

Fig. 1.5—*Samuel Watson, 'Brian Boroimhe at the battle of Clontarf', before 1867 (courtesy of the National Library of Ireland).*

northern cathedral. Already Brian had shown his reverence for the primatial see of St Patrick when, on his grand tour of the country in 1005, he had donated twenty ounces of gold to the altar there. As the battle ended, Brodar, a leading Viking, came upon the kneeling Brian and thought at first that he was a priest. On being informed that he was in fact the king, Brodar prepared to deal the fatal blow of an axe to the head of Brian, but not before the latter had mortally wounded Brodar by cutting off his legs with his sword. [1.5] In thus setting the violent death of Brian Boru in an enclave of prayer at a remove from the battle, the author stresses the credentials of the king as a martyr for Christianity at the hands of a leader whose men had 'no reverence, veneration, respect or mercy for God or for man, for church or for sanctuary'. The point is underscored by the reference to the battle's being fought on Good Friday.[15]

The murder of Brian from *Cogadh Gáedhel re Gallaibh*

Brodar then turned round and appeared with a bright, gleaming, trusty battle-axe in his hand, with the handle set in the middle of it. When Brian saw him he gazed at him, and gave him a stroke with his sword, and cut off his left leg at the knee, and his right leg at the foot. The foreigner dealt Brian a stroke which cleft his head utterly; and Brian killed the second man that was with Brodar, and they both fell mutually by each other.

CXV. There was not done in Erinn, since Christianity, excepting the beheading of Cormac Mac Cuilennain, any deed greater than this. In fact he was one of the three best that were ever born in Erinn; and one of the three men who most caused Erinn to prosper, namely, Lugh Lamha-fada, and Finn Mac Cumhaill, and Brian Mac Ceinneidigh. For it was he that released the men of Erinn, and its women, from the bondage and iniquity of the foreigners and the pirates. It was he that gained five-and-twenty battles over the foreigners, and who killed and banished them as we have already said. He was the strong, irresistible, second Alexander, for energy, and for dignity, and for attacks, and for battles, and for triumphs. And he was the happy, wealthy, peaceable Solomon of the Gaedhil. He was the faithful, fervent, honourable, gallant David of Erinn, for truthfulness, and for worthiness, and for the maintenance of sovereignty. He was the magnificent, brilliant Moses, for chastity, and unostentatious devotion.

Cogadh Gáedhel re Gallaibh, ed. J.H. Todd, pp 203, 205

Not only is Brian given the status of Christian martyr by the twelfth-century biographer in *Cogadh Gáedhel re Gallaibh* but he is also presented as a divinely approved imperial figure. We have already seen that, while he was venerating the church of Armagh in 1005, Brian had been inscribed by his chaplain in the Book of Armagh as 'Imperator Scotorum' or 'the Emperor of the Irish'. There were probably deliberate resonances herein of the title adopted slightly earlier by the Ottonian royal house, 'Imperator Romanorum' or 'Emperor of the Romans'. In marking his death in the *Cogadh*, the author refers to Brian as 'high sovereign of Erinn, and Albain, and of the Saxons, and Britons, and of the west of Europe'. Moreover, through comparisons made with Old Testament patriarchs—'Solomon of the Gaedhil', 'gallant David of Erinn' and 'the magnificent, brilliant Moses'—Brian's wisdom and epic leadership qualities are depicted and his *imperium* is viewed as holy. In an era of crusading holy wars against infidels, this contemporary portrayal of an Irish Christian emperor who vanquished heathens and restored peace and order in church and state through his perspicacious rule was entirely appropriate.[16] [1.6]

Fig. 1.6—The opening passage of Cogadh Gáedhel re Gallaibh, *as reproduced in J.H. Todd's edition, published in London in 1867.*

In keeping with the prestige of its slain victor, the battle of Clontarf is dramatised in *Cogadh Gáedhel re Gallaibh* through the evocation of supernatural phenomena. In common with the account in the Annals of Loch Cé, Brian's vision of the otherworldly Aibell (or Óebinn) of Craig Léith is conveyed, in this instance in the context of his preparation for death and arranging for his foretold successor, Donnchad, to see to the carrying out of his obsequies. There is narrated an additional apparition in the form of Dúnlaing Ua hArtacháin, who absented himself from a heavenly vision to fight beside Murchad, in the process foretelling the death of the latter, his father Brian, his son Tairdelbach and his cousin Conaing. Dúnlaing himself enters the fray to slay the Viking Cornabliteoc and 150 of his followers, before succumbing himself, as he predicted. An ominous atmosphere is conjured up by the spectre of birds of prey and demoniacal phantoms, including witches and goblins, hovering over the massed warriors on the battlefield. As they fought, thick clots of gore were blown by a bitter wind to stain their faces and their clothes. In a Macbethian effect, the arrows of the Scandinavians were said to be dipped in 'the blood of dragons and toads, and water-snakes of hell, and of scorpions and otters, and wonderful venomous snakes of all kinds'.[17]

The incantatory force of Brian's battle, as conveyed in the *Cogadh* in the early twelfth century, was strong enough to be represented in the Norse sagas 100 years or so later. Particularly in the saga of *Brennu-Njál*, but also in those of *Orkneyinga* and *Þorsteinn Siðu-Hallsson*, the battle of Clontarf figures in the adventures of Viking warriors such as Sigurd, earl of Orkney, Sitric, king of Dublin, and Brodar of Man. Composed from an eclectic *mélange* of sources, including accounts from Ireland and regions across the North Sea, the sagas capture the doom-laden nature of the events at Clontarf for Vikings and Irish alike, albeit as a coda or as incidental to their main stories. By the time these sagas were being compiled, their Scandinavian authors were looking back at their ancestors' engagement in political and military matters in the heavily intertwined parts of the northern sea world. There was also a keen awareness of the increasing significance of the battle of Clontarf in historical accounts and of the burgeoning of the reputation of the fallen victor, Brian Boru. It behoved the honour of self-respecting thirteenth-century Icelanders that their forebears had been associated with such storied events in Ireland, no matter how grim the memory. For the author of *Brennu-Njál's Saga* in particular, the Irish episode in 1014 was a deftly interwoven epilogue to a family story of suffering and vengeance, but in general the Norse writers brought a European perspective to bear upon the battle and its participants.[18]

In *Njál's Saga*, the link between the Irish imbroglio of early 1014 and the wider Viking world was in the figure of Sitric ('Silkenbeard') mac Amlaíb, the Norse king of Dublin, who was shown to have resorted to the court of Sigurd, earl of Orkney, to gain aid for his war against Brian Boru. There, with the prior approval of his mother, Gormlaith, Sitric offered her hand, as well as his kingdom, to Sigurd in return for assistance, which was duly forthcoming. In this further development of the family feud as background to the fighting, Gormlaith, the former wife of Brian, is presented as motivated by malice, to the extent that she urged Sitric on to 'spare nothing' in his enlisting of more Viking warriors against the high-king, including Brodar and Óspakr, two brothers, then in the Isle of Man. Sitric succeeded in recruiting Brodar, the eventual slayer of Brian, by duplicitously offering him the favours already promised to Sigurd—his mother as bride and the kingdom of Dublin. While the roles of villains and villainess in this episode of the *Saga* were thus cast with the depiction of Sitric, Brodar and Gormlaith, those of hero were assigned to, among others, Brian himself and also Óspakr, whose goodness contrasts with the evil of his brother, Brodar. Unlike the latter, who had reneged on his former Christianity, Óspakr was 'a heathen' but, as 'the wisest of all men', he refused to 'fight against so good a king'. Instead, he vowed to 'take the true faith' and to go to Ireland, where he joined the army of Brian at Clontarf. Very clearly the battle, as dramatised in *Njál's Saga*, was to be seen as a struggle between divine truth and renegade falsity.[19]

Within that drama, all of the remaining elements that have become part of the staple account of the battle of Clontarf down to the present were put in place, including the *mise en scène*, the characters and the action. Omens abound, not least the depiction of events as taking place within Holy Week 1014, with the battle itself being fought on Good Friday. It was Brodar who, acting upon a sorcerer's prediction that Brian would fall but win the day on the Friday while his enemies would all fall in fighting on preceding days, decided to do battle on the solemn feast. Before setting out for Ireland, Brodar's fleet had to contend with showers of boiling blood, flying swords and sharp-clawed ravens as auspices of a bloody clash and general perdition. In the description of the battle, the stress is on the Viking participants, who were formed up into three battalions, led by Brodar in his suit of impenetrable mail, Sigurd and Sitric, who is present on the battlefield in this account. These units were faced by their enemy counterparts under the command of Wolf the Quarrelsome (probably Cú Duilig, Brian's brother), Kerthialfad (Brian's foster-son) and Óspakr. The author narrates the individual jousts involving Scandinavians at the heart of the 'bitter' fighting in order to capture the mayhem, murder and magic of that day. Most calamitous to the Viking side was the loss of Earl Sigurd, who, despite a warning that all who bore his standard would be killed, had secreted it under his cloak and was promptly pierced through. As the Irish pursued the fleeing Vikings, Brodar saw

Gormlaith [Kormlada] as villainess from *Njal's Saga*

Then King Sigtrygg stirred in his business with Earl Sigurd, and
bade him go to the war with him against King Brian.

The earl was long steadfast, but the end of it was that he let
the king have his way, but said he must have his mother's hand
for his help, and be king in Ireland, if they slew Brian. But
all his men besought Earl Sigurd not to go into the war, but it
was all no good.

So they parted on the understanding that Earl Sigurd gave his
word to go; but King Sigtrygg promised him his mother and the
kingdom.

It was so settled that Earl Sigurd was to come with all his host
to Dublin by Palm Sunday.

Then King Sigtrygg fared south to Ireland, and told his mother
Kormlada that the earl had undertaken to come, and also what he
had pledged himself to grant him.

She showed herself well pleased at that, but said they must
gather greater force still.

Sigtrygg asked whence this was to be looked for?

She said there were two vikings lying off the west of Man; and
that they had thirty ships, and, she went on, "They are men of
such hardihood that nothing can withstand them. The one's name
is Ospak, and the other's Brodir. Thou shalt fare to find them,
and spare nothing to get them into thy quarrel, whatever price
they ask."

Now King Sigtrygg fares and seeks the vikings, and found them
lying outside off Man; King Sigtrygg brings forward his errand at

once, but Brodir shrank from helping him until he, King Sigtrygg, promised him the kingdom and his mother, and they were to keep this such a secret that Earl Sigurd should know nothing about it; Brodir too was to come to Dublin on Palm Sunday.

So King Sigtrygg fared home to his mother, and told her how things stood.

Njal's Saga, section 11, 153–5

that the tent which sheltered Brian (who had opted not to fight on a feast-day) was lightly guarded and opportunistically beheaded the Irish king, despite the efforts of Tadc, Brian's son, to shield him. Brodar himself was seized and tortured to death by disembowelling, adding to the Viking dead, who included Earl Sigurd, Asmund the White, Halldor, son of Gudmund, and Erling of Straumey.[20]

Perhaps the most atmospheric and mesmerising aspect of the *Saga*'s evocation of the day of battle is the inclusion of a number of visions of doom in places far to the north of Ireland, most notably the *Darraðorljóð* (or 'Daurrud's song'). The latter is a Valkyries' incantation memorised by one Daurrud in Caithness on Good Friday 1014, after he saw twelve riders disappear into a bower. Looking in, he witnessed women weaving men's entrails on a loom weighted by human heads, with a shuttle made of swords and reels made of arrows. In stanzas beginning

'Wind we, wind swiftly
Our warwinning woof'

they chanted, as they wove, of the deaths of warriors in a gory battle, including a mighty king (Brian) and an earl (Sigurd), and of the survival of a young king (Sitric). In the Faroe Islands a similar apparition was envisioned by Brand Gneisti. When a priest in Svínafell in Iceland was saying Mass that day a drop of blood fell on his stole, while a colleague in the same region saw a deep sea containing horrible sights opening up beside the altar. One Hareck in the Orkneys thought that he met with Earl Sigurd and some men, and together they rode under a brae and were never seen again. And Earl Gilli of the Southern Isles dreamed that he was visited by Hostfinn, who told him of the death of Sigurd and that Brian fell 'but kept his kingdom'.[21]

Visions of doom from *Njal's Saga*

At Swinefell, in Iceland, blood came on the priest's stole on
Good-Friday, so that he had to put it off.

At Thvattwater the priest thought he saw on Good-Friday a long
deep of the sea hard by the altar, and there he saw many awful
sights, and it was long ere he could sing the prayers.

This event happened in the Orkneys, that Hareck thought he saw
Earl Sigurd, and some men with him. Then Hareck took his horse
and rode to meet the earl. Men saw that they met and rode under
a brae, but they were never seen again, and not a scrap was ever
found of Hareck.

Earl Gilli in the Southern isles dreamed that a man came to him
and said his name was Hostfinn, and told him he was come from Ireland.

The earl thought he asked him for tidings thence, and then he
sang this song:

> "I have been where warriors wrestled,
> High in Erin sang the sword,
> Boss to boss met many bucklers,
> Steel rung sharp on rattling helm;
> I can tell of all their struggle;
> Sigurd fell in flight of spears;
> Brian fell, but kept his kingdom
> Ere he lost one drop of blood."

Those two, Flosi and the earl, talked much of this dream. A week
after, Hrafn the Red came thither, and told them all the tidings
of Brian's battle, the fall of the king, and of Earl Sigurd, and
Brodir, and all the Vikings.

Njal's Saga, section ii, 155–6

38

The extended coverage of the events of Holy Week 1014 in *Njal's Saga*, as well as the briefer mentions in other literary works emanating from the Scandinavian milieu in the thirteenth and fourteenth centuries, attests to the fame of Brian Boru and, by extension, the battle of Clontarf in northern Europe in the later Middle Ages. Despite the defeat sustained by the Vikings on the battlefield, the image of Brian presented is of a good and holy king who attracted the pagan Óspakr to convert to Christianity and refused to fight on a hallowed day. Moreover, at the moment of his death, his blood effects a miraculous healing of Tadc's severed hand, and his own decapitated head is restored to his trunk for the laying out of the body. Óspakr's brother, Brodar, who reneged on his faith and slew the king, is shown as paying a terrible price for his apostasy and hatred of Christianity. Unlike the *Cogadh Gáedhel re Gallaibh*, which sees the conflict between Irish and foreigners in black and white tones, *Njal's Saga*'s hues are more subtle in demonstrating goodness on both sides, but there is no doubt about its burnishing of the credentials of King Brian Boru for martyrdom. The terrain where the battle was fought and Brian died is very lightly sketched, references to a river and to a wood close to Brian's refuge being the only guides to the topography outside the burg (or town) of Dublin, where battle was joined. Dubbed 'Brian's battle' rather than the battle of Clontarf, the conflict was deemed to be important because of its proximity to the kingdom of Dublin, a strategic hub for Scandinavian maritime hegemony.[22]

Extract from Daurrud's song from *Njal's Saga*

THE WOOF OF WAR.

> See! warp is stretched
> For warriors' fall,
> Lo! weft in loom
> 'Tis wet with blood;
> Now fight foreboding,
> 'Neath friends' swift fingers,
> Our grey woof waxeth
> With war's alarms,
> Our warp bloodred,
> Our weft corseblue.

This woof is y-woven
With entrails of men,
This warp is hardweighted
With heads of the slain,
Spears blood-besprinkled
For spindles we use,
Our loom ironbound,
And arrows our reels;
With swords for our shuttles
This war-woof we work;
So weave we, weird sisters,
Our warwinning woof.

Wind we, wind swiftly
Our warwinning woof
Woof erst for king youthful
Foredoomed as his own,
Forth now we will ride,
Then through the ranks rushing
Be busy where friends
Blows blithe give and take.

So cheerily chant we
Charms for the young king,
Come maidens lift loudly
His warwinning lay;
Let him who now listens
Learn well with his ears
And gladden brave swordsmen
With bursts of war's song.

Now mount we our horses,
Now bare we our brands,
Now haste we hard, maidens,
Hence far, far, away.

Njal's Saga, section 11, 155–6

1 Máire Ní Mhaonaigh, *Brian Boru: Ireland's greatest king?* (Stroud, 2007), 65, 76–7, 99; John Ryan, 'The battle of Clontarf', *Journal of the Royal Society of Antiquaries of Ireland* [hereafter *JRSAI*] **68** (1938), 32–7; James H. Todd (ed.), *Cogadh Gáedhel re Gallaibh: the war of the Gaedhil with the Gaill, or the invasions of Ireland by the Danes and other Norsemen* (Dublin, 1867) [hereafter *CGG*], 193; Darren McGettigan, *The battle of Clontarf, Good Friday 1014* (Dublin, 2013), 93–4.

2 Ní Mhaonaigh, *Brian Boru*, 99; Samuel Haughton, 'On the time of high water in Dublin Bay on Good Friday the 23rd April 1014 the day of the battle of Clontarf', *PRIA* 7 (1857–61), 495–8.

3 McGettigan, *Battle of Clontarf*, 89.

4 Ryan, 'Battle of Clontarf', 2–5; Ní Mhaonaigh, *Brian Boru*, 53–99; Clare Downham, 'The battle of Clontarf in Irish history and legend', *History Ireland* **13** (5) (2005), 21–3.

5 Ní Mhaonaigh, *Brian Boru*, 12, 15, 30, 53, 127.

6 Ryan, 'The battle of Clontarf', 2–3; Ní Mhaonaigh, *Brian Boru*, 37–9, 54–9; McGettigan, *Battle of Clontarf*, 18–25.

7 *Annals of Innisfallen* [hereafter *AI*], *s.a.* 1014; *Annals of Ulster* [hereafter *AU*], *s.a.* 1014; *Chronicon Scotorum* [hereafter *CS*], *s.a.* 1014; *Annals of Loch Cé* [hereafter *ALC*], *s.a.* 1014; Ní Mhaonaigh, *Brian Boru*, 54–7; Ryan, 'The battle of Clontarf', 16–17, 25–8; McGettigan, *Battle of Clontarf*, 80–2, 98.

8 Ní Mhaonaigh, *Brian Boru*, 57–65; *ALC, s.a.* 1014.

9 This work was published in a scholarly edition in 1867 by James H. Todd (see note 1, above); Ní Mhaonaigh, *Brian Boru*, 45–6, 66–79.

10 *CGG*, 138–41.

11 *Ibid.*, 153, 159, 161, 195, for example; for Sulcóit and Glenn Máma, *ibid.*, 77–81, 109–13.

12 *Ibid.*, 133–9.

13 *Ibid.*, 142–7, 191–3; Seán Duffy, 'Brian Bóruma [Brian Boru] (*c.* 941–1014)', in H.C.G. Matthew and B.H. Harrison (eds), *Oxford Dictionary of National Biography* (61 vols, Oxford, 2004) [www.oxforddnb.com, accessed 6 November 2010].

14 *CGG*, 159–97.

15 *Ibid.*, 135, 153, 197–203, 211.

16 Ní Mhaonaigh, *Brian Boru*, 30; *CGG*, 205.

17 *CGG*, 159, 171–5, 183–5, 201.

18 See A.J. Goedheer, *Irish and Norse traditions about the battle of Clontarf* (Haarlem, 1938); Ní Mhaonaigh, *Brian Boru*, 79–97.

19 *The story of Burnt Njal (Njal's Saga)*: The Online Medieval and Classical Library, no. 11, produced, edited and prepared by Douglas B. Killings, part 11, sections 153–5 [http://omacl.org/Njal/, accessed 8 February 2011].

20 *Ibid.*, part 11, sections 155–6.

21 *Ibid.*, section 156.

22 *Ibid.*

CHAPTER TWO

'That field of glory':
how Clontarf became famous

I N HIS MEMOIR of literary Dublin in the 1940s and 1950s, John Ryan recalled in
dialogue form his attempt to present a visiting poet from Denmark to Patrick
Kavanagh:

> 'Me: May I introduce Ole Sarvig, the distinguished ...
> P.K.: Whaaa?
> Ole: I am being Ole Sarvig, Danish poet and ...
> P.K.: You dirty —!
> Ole: (much distressed) Why for you call me such a horrible thing?
> P.K.: You killed our last Árd Rí!'[1]

Although the Dane was being blamed erroneously for his ancestors' slaying of
the last high-king of Ireland (who was, in reality, Ruaidhrí Ua Conchobair), the
Irish poet's heart was in the right place. Kavanagh was remembering the story of
the death of Brian Boru (who aspired to be high-king of Ireland) at the battle of
Clontarf in 1014 and taking offence on behalf of the Irish nation. One of the most
vivid images from Irish history as taught in school, after all, was that of the aged
King Brian kneeling in prayer in his tent at the end of the day of the battle, and
being rushed at and beheaded by Brodar the Viking. Although Brodar himself
was promptly killed and the army of Brian was believed to have prevailed over the
Viking enemy, in popular perception the death of the Christian warrior-king has
tended to overshadow the events of the battle.

Based on the literary foundations of *Cogadh Gáedhel re Gallaibh* and the
Scandinavian sagas, writers and artists have constructed the legend of Brian
Boru and the battle of Clontarf in a whole series of histories, epic poems, dramas,
novels and paintings down to the present. From the late Middle Ages onwards,
the iconic status of Brian has been moulded by different generations and
communities to suit the political and cultural needs of their times. While Gaelic

scholars promoted the image of Brian as the scourge of invaders for their political patrons, commentators among the more recently arrived Anglo-Normans tended to see the battle in 1014 as a victory for the modernising influences of newcomers, i.e. the Vikings. After the Reformation, when political and religious identities became more sharply divided, Catholic writers perceived Brian Boru as a model of Counter-Reformation sainthood and an ideal of kingship, whether based on the assent of the conquered or the election of the estates. Through the medium of antiquarian and romantic tales in the eighteenth century, the version of Brian Boru in popular consciousness fitted well into the nationalism of Daniel O'Connell and the Young Ireland movement by the 1840s. By the time of his apotheosis in the artistic and historical works of patriotic writers and artists, culminating in the Irish literary renaissance, Brian was eminently suited to the role of symbol of an independent Ireland. Meanwhile, a more scientific approach to the literary, topographical and archaeological evidence from the late nineteenth century onwards has engendered scholarly revision of the history of the battle. While the outcome may be a more balanced treatment of Clontarf in all of its aspects in contemporary historiography, the resonances in the popular histories have been somewhat muted and Brian's popularity remains undiminished to this day.

The uses of the history of Brian and Clontarf

For his Gaelic descendants, the self-styled Uí Briain, the desire to emulate a great ancestor was reflected, as we have seen, in the construction of an idealised biography, *Cogadh Gáedhel re Gallaibh*, and in the veneration of artefacts associated with him, such as his sword and his drinking-horn. The power of the Uí Briain declined, both nationally and regionally, because of the rise of rival dynasties, most notably the rulers of Connacht, the Uí Conchobair (O'Connors), but also because of the irruption of the Normans into north Munster. In the work of the bardic poets of the family, there was expressed the need for a saviour, 'the like of Brian' (*samhail Briain*), who would repel the invaders and restore Uí Briain pride. It is significant that in this poetry the Normans were dubbed *gaill* (foreigners), as the Vikings had been, allowing for a continuation in the general Gaelic literature of the concept of contention between native and invader. In that context, the deeds of Brian Boru, and especially his perceived victory over the *gaill* at Clontarf, remained extremely relevant as a galvanising force down to the sixteenth century.[2]

By contrast, writers from a Norman or English background tended to downplay the significance of Brian's achievements and instead to enhance those of the Vikings. Perhaps a clue to this approach may be found in the nomenclature used of the Scandinavians by some of these commentators in the Tudor period, such as Edmund Campion, Raphael Holinshed and Meredith Hanmer. They conflated the terms 'Danes', 'Norway-men', 'Ostmanni' and 'Easterlings' under the name 'Normans', thus creating a perception of a continuum with the newcomers who arrived in England in 1066 and in Ireland from 1169. Coupled with this homogenising designation was the evidence adduced from the work of Giraldus Cambrenisis, the great chronicler of the Norman conquest of Ireland, of the benign influence of the Vikings (or 'Ostmen') in civilising the Irish through the construction of towns and the fostering of trade. In the first part of the history of Ireland in Holinshed's *Chronicles* (1577) the battle of Clontarf is mentioned in passing and then as a *lieu de mémoire* of Scandinavian military and commercial power ('onely a memory is left of their field in Clantarfe'), their victory being implied in the continuation: 'where diverse noble Irish men were slayne, that lye buryed before the Crosse of Kilmaynam'. The section of the *Chronicles* composed by the Dublin historian Richard Stanihurst gives more detail, making reference to the Ostmanni of Ostmantowne (later Oxmantown) who 'discomfited at Clontarfe in a skyrmishe divers of the Irishe'. He goes on to name the notable Irish who died there as 'Bryanne Borrough, Niagh [Miagh or Murchad] mack Bryen, Tady O Kelly, Dolyne Ahertegan [and] Gylle Barramede' and avers that they were interred at Kilmainham, 'over against the great crosse'.[3]

In a chronicle produced in the Pale region around Dublin in the 1560s and 1570s, dubbed the 'Book of Howth', the compiler, who was Irish-born of English stock, presents a very different version of the causes and outcome of the battle of Clontarf to those found in the Gaelic and Viking sources. According to this writer, the *casus belli* was the offence caused to one known as the white merchant of Dublin, the fourth son of the king of Denmark, who had consigned his beautiful Irish wife to the care of King Brian Boru while he ventured abroad to trade. During his absence, Murchad, Brian's son, began an affair with her, which was discovered when the merchant returned to his house in Dublin to find the pair in bed together. Vowing vengeance within a year, he collected a strong force of Danes to confront the army of Murchad and Brian in battle at Clontarf. In the ensuing fray, the Danes were initially forced to retreat but regrouped and eventually won the day. In giving reasons for Brian's defeat, the compiler of this account reveals a topographical awareness of the battle site. The Irish king was at fault firstly in rushing into battle before the arrival of 7,000 reinforcements led by his son, Donnchad; secondly, he deployed his army unwisely, placing his strongest unit, the cavalry, on the wing next to the shore, the surface of which was too soft for the horses to gain a firm footing; and thirdly, the Danes and 'Normans' were superior in their strategy and weaponry, using battles of footmen, spearmen, archers and slingers. Aside from knowledge of the shoreline of the bay, the 'Book of Howth' compiler conveys a fairly credible picture of the landscape, references being made to a great wood to the north of a 'stynging' or stinking stream, the scene of much of the action. Besides 'the field and his life', the king lost 11,000 men and his son, according to this narrative.[4]

In this Anglo-Norman and English version of the events of 1014, the defeat of the Irish by newer arrivals, who were deliberately called 'Normans', was clearly established. The famous Irish king Brian Boru is either not mentioned or presented as a defeated leader, while the Scandinavians come across as superior in military tactics and equipment. The broader context for the battle is the reforming influence brought to bear upon the indigenous community by the newcomers from Denmark and Norway, who planted their civic and commercial institutions among the Irish for their betterment. Far from being pagans, moreover, these settlers were seen as patrons of church-building, while the Irish receive little credit for the practice of Christianity. There are, in this revised narrative, resonances for the reforming milieu of the later sixteenth century in Ireland, when these accounts were produced. The descendants of the later Norman settlers in Ireland, among whom the 'Book of Howth' was produced, were very conscious of their role as bringers of civility to the Gaelic inhabitants through the diffusion of English mores and culture throughout the island. For the newly arrived English in Elizabethan Ireland, such as Campion and Hanmer, a colonial approach to the reform, if not the conquest, of Ireland was premised on the presentation of the Irish as inferior to other civilisations but susceptible in lesser or greater measure to the reforming influences of newcomers.[5]

A strong counterblast to such a perception marked the work of Geoffrey Keating, a Gaelic scholar of Norman background in Munster in the seventeenth century, whose *Foras feasa ar Éirinn* came to exert great influence on modern Irish literature and learning. Taking issue directly with the Anglophile Elizabethan writers, including Campion, Stanihurst and Hanmer, Keating set out to show in his history of Ireland the vibrancy of Gaelic civilisation as the driving force of a modern Irish Catholic nation. Using the career of Brian Boru, among other aspects of Ireland's past, and leaning heavily on the account in *Cogadh Gáedhel re Gallaibh*, Keating provided a suggestive template for the triumph of an indigenous ruler over foreigners, while establishing an era of Christian peace and justice. Brian was, for him, a model of ideal kingship that rested on the notion of the consent of the political élite, elicited because of his valour and powerful actions rather than by any hereditary right. The righteous assertion of sovereignty by a worthy monarch fostered an era of legality and justice, those who had been unjustly dispossessed of land by the Vikings (or 'Lochlannaigh') being restored to their proprietorship. Patronage of the church and learning was also a central feature of Brian's reign. The evidence of Catholic reform within a framework of legitimate monarchy in Ireland had deep resonances for the era of the Counter-Reformation in which Keating wrote. At the time, a member of the Scottish Stuart dynasty, rather than an Irish-born prince, ruled as king of Ireland, and Keating, among other Irish commentators, was prepared to give his loyalty to him. Indeed, Keating interwove the pedigree of the Stuart kings with that of Brian Boru, in a common descent from the race of Éibhear.[6]

Keating's treatment of the battle of Clontarf is relatively brief, the role of Gormlaith as *agent provocateur* being emphasised, but, apart from the listing of all of the participants on the side of Brian, the details of the fighting are scant enough. The death of Brian at the hands of Brodar is noted, as is the total of 13,800 casualties on the side of the Vikings and Leinstermen. As a coda, Keating adverted to the role of Máel Sechnaill, king of Meath, as spectator in order to underline the seriousness of his reneging on Brian's army in the field. Máel Sechnaill gives a dramatic but self-serving account as an eyewitness of the battle, unable to participate as the weapons of his soldiers were tangled up in the wisps of hair from dead warriors' heads and beards blown from the battlefield. His treachery is shown to be of a piece with the behaviour of one who, as high-king, had given himself up to 'luxury and comfort and ease', while Brian had undertaken the 'labour and hardship of expelling the Lochlannaigh'.[7]

For eighteenth-century Catholic historians who published works in English, Keating's *Foras feasa* (which itself appeared in print in 1723) proved to be extremely evocative. Writers such as Hugh McCurtin, James MacGeoghegan, Sylvester O'Halloran and Charles O'Conor were inspired by the example of Brian Boru's triumph over the Vikings at Clontarf in their own aspirations to political and religious liberties.[8] They conceived of his kingship of Ireland in terms of the contemporary discourse of elective monarchy, validated by the consent of the estates of the realm.[9] As scourge of the inhuman and pagan Danes, Brian fitted very well the profile of deliverer of his country from bondage and injustice. In particular, his restorative and just reign could be seen to contrast with the oppressiveness of the Penal Law regime, which deprived Roman Catholics of their landowning and civil rights. In this respect, the most vivid symbolism of dedicated secular and religious leadership is to be found in O'Halloran's *History of Ireland* in the portrayal of Brian before the battle of Clontarf, riding up and down between

Geoffrey Keating on Máel Sechnaill observing the battle

The following is the account of the Battle of Cluain Tarbh which Maolseachlainn son of Domhnall, king of Meath, gave a month after the battle was fought; for the clan Cholmain were asking him for tidings of the battle. Thereupon Maolseachlainn said that he had never seen such a battle or an approach to it. "For," said he, "if God's angel from heaven were to give you an account of it his account would seem incredible. Now I and my host were looking at them at the distance only of a fallow field and fences. But when these battalions had faced one another and stood breast to breast, they set to flail and to lash one another; and like unto a heavy flock of white sea-gulls over the coast, when the tide is coming up into the land, were the white showers of shields above their heads; and if we wished to go to the assistance of either side it was not in our power to do so, for our lances and our arms were bound and fastened above our heads by the firm closely set wisps of hair which the wind blew to us from the heads and beards of the warriors as they were being hacked and cut down by the edge of the swords and strong weapons on every side, so that we found it difficult to keep the handles of our weapons from getting entangled in one another. And we thought that those who were in the fight did not suffer more than we did who had to look on without running wild and mad."

Observe, O reader, that though it was as part of the host of Brian that Maoilseachlainn and the men of Meath came to the field of battle, still through a plot between himself and the Lochlonnaigh, he did not come into the battle array amongst Brian's host, but what he did was to remain with his host beside the battle, as the Lochlonnaigh had directed him.

Geoffrey Keating, *Foras feasa ar Éirinn*, ed. D. Comyn and P.S. Dineen

(4 vols, London, 1902–14), iii, pp 285–7

the massed ranks, brandishing a crucifix in one hand and a sword in the other, and exhorting his men to fight for 'their religion and their country'.[10] His holy death crystallised the appeal of this saintly king for eighteenth-century Catholics. [2.1]

Contemporary literary and antiquarian works by both Protestants and Catholics in English and Irish paralleled and intertwined this expressive pen-portraiture of Brian by eighteenth-century Catholic historians. One important movement was that of Gaelic scribes of a mostly Munster background (and

Brian as a crusading king in O'Halloran's history

Brian rode through the ranks with a crucifix in one hand, and his drawn sword in the other. He exhorted them as he passed along, "to do their duty as soldiers and Christians, in the cause of their religion and their country. He reminded them of all the distresses their ancestors were reduced to, by the perfidious and sanguinary Danes, strangers to religion and humanity! That *these* their successors waited impatiently to renew the same scenes of devastation and cruelty, and, by way of anticipation, (says he), they have fixed on the very day on which Christ was crucified, to destroy the country of his greatest votaries; but that God, whose cause you are to fight this day, will be present with you, and deliver his enemies into your hands." So saying, he proceeded towards the centre to lead on his troops to action; but the chiefs of the army with one voice requested he would retire from the field of battle, on account of his great age, and leave the gallant Morrogh the chief command.

Sylvester O'Halloran, *A general history of Ireland* (1778), pp 262–3

Fig. 2.1—P. O'Byrne, 'Brian Boru, king of Ireland (941–1014)', 1910 (courtesy of the National Library of Ireland).

hence sympathetic to the O'Briens of Thomond) who produced, among other works, a prose tale entitled *Cath Cluana Tarbh*, thus privileging the place-name in a title for the first time.[11] That the tale was extremely popular is attested to by its survival in over 80 manuscript copies from the eighteenth and nineteenth centuries. *Cath Cluana Tarbh* drew heavily upon *Cogadh Gáedhel re Gallaibh* and *Foras feasa ar Éirinn*. Its various versions contained most of the established elements of the narrative that had evolved since the Middle Ages, including, for example, Gormlaith's role as instigator of the battle, Máel Sechnaill's treachery and the supernatural experiences of the participants. This account is very close to those in other eighteenth-century compilations, such as the 'Dublin' Annals of Innisfallen and the *Leabhar Oiris*. The 'Dublin' Annals of Innisfallen were written under the patronage of John O'Brien, bishop of Cloyne and Ross from 1748 to 1769, whose antiquarian studies had piqued his pride in his Munster ancestry.[12] While the battle of Clontarf was thus being romanticised in story or being presented as 'real and true' history,[13] the pursuit of genealogy, archaeology and textual study by mutually supportive scholars from Gaelic and Anglophone backgrounds was eventually to make feasible a more scientific analysis of the sources for the battle in 1014. Emblematic of this trend was the eventual publication of *Cogadh Gáedhel re Gallaibh* in 1867 by the Irish Archaeological Society under the editorship of James H. Todd, a Church of Ireland clergyman.[14]

The burial of Brian in Armagh from *Cath Cluana Tarbh*

The community of Swords came the following day and carried the bodies of Brian and Murchadh, and from there to Duleek and from there to Louth, and Maol Muire son of Eocha, primate of Armagh, came with his clergymen to Louth to get those bodies and they carried them to Armagh. The clergymen spent twelve nights' vigil over those bodies with hymns, psalms and canticles, and Brian son of Cinnéide, i.e High King of Ireland and Octavian Augustus of the Gaels, was buried after reigning for thirty-seven years as King of Munster and twelve years as King of Ireland, and he was buried in a separate shrine on the northern side of the church of Armagh, and the body of Murchadh son of Brian and the head of Connaing son of Donn Cuan and the head of Mothla son of Faolán in another shrine on the southern side of the church.

Cath Cluana Tarbh, ed. Méidhbhinn Ní Úrdáil (London, 2011), p. 125

A medieval 'Liberator'

It was mainly through the medium of literary works and educational texts that popular consciousness of Clontarf was awakened in the century before Daniel O'Connell selected the location for his climactic monster meeting in 1843. In 1715 there had been published Sarah Butler's novel *Irish tales*, which interwove the story of the events leading to Brian Boru's 'most bloody and terrible' fight in 1014 with the love story of Dooneflaith, the daughter of Máel Sechnaill, and Murchad, son of Brian. Based on Keating's then manuscript account in *Foras feasa ar Éirinn*, the novel reads on one level as a romantic love story against a violent backdrop but on another as a model for the successful expulsion of repressive invaders, from the perspective of an author who supported the cause of the exiled Stuart monarchy.[15] Another literary perspective on the battle occurred in Thomas Gray's poem 'The fatal sisters', which is the English poet's version in sixteen stanzas of the *Darraðorljóð* (or 'Daurrud's song'), published in 1769. Referring to an unnamed Irish battle as the occasion for this incantation of the Valkyries in distant Caithness, Gray was anxious to reproduce therein a Nordic style of poetic expression, as later recognised by Sir Walter Scott.[16]

While the landscape of the battle may have been anonymous in Gray's poem, the linking of momentous events to a specific place may be seen quite clearly in the literary, artistic and poetic descriptions of Clontarf from the turn of the eighteenth century. Drawn by the beauty of the locale and its growing popularity as a seaside resort close to Dublin, a series of visitors commented on Clontarf as part of their Irish travel writings. Most merely accepted the fact that the district was where the battle was fought and then proceeded to give longer or shorter summaries of the mythologised events from their distinctive perspectives. For example, Richard Lewis, in *The Dublin guide* of 1787, wrote that Clontarf, a very large and pleasant village, was where the last battle was fought between the Irish and the Danes, and concluded by proclaiming that the great Brian Boru gloriously fell, like an immortal Gustavus Adolphus or the intrepid General Wolfe, at the moment of supreme success. Similarly, Charles Topham Bowden, in *A tour through Ireland* of 1791, visited Clontarf, 'so memorable for the defeat and consequent expulsion of the Danes'. He affirmed that 'in that important battle, the great Brian Boru received his death wound', adding the antiquarian information that 'the grave of this warrior was lately discovered in a burying ground west of the city'.[17] Landscape painters chose Clontarf as a subject for their works, using the castle (in the case of the paintings by Thomas Snagg and J.M.W. Turner in 1805

Brian Boru in the classroom

Which of the Irish Monarchs chiefly signalized himself against [The Danes]?

Brien Boirumhe or Boru who from being King of North Munster was advanced to the monarchy on account of his extraordinary qualities and princely endowments.

In what memorable battle were the Danes finally subdued?

In the battle of Clontarf fought on Good Friday 1014. Brien then in his eighty-eighth year would have led on his troops to conquest had not the entreaties of his friends prevailed on him to retire to his tent.

What became of the gallant chieftain?

A party of the Danes having entered his tent, the aged Monarch slew three of them but received his death from a fourth.

What was Brien's character?

He adorned the throne by every princely Virtue, cultivated the Arts and Sciences, was a celebrated Hero Scholar and Statesman and, what is still more estimable, he was a good Christian.

A sketch of Irish history compiled by way of question and answer
for the use of schools (1815), p. 10

and 1817 respectively), the Charter School (in the painting by William Ashford in 1794) and the Sheds of Clontarf (in John Laporte's work of 1796) as foregrounds for their scenes.

In 1822 William Hamilton Drummond, the poet and librarian of the Royal Irish Academy, published his two-part poem *Clontarf*. In the preface he reflected on the role of 'loco-descriptive poetry', declaring that beauty of scene was not enough for the reader's delectation but that the actions of human beings stamp true importance on every celebrated region. These he proceeded to show in the second part of the poem, which is a stirring rendition of the fighting, encapsulating many of the motifs already identified in previous literature, Brian exhorting his warriors to strive 'for God and Erin'. Drummond also included his version of the lament of the 'sisterhood' or Valkyries who wove their fabric with human entrails. In a 'historic retrospect', the poet revealed his disdain for those of both Norman and Gaelic origin who sold the country's freedom in succeeding centuries, and he ends by invoking the names of Grattan and Wellesley, the duke of Wellington, as representing the best hope for his country's reform. The first part of the poem, by contrast, contains a fine pastoral evocation of the beauty and topography of the district from personal reconnaissance. The author's preface on Clontarf is based on antiquarian and historical research, drawn from Charles Vallancey's *Collectanea*, the annals of Tighernach and Innisfallen and the *Chronicon Scotorum*. Also cited were Edward Ledwich and other antiquarians, who speculated that the vortex of the battle was not in fact in Clontarf but either in Finglas, at the hill of Knockbrise, or in the vicinity of Rutland (later Parnell) Square, where a 'vast human debris' of bones as well as weapons had been discovered. Drummond attests, however, to the local tradition among the inhabitants of Clontarf that the battle had been fought in the vicinity of the Sheds of Clontarf, and he mentions the finding near Clontarf by Thomas Cornwall shortly after 1690 of Brian Boru's sceptre, upon which Dean Richardson discovered characters associated with the king.[18] A contemporary equivalent of Drummond's poetical description in the genre of historical painting

Fig. 2.2—Hugh Frazer, 'The battle of Clontarf', 1826
(courtesy of Isaacs Art Centre, Hawaii).

is the work by Hugh Frazer, 'The battle of Clontarf', completed in 1826, which conveys a sense of topographical verisimilitude. Behind the left foreground, in which Brian is shown in his tent, raising his arm as if in blessing of his troops, there appears a promontory, similar to the Howth peninsula. [2.2]

A very different kind of patriotic sentiment to that of Drummond impelled the movement headed by Daniel O'Connell and Young Ireland, which set the history of Brian Boru and the battle of Clontarf in the context of an Irish struggle for liberation from foreign enslavement. As a prelude to the meeting to be held at Clontarf in 1843 in the campaign for the repeal of the Union, newspapers, including *The Nation*, the journal of Young Ireland, engaged in raising public awareness of the significance of the battle through a series of articles and poems. The focus of the planned event was Conquer Hill, a slight eminence or sandbank in the extensive fields to the east of the district, between Clontarf Sheds and Dollymount, which was depicted for the first time on the Ordnance Survey map of 1843.[19]

Despite the failure of the proposed assembly to go ahead, the place of the battle in the history of Irish nationalism was assured. About this time Thomas Davis advocated among Irish artists, as part of an agenda of national regeneration, a

THE BATTLE OF CLONTARF, APRIL 23rd, 1014.

Fig. 2.3 — W.H. Holbrooke, 'The battle of Clontarf, 23 April 1014', dedicated to William Smith O'Brien, MP, before 1848 (courtesy of the National Library of Ireland).

programme of historical paintings of key events, including Brian reconnoitring the Danes before the battle of Clontarf and the last of the Danes escaping to his ship. About 1845 there appeared in *The pictorial history of Ireland* by W.H. Holbrooke a large historical illustration depicting the battle of Clontarf.[20] [2.3] In 1843, the year of the cancellation of the monster meeting, John Augustus Shea published in New York a long narrative poem, *Clontarf, or the field of the green banner*, in which Brian Boru, monarch of the isle of saints, appears as an exemplar for the overthrow of 'vassalage to a foreign throne' in the name of 'our country's right'. Moreover, America, the poet's adopted land, is called upon to assist the cause of Irish freedom in the present.[21]

The name 'Clontarf' was developing a mystique so powerful that it was appropriated by patriotic Irish people at home and throughout the diaspora in the nineteenth century. At least two townships named Clontarf were established in both North America and Australia: a village in eastern Ontario in Canada, a town in Minnesota in the United States, and two coastal suburban enclaves near

---

An Irish exile, inspired by the victory at Clontarf, appeals for American aid for the struggle for freedom

And shall the Island of their birth,
   'Gainst slavery leagued, a slave remain,
Or, " 'mid the nations of the earth,"
   Uprising from the oppressor's chain,
Resume her place? It is with thee
   To say how long these things shall be.
Yes! Yes! to thee, and to thy race,
   America! I urge my plea;
Thy land is Freedom's dwelling place,
   And such may it for ever be:
She tells her tale of woes to thee;
To whom can she look up for aid,
   If not the victorious free,
Whom Freedom her vice-gerents made?

John Augustus Shea, *Clontarf; or the field of the green banner: an historical romance* (New York, 1843), pp 126–7

---

the Australian cities of Brisbane in Queensland and Sydney in New South Wales. It was in the suburban village of Clontarf, near Sydney, as we have seen, that an assassination attempt was made on Prince Alfred, Queen Victoria's eldest son, in March 1868. [2.4] The building of the town of Clontarf, Minnesota, on the edge of the prairie was overseen by Bishop John Ireland, whose family had fled the Great Famine in 1849. The symbolism for this pioneering figure of Catholicism in the American mid-west was no doubt potent: the victor in the battle of 1014 was hailed as a Christian emperor who had overcome the forces of paganism.

A confluence of scholarly streams in the second half of the nineteenth century gradually made possible a more scientific treatment of the study of the battle, including the location of the hostilities. The work of the Celtic and Archaeological societies, both as separate associations and then conjoined after 1854, aimed to highlight the cultural and political achievements in Ireland's Early Christian and medieval past. Owing to the efforts of the scholars engaged on the Ordnance Survey, a detailed study of local geography and place-names was embarked upon. All of these strands were interwoven in the work of James H. Todd, a Church of Ireland clergyman, who edited for publication one of the most influential medieval sources for the battle of Clontarf, *Cogadh Gáedhel re Gallaibh*.

Fig. 2.4 — The attempted assassination of Prince Alfred at Clontarf, New South Wales, 1868 (Illustrated Australian News, State Library of Victoria).

Todd had an impressive record of publication in the ecclesiastical field prior to his steering of the *Cogadh* into print under the auspices of the Master of the Rolls in 1867. He drew upon a wide range of annals, genealogies and secondary sources, among which those by George Petrie, John O'Donovan, Eugene O'Curry, William Reeves and Charles Haliday were expressly acknowledged.[22]

As part of his research for his edition of *Cogadh Gáedhel re Gallaibh*, Todd enlisted the scholarly assistance of Dr Samuel Haughton, professor of geology in Trinity College, Dublin. He asked Haughton to calculate the time of the high tides in Dublin Bay on 23 April 1014, the putative date of the battle. Using formulae which he had adopted in a series of other studies on tidal patterns, Haughton was able to confirm that high water occurred on the northern shoreline at 5.30am and 5.55pm on Good Friday 1014, without being prompted about the details in the medieval writer's account. The findings were published in the *Proceedings of the Royal Irish Academy* in 1861, along with Todd's own response to them. In the editor's view, the expert confirmation vindicated the use of *Cogadh Gáedhel re Gallaibh* as a reliable source, asserting as it did that the battle began at sunrise (calculated also at 5.30am) as the tide flowed, and ended with the rout of the defeated Danes and their attempted flight at the return of high water which carried their ships out to sea. Todd in his article (which contains a concise history of the causes of the battle, drawn from the Irish source as well as the Scandinavian saga of Burnt Njal) also squares the information about the wind direction and the location of the Irish army at Dubhgall's Bridge with the detail of Viking non-participants watching the battle from the citadel of Dublin.[23]

It was that latter episode of the dramatic witnessing of the fighting from the battlements of Dublin upon which the central thesis of an article by Thomas O'Gorman on the site of the battle of Clontarf was premised. Published in 1879 in the *Journal of the Royal Historical and Archaeological Society of Ireland*, O'Gorman's was the first dedicated study of the site of the battle. Based very firmly on Todd's edition of *Cogadh Gáedhel re Gallaibh*, and also adducing the narrative in *Njal's Saga*, O'Gorman's analysis rejected the tradition of the main fighting having occurred to the east of the Tolka, in the area between Marino Crescent and Conquer Hill. He was persuaded not only by the fighting being visible from Dublin but also by the more contemporary appellations of the battle as 'Brian's battle' or 'the battle of the fishing weir of Clontarf' (supposedly the site of present-day Ballybough bridge). The author posited the theory, based mostly on *Cogadh Gáedhel re Gallaibh*, that the latter feature was where the wings on the east of the battle line were drawn up, the central parts being in the area of Mountjoy Square, and fighting on the westerly flank taking place around Oxmantown and the Liffey bridge. Adducing the toponymic evidence from the *Cogadh* of Dubhgall's Bridge, Tomar's Wood and the fishing weir, O'Gorman lines up the forces in the district between Dublin and the Tolka, with the eastern and central sections of the battleground being visible from the city. As supplemental evidence for such a scenario, the author refers to Edward Ledwich's article in the *Dublin Magazine* of 1763 attesting to the discovery of vast quantities of human bones during the laying out of the Rotunda Gardens in Rutland Square, and archaeological finds of weaponry detailed by J.C. Walker in his work *Historical memoirs of the Irish bards* of 1788. He did concede to local tradition, however, in envisioning a running fight at the conclusion of the battle that might have taken in areas of Clontarf as well the shoreline towards Howth, and he was definitely convinced by Samuel Haughton's scientific research into the tides in Dublin Bay.[24]

Thus, just as the patriotic overtones of the name of Clontarf were being universally recognised and it was becoming established as a national shrine, historical and antiquarian research seemed to break the connection between the battle and the district. This came at a time when Clontarf was embracing its identity, first as a seaside suburb and then as a township. Rapid development at

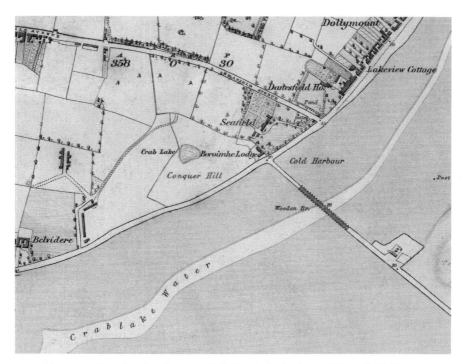

Fig. 2.5—Map showing Conquer Hill, Boroimhe Lodge and Danesfield House, Dollymount (Ordnance Survey map, 1837–43).

the shoreline at Dollymount with the construction of the Bull Wall and to the west of the district with the building of the railway embankment gave rise to archaeological finds, including coins, axes and swords. Opposite the Bull Wall had been erected two mansions called Boroimhe Lodge and Kinkora in the 1830s. [2.5] The presence of at least two sepulchral tumuli, of probable Bronze Age origin, in the neighbourhood, as noted by O'Gorman in his article, tended towards a confounding of chronological divisions, especially when joined with speculation about the Scandinavian provenance of the unearthed treasures. O'Gorman also noted, in a similarly sceptical vein, the designation of a drinking fountain on Castle Avenue as Brian Boru's Well, over which a decorative metal plaque had been erected by public subscription in 1850. Local pride was fuelled by excursions such as those of the Irish Historical and Antiquarian Society in 1886 and 1895, led by Mr Petrie Byrne, to the sites associated by tradition with the battle.[25] [2.6]

Speculation as to the place of burial of those who fell in the battle, about which there were many legends, came to centre on Clontarf, as the locale embraced the link with the battle site more closely. Variously thought to be sited in Kilmainham, modern Parnell Square and Glasnevin,[26] the main graveyard of the dead of Clontarf was putatively transposed to the Conquer Hill area in the early

Fig. 2.6—Decorative metal plaque erected by public subscription over Brian Boru's Well, Castle Avenue, 1850.

twentieth century. In 1907 controversy flared in Clontarf when an employment scheme was proposed by Dublin Corporation for the levelling of the tumulus called Conquer Hill for development. Close by, Brian Boru Street and Brian Boru Avenue had recently been built. A meeting of protesters in Clontarf Town Hall succeeded in getting the lord mayor to call off the work, as it was claimed that many of those who fell in the battle of Clontarf were buried underneath this mound. Antiquarians and local historians, including Weston St John Joyce, joined in the controversy, which resulted in a formal inspection by the city engineer and a veterinary surgeon. It was found that the hill contained animal bones of not more than 100 years' antiquity, and was composed of stratified levels of material heaped up from the cleaning of drains. Undeterred, a body called the Clontarf Improvements Association approached Dublin Corporation in 1910 for permission to lay out a monument in the district in the form of a drinking fountain, surmounted by a Celtic cross, and statues of Brian, Máel Sechnaill, Sitric and Sigurd, with an inscription in Latin, Danish, English and Irish. Although funding of up to £700 was collected for the project, the proposed memorial for the ninth centenary of the battle was not erected.[27]

In May 1914 a national committee, comprising mostly civic representatives, planned a military display, a pageant and other cultural events to commemorate the 900th anniversary. Sensitive to the contemporary debate about Home Rule, the planners of the celebrations envisaged them as being inclusive of unionists and nationalists, and as transcending religion and politics. The nearest approach to a 'state of the art' synopsis of Clontarf studies in 1914 was Thomas J. Westropp's series 'The hero of Clontarf' in *The Irish Monthly*, which, while adding to the glorification of Brian Boru, would have offended local sensitivities with its reference to the 'carman's tale' of Brian Boru's Well and the 'so-called' battle of Clontarf.[28]

Meanwhile, the popular veneration of Brian Boru as hero continued. The artist James Ward included a panel depicting Brian Boru addressing his troops before the battle of Clontarf in his series of frescoes executed to adorn the cupola of the City Hall, Dublin, unveiled in 1919. This decorative enterprise at the seat of civic government celebrated episodes in Irish Christian history and the struggle for national independence, many of them Dublin-related. [2.7] In 1920 Revd J.B. Dollard composed a patriotic play in four acts, *Clontarf: an Irish national drama*, which, while acknowledging the bravery of the Vikings, celebrated Ireland's status as a 'proud, inviolate nation'. In the decades after the establishment of the Irish Free State, Brian Boru remained a potent symbol of Irish independence and Clontarf was seen as the climax of a successful struggle for the deliverance of the country from the thrall of the invaders. There was

Fig. 2.7—James Ward, 'Brian Boru and the battle of Clontarf': mural at City Hall, Dublin, 1919 (© Dublin City Council, courtesy of Dublin City Library and Archive).

continued in the textbooks used in the classrooms the heroic tale of Brian and his battle as narrated in the nineteenth century, for example in Rebecca Helena Hime's poem *Brian Boru and the battle of Clontarf*, published in 1889, with the purpose of commemorating 'the deeds of the great Brian, such that boys and girls might care to read'. Schoolbook accounts in the decades after 1922 presented the Irish king as a national hero, while the treatment of the Scandinavians was, in the main, derogatory. [29]

As an antidote to the 'legendising', there emerged in 1938 two important scholarly studies of the battle and its sources. In that year John Ryan's article entitled 'The battle of Clontarf' was published in the journal of the Royal Society of Antiquaries of Ireland. Based on a thorough analysis of all the relevant Irish annals, chronicles and literary tales, as well as the saga of Burnt Njal, Ryan's study contained as balanced and solid an account of the battle, its participants, its causes and main protagonists as the contemporary state of Irish historical studies would allow. Among his conclusions is the 'revolutionary' one (as he lightly calls it) that the battle of Clontarf was fought at Clontarf. Unfortunately, Ryan did not have access to a book published in the same year by A.J. Goedheer, entitled *Irish and Norse traditions about the battle of Clontarf*, though he did use the recent edition of *Njal's Saga* published in Dublin in 1933 under the title *Brian's battle*. Goedheer performed a valuable service in reviewing the Irish sources from an outsider's perspective. In tracing the genesis of the Scandinavian sagas, he contextualised *Njal's Saga* and effectively placed the story of Clontarf in its North

Sea context. Goedheer's work was an antidote to the insularity thitherto of the tradition of scholarship associated with the battle of Clontarf.[30]

From the 1960s onwards, a scholarly reappraisal of the pre-Norman period in Ireland has resulted in the emergence of a much more nuanced picture of Brian Boru, the Vikings and the place of the battle of Clontarf in medieval history. In the academic discourse, many of the legends have been jettisoned and an alternative version of the events is slowly being adumbrated. Among the aspects of the period that have been subjected to more rigorous analysis are the political situation in Ireland in the tenth and eleventh centuries, the literary and historical sources, the Scandinavian presence in Ireland, the role of Dublin as an economic and administrative centre, the military realities of eleventh-century battles, and the wider context of the north-western archipelago and maritime area for an appreciation of strategies of power.[31] Elements of this new synthesis coexist with the popular version of the story of Brian and Clontarf. This is evident in such cultural works, artefacts and events as Morgan Llywelyn's prize-winning novel *Lion of Ireland* (1981), a most entertaining read, the set of four Irish postage stamps issued in 2002 to commemorate Brian's attainment of the high-kingship, and the planning of a much-anticipated film, a new life of Brian, which excites speculation in the blogosphere as to a possible casting for the lead role of hero ...

Clontarf has become synonymous with national pride because of its association with the war of the most famous Irish king, Brian Boru. From the early modern period the place itself has been denominated in the titles of histories, novels, poems and dramas. Its centrality in the national mythology of resistance to foreign rule was firmly established with its choice as a site for a monster meeting in 1843, and the abandonment of that event did not diminish its symbolic importance. The reasons for Clontarf's becoming a vortex of battle in 1014 have to do with its close proximity to Dublin—as a seat of power, as a commercial hub, as a port with many Irish Sea connections—and this association continued to be vital in the history of the district from the twelfth century onwards, whether as a village and suburb or as a focus of national events.

---

1 John Ryan, *Remembering how we stood: bohemian Dublin at the mid-century* (Dublin, 1987), 104.

2 Ní Mhaonaigh, *Brian Boru*, 101–20 (references to the sword and drinking-cup at pp 108 and 118 respectively; the so-called 'Brian Boru's harp', now preserved in Trinity College, has a later medieval provenance). See also *idem*, 'Brian Bórama (Bóruma, Boru)' [www.dib.cambridge.org. jproxy.nuim.ie/, accessed 11 October 2012].

3 Giraldus Cambrensis, *Topographia Hibernica*, pp 186–8 in J.F. Mimock (ed.), *Giraldi Cambrensis opera*, vol. v (London, 1867); A.F. Vossen (ed.), *Two bokes of the histories of Ireland compiled by Edmund Campion* (Assen, 1963), 82–4; Raphael Holinshed, *Chronicles of England, Scotland, and Ireland* (London, 1577), iii, 19–20; Richard Stanihurst, 'Description of Ireland', in L. Miller and E. Power (eds), *Holinshed's Irish Chronicle 1577* (Dublin, 1979), 47.

4 'The book of Howth', in J.S. Brewer and W. Bullen (eds), *Calendar of Carew Manuscripts* (6 vols, London, 1867–73), vol. v (1873), 24–6; see also Valerie McGowan-Doyle, *The book of Howth: Elizabethan conquest and the Old English* (Dublin, 2011).

5 For Hanmer on Clontarf see James Ware (ed.), *The historie of Ireland, collected by three learned authors, viz. Meredith Hanmer, Edmund Campion and Edmund Spenser* (Dublin, 1633), 182–5.

6 Geoffrey Keating, *Foras feasa ar Éirinn: the history of Ireland* [hereafter *FFÉ*], ed. David Comyn and P.S. Dineen (4 vols, London, 1902–14), iii, 245–65; for Keating see Bernadette Cunningham, *The world of Geoffrey Keating: history, myth and religion in seventeenth-century Ireland* (Dublin, 2000), 68, 126, 145.

7 *FFÉ*, iii, 273–7, 285–7.

8 For an overview of this period see Clare O'Halloran, 'The triumph of "virtuous liberty": representations of the Vikings and Brian Boru in eighteenth-century histories', *Eighteenth-century Ireland* **27** (2007), 151–63; the names of the main works on Irish history by these authors are Hugh McCurtin, *Brief discourse in vindication of the antiquity of Ireland* (1717), James MacGeoghegan, *History of Ireland* (1758–62), Sylvester O'Halloran, *General history of Ireland* (1778), and Charles O'Conor, *Dissertations on the history of Ireland* (1753; 2nd edn 1766).

9 See O'Halloran, *General history of Ireland*, iii, 291.

10 *Ibid.*, iii, 236–7.

11 Meidhbhín Ní Úrdail (ed.), *Cath Cluana Tarbh: 'The battle of Clontarf'* (Dublin, 2011).

12 Meidhbhín Ní Úrdail, '*Annala Inse Faithleann* an ochtú céad déag agus Cath Chluain Tarbh', *Eighteenth-century Ireland* **20** (2005), 104–19.

13 *Ibid.*, 107.

14 For the context see Damien Murray, *Romanticism, nationalism and Irish antiquarian societies, 1840–80* (Maynooth, 2000), 62–4; in 1832–3 a translation of 'Cath Cluana Tarbh' appeared in *The Dublin Penny Journal*, vol. 1, no. 7 (1832), edited by the antiquarian John O'Donovan (pp 133–6).

15 See Sarah Butler, *Irish tales* (ed. Ian Campbell Ross, Aileen Douglas and Anne Markey) (Dublin, 2010).

16 Thomas Gray, *The fatal sisters* (1769) [http://www.thomas.gray.org/, accessed 8 February 2011]; 'Norn—the language of Orkney', 1814: Orkneyjar: the heritage of the Orkney islands [http://www.orkneyjar.com/Orkney/norn_scott.htm, accessed 8 February 2011].

17 Richard Lewis, *The Dublin guide, or a description of the city of Dublin and the most remarkable places within fifteen miles* (Dublin, 1787), 109–10; Charles Topham Bowden, *A tour through Ireland* (Dublin, 1791), 80.

18 William Hamilton Drummond, *Clontarf, a poem* (Dublin, 1822), especially pp x–xiv.

19 See Elizabeth Parker, '"Ourselves alone": history, nationalism and *The Nation*, 1842–5', *Voces Novae: Chapman Historical Review* **2** (2) (2011) [www.journals.chapman.edu/ojs/index.php/VocesNovae/article/view/198/537, accessed 9 May 2013].

20 Cyril Barrett, 'Irish nationalism and art, 1800–1921', *Studies* **64** (1975), 397; Thomas Davis, 'Hints for Irish historical paintings', in T.W. Rolleston, *Thomas Davis: selections from his prose and poetry* (London, 1890) [www.gutenberg.org/files/21210-h/21210-h.htm, accessed 7 June 2012].

21 John Augustus Shea, *Clontarf, or the field of the green banner: a historical romance* (New York, 1843); P. Cudmore's poem, in *The battle of Clontarf and other poems* (New York, 1895), presented the events as 'a victory of Christianity and Ireland's independence over foreign invaders, paganism and barbarism'.

22 Murray, *Romanticism, nationalism and Irish antiquarian societies*, 35–7, 50, 62–4; CGG, cciv–v.

23 Haughton, 'On the time of high water in Dublin Bay', 495–8; J.H. Todd, 'On the history of the battle of Clontarf', *PRIA* 7 (1857–61), 498–511.

24 O'Gorman, 'On the site of the battle of Clontarf'.

25 *Ibid.*, 169–70; *Freeman's Journal* [hereafter *FJ*], 10 May 1886, 23 September 1895.

26 Holinshed, *Chronicles of England, Scotland, and Ireland*, iii, 19–20; O'Gorman, 'On the site of the battle of Clontarf', 181; Tony O'Doherty, *A history of Glasnevin* (Dublin, 2011), 14–15.

27 *Irish Times* [hereafter *IT*], 3, 7 and 9 January 1907; 5 and 22 June 1910.

28 *IT*, 30 May 1914; T.J. Westropp, 'The hero of Clontarf', *Irish Monthly* **42** (1914), 133–41, 177–89, 246–59.

29 Philip McEvansoneya, 'History, politics and decorative painting: James Ward's murals in Dublin City Hall', *Irish Arts Review Yearbook* **15** (1999), 142–7; J.B. Dollard, *Clontarf: an Irish national drama in four acts* (Dublin, 1920); Rebecca Helena Hime, *Brian Boru and the battle of Clontarf* (London, 1889), 7.

30 Ryan, 'The battle of Clontarf'; Goedheer, *Irish and Norse traditions about the battle of Clontarf*.

31 For a flavour of this new historiography see, besides the works of Ní Mhaonaigh, Downham, Ní hÚrdáil and McGettigan cited above, Donnchadh Ó Corráin, *Ireland before the Normans* (Dublin, 1972); Colmán Etchingham, 'North Wales, Ireland and the Isles: the Insular Viking zone' *Peritia* **15** (2001), 145–87; Mary Valante, *The Vikings in Ireland: settlement, trade and urbanisation* (Dublin, 2008); John Bradley, 'Some reflections on the problem of Scandinavian settlement in the hinterland of Dublin during the ninth century', in J. Bradley, A.J. Fletcher and A. Simms (eds), *Dublin in the medieval world: studies in honour of Howard B. Clarke* (Dublin, 2009), 39–62; and Seán Duffy, *Brian Boru and the battle of Clontarf* (Dublin, 2013).

CHAPTER THREE

Making of a manor: Clontarf under the Knights Templar, 1172–1312

The formation of the manor of Clontarf

T HE ATMOSPHERE OF medieval Clontarf can best be savoured today by a walk within the ambit of the castle and the neighbouring graveyard with its ruinous church. Nestling now within the sharp bends of Castle Avenue, and separated from each other by a stone wall, the castle and church were once at the heart of the medieval manor and village of Clontarf. Although the present buildings are mainly of post-medieval date, the very shape of the surrounding roads conveys the layout of the manorial demesne. But instead of the suburban avenues that radiate out today, the precincts of the medieval castle were occupied by farms, pastures and woodlands that stretched north to Killester and Raheny and southwards towards the sea. The uninterrupted view then of the bay of Dublin would have suggested the openness of Clontarf to the outside world, as a small merchant community at the coast developed trading links with other ports. A distant prospect of the spires of Dublin bespoke the separateness of Clontarf as a village, and yet its economic and social connections with its urban neighbour were always strong. Moreover, through its association with the great military orders of the Middle Ages—first the Knights Templar and then the Knights Hospitaller of St John of Jerusalem, who were the successive landlords of medieval Clontarf—the district was inevitably brought into the mainstream of Irish and European affairs.

Manor, village, port: these integral features of the period of Anglo-Norman settlement all combined to fashion the abiding character of Clontarf. That there was a community living in the area before 1172 seems clear from the reference to the granting of a 'vill near Dublin called Clumtorp' to the Knights Templar by Henry II about that year.[1] There was reputed to be an old ecclesiastical centre in the district, which may have become the site for the Templars' church,[2] while the presence of a fishing community is suggested by the weir on the Tolka River at the time of the battle of Clontarf. It is quite possible that after 1014 the burgeoning Hiberno-Norse town of Dublin spawned an outpost in the form of a coastal station at Clontarf, whose personnel formed themselves into a village community supplying the townsfolk with fish and agricultural produce.[3] The Christianised Vikings may have patronised an existing church building in this area of Fingal (from the Irish name 'Fine Gall', the territory of the Gall), as happened at Howth, for example, and some may have lived in its immediate vicinity. Likely too is a significant presence of Gaelic people: although the evidence for Gaelic habitation in the hinterland of Dublin is problematic, the mobility and adaptability of those of Irish background has been amply demonstrated.[4] Perhaps the most intriguing sign of the cultural interplay between Scandinavian and Gaelic before the arrival of the Normans is the dual form of the place-name: 'Cluain Tarbh', an old name dating back to at least the eighth century and meaning 'meadow of bulls', appears in the Irish-language sources, and 'Clumtorp', 'Clumtorf', 'Clumpthorp' and 'Clenmthorp', Norse-sounding versions, are used in the repeated recording of the grant of the 1170s to the Knights Templar.[5]

The Normans, like the Vikings, came to Ireland as conquerors and fighters but quickly settled down as town-dwellers, landlords and farmers. Clontarf was a prime location for settlement, with its fertile agricultural lands, and its anchorage and harbour in close proximity to Dublin. In this favoured milieu, the Anglo-Norman feudal system was given every chance to flourish. Agrarian and marine resources could sustain a thriving manorial community, and trade in surpluses could be carried on with the nearby city and more remote places. The choice of the Knights Templar to establish social, economic and religious institutions in the area reflected their reputation as organisers of territories for their patron-rulers, even at a remove from the holy places of the Middle East where they performed their principal functions as crusaders. Under the auspices of the Knights Templar, not only was the village of Clontarf nurtured but also the links between the inhabitants and the neighbouring town of Dublin and the wider world were forged.

Clontarf was the subject of a royal grant shortly after King Henry II seized control of the Norman invasion of Ireland after 1171. That he included Clontarf among a select number of properties for special conferral upon his retainers attests to the strategic value of the district. Its openness to the sea as well as its closeness to Dublin bestowed an importance upon it as a seat of loyalty to the king's regime. The grant was made by Henry to the Knights Templar at Avranches in Normandy between 1172 and 1177.[6] The reference was to 'a vill near Dublin called Clumtorp with its appurtenances', by which was meant existing legal rights attached to the lands. The choice of the Knights Templar as the grantees was a sign of their privileged standing in the king's entourage. By endowing the Templars with these lands Henry was ensuring both spiritual and temporal benefits: the prayers of the members of the order for the king's soul were a condition of this conferring of Clontarf, but, more immediately, by designating the great crusading brotherhood as the lords of that place Henry was assuring the secure and productive management of the lands.[7]

Grant of Clontarf to the Knights Templar

1190: Grant in frankalmoign and confirmation to the Knights Templars of gifts made to them by Henry II of lands in England; and of the following tenements, lands and possessions in Ireland:- mills in Waterford; mills in Wexford; the vill of **Clumtorf** ...

Calendar of documents relating to Ireland, 1171–1251, p. 13

1227: Grant in frankalmoign and confirmation to the Knights Templars, of gifts made to them by King Henry II of lands &c in England; and of the following tenements, lands and possessions in Ireland:- mills in Waterford, mills in Wexford, the vill of **Clumtorp** ...

Calendar of documents relating to Ireland, 1171–1251, p. 225

1281: Inspeximus and confirmation of charter of Henry III (1227), granting and confirming to the Knights Templars lands in England, and the following mills, vills, lands and possessions &c in Ireland, namely:- the mills of Waterford, the mills of Wexford, the vill of **Clumpthorp** ...

Calendar of documents relating to Ireland, 1252–84, p. 368

1287: Grant to the Brothers of the Temple to defend the Holy Land of Jerusalem, of mills on the water near Waterford, which water is called Polwaterfoure, mills on the water near Waterford, which is Innermictam; a vill near Dublin called **Clenmthorp** with its appurtenances ...

Calendar of documents relating to Ireland, 1285–92, p. 329

Who were the Knights Templar? The Order of the Temple had been established 60 years previously to defend the crusader kingdom of Jerusalem after the First Crusade. The fraternity of knights evolved into a religious order with vows and a monastic rule. The principal headquarters of the new order were on the Dome of the Rock in Jerusalem, where stood the Aqsa palace, known to the crusaders as the Temple of Solomon. The main functions of the Knights Templar, as they became known, were to defend the crusader states against Moslem attack and to protect pilgrims from Europe to the Holy Land. They spread rapidly throughout eastern, central and western Europe, establishing houses and castles on lands donated by rulers. When located away from the front line of Palestine, the Knights lived peaceably for the most part (except in the Iberian peninsula, where they were engaged in fighting the Moors) as farmers, gathering income for the effort against the infidels. By patronising the Order of the Temple, the European leaders were ensuring not just a supply of funds for the crusading ventures of the Knights but also the stability of their homelands, particularly in frontier zones. Although Clontarf was already a settled district, its take-over by the Knights Templar in the 1170s assured Henry II and his successor lords of Ireland of a bastion of security on the outskirts of the seat of government there.[8]

Unlike the other great knightly order that arrived in Ireland with the Normans, the Hospitallers of St John of Jerusalem, the Knights Templar were decentralised in their national organisation. Both orders had their headquarters in the holy city of Jerusalem, but whereas the Knights Hospitaller became divided into national units or 'langues' (tongues), ruled by priors, the Templars were only loosely grouped throughout Europe. And while Kilmainham was recognised as the centre of the Hospitallers' Irish organisation, there was no official headquarters among the houses, called commanderies or preceptories, of the Templars. Although Clontarf was the main Dublin property of the Knights Templar, it did not have any special standing as an administrative hub. And yet *de facto* its closeness to the seat of government enhanced the status of the members of the Clontarf commandery. The first person we can positively identify with the district is Walter, Templar and master of 'Cluntarf', listed as a witness to deeds of St Mary's Abbey, Dublin, in 1186. Other references to personnel at Clontarf suggest that it was a key institution in the order's set-up, and indeed in the mainstream of colonial life.[9]

Though printed 600 years after the Templars' arrival in the area, the most detailed early modern map of Clontarf—that by John Rocque—gives us an indication of the shape of the medieval manor. [3.1] At the northern end of a village street that led down to the sea were the principal manorial residence (or castle) and the church, situated about 150 metres apart, as they had been since

Fig. 3.1—Extract from John Rocque's An actual survey of the county of Dublin *(1760), showing the central location of Clontarf Castle and demesne in the district, and the pattern of fields on the manor (courtesy of the Royal Irish Academy).*

the building of the original structures in the twelfth or thirteenth century. These had been significant poles of influence within the community for many centuries thereafter. Described by most modern sources as a castle from its earliest construction, the original house of the Knights may have been in reality a large fortified residence, in accordance with the normal style of Templar preceptory in Britain and Ireland. On the other hand, there were almost 100 'castles', large and small, in the Dublin region by the late Middle Ages, though not all were of stone. The problem in categorising the Clontarf manor-house arises from the fact that no information about its construction survives, and most of the original building was cleared away in the reconstruction of Clontarf Castle in the 1830s. [3.2] Archaeological excavations carried out at the time of the recent refurbishment of the castle in 1996–7 found little trace of the Templars' castle, though a western boundary wall of the demesne complex was discovered. The only written evidence for the nature of residence at Clontarf comes at the end of the Middle Ages, when it was equated to a hall and two towers, one of them probably the square 'keep' or main defensive structure of the original building, which survived in part until the nineteenth century. In any case, whether called a 'house' or 'castle', the principal residential seat of Clontarf was occupied by a sequence of landlords down to the twentieth century.[10]

Fig. 3.2—Drawing of Clontarf Castle as it was before the restoration of the 1830s
(Dublin Penny Journal, 1834).

The old, now ruinous church at Clontarf is the successor building to at least two others that have stood on the site, possibly stretching back to the Early Christian period, but the church of the Knights Templar is the first certain ecclesiastical structure. [3.3] Built about the same time as their preceptory or castle, the chapel building was located very close to the centre of the manor, as was the Norman fashion. Although there is no drawing of the original building, it is likely to have been small, and certainly within the footprint of the present ruins. While some Templar chapels were architecturally elaborate, the church at Clontarf is likely to have been built in a plain vernacular style, similar to that of the Knights at Rincrew, Co. Waterford, for example, for which there is an illustration of the original in ruins. [3.4] The advent of the Normans helped to consolidate the formation of parishes within the areas colonised, with the construction of hundreds of new churches from about 1200. As well as being the chapel of the Order of the Temple at Clontarf, the new church building became the place of worship for the newly formed parish of Clontarf, which was to be run by the Knights, almost independently of the archbishop of Dublin. For 700 years the parishioners of Clontarf assembled at the church in the castle precincts for religious services and ceremonies." [3.5]

Fig. 3.3—Ruins of the church at Clontarf of 1609, built on the site of the church of the Knights Templar (original watercolour).

Fig. 3.4—Drawing by Daniel Grose of the Templar church at Rincrew, Co. Waterford, c. 1800, which gives possible indications of the size and style of the Knights' church at Clontarf (courtesy of the Irish Architectural Archive).

Fig. 3.5—View of the ruined 1609 church, with the top of the restored medieval tower of the castle, showing the contiguity of the poles of manorial influence.

Rocque's map of Clontarf also showed the pattern of field boundaries, probably of ancient date, spreading out from the castle/church nucleus. We see here very clearly the traces of the Knights' organisation of a manor, or basic unit of feudal society, at Clontarf. Throughout their estates in Europe, they turned to agriculture to produce funds for their military activities in the east, enjoying a reputation for productive farming. Thus, by turning the district into a profitable economic unit and settled village, the Knights set the character of Clontarf. Of the original royal grant of 1,190 acres, the Knights concentrated on the development of an agrarian estate or manor of just under 400 acres. A demesne of 88 acres clustered around their manor-house was farmed by the Knights themselves, while the rest of the fields, comprising large and small farms, were rented out to tenants and worked by the families dwelling on the manor, who rendered labouring duties such as ploughing and reaping on the demesne lands in lieu of rent. The bulk of the manorial estate was made up of arable lands, while the balance consisted of pasture, meadow and woodland. A stand of timber, called the Priorswood, survived into the early modern period but had disappeared by the time of the 1760 survey. The cottages in the nucleated village that grew in the vicinity of the manor-house housed the peasant families, as well as some craft-workers and fisherfolk, though the latter may have formed their own community at the shore slightly to the east. As lords of the manor, the Knights were entitled not only to labour dues, such as reaping and sowing, but also to fees for use of the mill at Clontarf, and possibly for the anchoring of ships off the coastline.[12]

Of the approximately 400 acres actually farmed (excluding woodland and scrubland), 75% of the lands of the manor of Clontarf were outside the demesne of the Knights and therefore worked by their tenants. At least a couple of large farms were formed, to judge by later references to 'Busshells Farme' and 'Whitefferme'. From an enquiry of 1308, on the occasion of the suppression of the order, we find that the bulk of the manorial territory was under the plough. Half of the fields (170.5 acres in extent) were given over to the cultivation of wheat, oats were grown on 154.5 acres, while two areas of eight acres were devoted to barley and legumes (peas and beans) respectively. As elsewhere, the Knights probably encouraged the most advanced agricultural techniques on their lands in Clontarf, including crop rotation, and crop surpluses would be sold to merchants from the neighbouring city and farther afield. The existence of a granary among the buildings near the castle attests to the centrality of grain-growing on the manor, and the mill in Clontarf allowed for the processing of cereals in the locality. Clontarf was one of the few areas documented in the vicinity of Dublin in which barley-growing was carried out. Given the prevalence of wheat for

---

Corn, livestock and meat on the farm of the Knights, 1308

100 quarters of wheat at 5s a quarter

120 quarters of oats at 40d a quarter

20 quarters of beans and peas at 4s a quarter

30 oxen for the 5 ploughs

10 plough-horses

14 horses, including a ferraunt and a palfrey

10 cows and a bull in the cow-house

60 sheep

100 pigs

10 beef carcasses in the larder

12 bacons

G. MacNiocaill, 'Documents relating to the suppression of the Templars in Ireland',

Analecta Hibernica 24 (1967), p. 188

---

flour and bread-making, the barley crop was probably used for malting and the brewing of beer. The oats grown at Clontarf could be turned into human foods when baked or stewed, used in the brewing of inferior ale or given to animals as fodder. Legumes—beans and peas—were also important for human and animal consumption, and their cultivation moreover played a vital part in boosting the fertility of the soil.[13]

On the pasture and meadow lands of Clontarf, the Templars promoted animal husbandry on the demesne and manor. As knights they were experienced horsemen, and at Clontarf in 1308 they possessed a number of steeds. Besides the ten plough-horses ('affers'), which, along with 30 oxen, were used to pull their five ploughs, there were nine cart-horses and two packhorses for working around the farm. The master of the order had an iron-grey warhorse worth £20 in his stable, and there were in addition four other horses, including a palfrey, for the use of the brothers. Apart from the beasts of burden in the stables and behind the plough, there were herds and flocks in the meadows and pastures. There was a cowhouse accommodating ten cows as well as a bull, and the fact that the larder contained four stone of cheese suggests that the herd may have been kept for dairying purposes. Clontarf manor had a large flock of sheep, numbering over 200 in 1308, which yielded meat and skins as well as wool, of which there were five stone in the storehouse. A hundred pigs were kept on the manor, producing meat, there being twelve sides of bacon in the larder in 1308. The produce of the land and herds thus gave rise to domestic and commercial activities in manorial life, including cheese-making, drying of hides, wool-gathering, and preparation and cooking of food, as well, perhaps, as brewing. In the sixteenth century, and possibly beforehand, there was a dovecote among the complex of buildings on the Clontarf manor-house site, where doves and pigeons were kept for eggs and meat. References to the keeping of warrens on the lands of Clontarf and the consumption of rabbit, especially on festive occasions, date from slightly later than the period of the Templars' tenure.[14]

There is no mention of fishing in the inquiry of 1308 but, as well as farming the area, the Knights were doubtlessly involved in developing the port of Clontarf which grew up as a satellite, coastal village on the manor. Two members of the Order, Galfridius Templarius and Henricus le Templer, were members of the Dublin guild merchant in the mid-thirteenth century, both presumably attached to the Clontarf preceptory as the only Dublin house of the Templars. Brothers in general were entitled to become free of the guilds in towns and to engage in trade, the profits to be channelled into their mission to the Holy Land. To facilitate this commitment, the Knights took an interest in ports in order to build up shipping links to their principal fleets, based abroad in France and Britain. Control over the maritime reaches of the Clontarf district was important for the order, not just for the fisheries but also for the dues paid by vessels putting in at the pool of Clontarf, one of the deeper anchorages in Dublin Bay, no doubt one of the 'appurtenances' of the vill of Clontarf referred to in Henry II's grant of the 1170s. That there was a mercantile community at Clontarf by the mid-thirteenth century is attested by the enrolment of two merchants of Clontarf in the Dublin guild merchant, Patricius Faber de Cluntarf in 1243–4 and Rogerus, son of Ricardus Blund de Clontarf, in 1261–2. By the early fourteenth century, then, two communities had grown up on the manor of the Knights, one based largely on farming and centred on the castle, and the other drawing its livelihood from fishing and trade, located along the shoreline in the lea of the headland of Clontarf.[15]

The trials of the Templars

The picture of Clontarf that emerges by the early 1300s is of a settled and thriving community centred on the Knights' castle and church, with a growing coastal hub. With their extensive freedoms from the payment of tolls at markets and fairs and tithes to the church, the Knights evidently prospered there, as the value of their preceptory at its dissolution compared very favourably to the more lucrative Templar manors in the west midlands of England. As was the case with Templar communities throughout Europe, the order in Clontarf probably had permission to hold periodic fairs and markets that would have provided a focal point for the commercial and social life of the district. That it was the principal residence of the masters of the order in Ireland from the time of Walter of Cluntarf in the 1180s, as well as its *de facto* headquarters, added prestige to the north Dublin preceptory (which also had its own superior or preceptor). The Knights, the fully fledged members of the order, would have been familiar figures as they rode through the district of Clontarf, dressed in their white robes with red crosses and sporting long beards. They differed from conventional knights in their having taken vows of poverty, chastity and obedience, and in their dedication to the defence of the Christian church. Most may have been from a noble and Norman background, such as Robert de Pourbriggs, who was among those interrogated at the trial of 1308. The sergeant-brothers of the order, both soldiers and servants, who functioned as defenders of the preceptory and as grooms and agrarian workers respectively, were normally below the knightly rank and could, for example, belong to the municipality of Dublin. There may have been some knight pensioners or other lay people who had residential rights on the manor on account of their having

Fig. 3.6—A Knight Templar
(*James Ware*, Whole works of Sir James Ware concerning Ireland *(Dublin, 1764))*.

served as Knights or donated land and wealth to the community. In addition to the lay members, there were priests or chaplains of the order who served the local church and ministered to the spiritual needs of the community.[16] [3.6]

The parish of Clontarf was formed under the auspices of the Knights Templar. They had the right to appoint the parish priest or rector, and they gathered in income from tithes on the manor. A curate could be hired to serve the parish, being paid a small stipend. One of their privileges was freedom from the jurisdiction of the local ecclesiastical metropolitan, the archbishop of Dublin. The church appears to have been well maintained and equipped, according to the inventory of 1308. Among the liturgical books listed were a French-language version of the Gospels, a missal, a troper, a psalter, a manual (or guide to sacramental practice) and a gradual (a service book). The sacral vessels included two chalices, of which one was gilt, and two altar vessels, one of which was silver, while the range of sacred vestments, such as three chasubles, four albs, four amices (or copes), two stoles, three maniples and three girdles, suggests that more than one celebrant would have been able to say Mass simultaneously, one possibly at a side altar. We know the name of at least one priest who served as rector of Clontarf—a man of Norman background called de Botiller around 1300. There may also have been in existence at Clontarf a confraternity of supporters of the order who shared in the spiritual benefits of the worshipping community in return for donations of money and property.[17]

Religious objects in the church at Clontarf, 1308

A French book of the Gospels and a book of Brutus the Englishman

A troper, a psalter, a manual and a gradual

3 chasubles, 4 amices, 2 stoles, 3 maniples, 3 zones [belts or cinctures], a manutergium [sacred towel], an auricularium [confessional stole?] and a corporal [cloth for the Eucharist]

A chalice worth 1 mark

A wooden communion cup

A gilded chalice worth 20 shillings

A silver vessel with feet worth 2 marks

G. MacNiocaill, 'Documents relating to the suppression of the Templars in Ireland',

Analecta Hibernica 24 (1967), p. 215

Not surprisingly, given the wide-ranging privileges and exemptions enjoyed by the order, the Templars were to become the objects of jealousy on the part of religious and secular rivals in Ireland. These generous perquisites included commercial rights such as freedom from customs levies, relief from feudal and military services, and extensive local jurisdiction over trade and justice, as well as independence of diocesan ecclesiastical supervision. Originally granted by state and church to bolster the Knights' capacity to wage war in the Holy Land, the range of privileges was eventually seen to place them at an unfair advantage *vis-à-vis* other landlords and orders, and the result was a series of cases in the courts. A dispute over land with the Cistercian abbot of Dunbrody, Co. Wexford, for example, dragged the Templars through the courts in Ireland and England for a decade from 1279, and involved a testing of their royal grants to Clontarf and all of their other manors. In another case, a lay suitor, Matilda le Botiller, took action at law against the rights of the Templars to appoint a priest in the parish of Carlingford on their manor of Cooley, raising questions about their advowsons (rights of presentation to church benefices) in general. Although the Knights Templar may have won these and other cases, their vindication bred deeper resentment among those who envied their success.[18]

The trend of international events turned against the Templars, as the order was ousted from the Holy Land with the loss of its headquarters at Acre in 1291, leaving them more vulnerable throughout Europe to the jealous claims of their religious and secular enemies. Among the former were the Knights Hospitaller of St John of Jerusalem, with whom a possible merger was mooted in the 1290s after the expulsion from Palestine, but this scheme was stillborn. The Templars' most implacable foe was the French king, Philip IV, who determined on their destruction, motivated by jealousy of their perceived wealth and resentment at their exempt status within the French church. On foot of a damning list of charges drawn up against the order, which was accused of practising heresy, idolatry, immorality and impiety, Philip ordered the arrest and imprisonment of all of the Knights in France in 1307, and, having been subjected to torture, most confessed their guilt. After a series of show trials, a number of Knights, including the master of the order, Jean de Molay, were condemned to burn at the stake for heresy. Philip put pressure on Pope Clement V, a Frenchman who moved the papal court to Avignon in 1309, to order the arrest and trial of the Knights Templar in territories throughout Europe.[19]

Reluctantly, King Edward II decreed that the Knights Templar in England and Ireland be rounded up in early 1309. On 3 February the Irish Knights of the Temple were arrested and imprisoned in Dublin Castle, and their lands and possessions confiscated. Local juries were deputed to make inventories of properties of the Knights, including those of Clontarf, while the captive Knights were subjected to a comprehensive interrogation about their beliefs and practices. The details and valuing of all the goods and estates of the order revealed that the Knights lived modestly and were not possessed of fabulous riches, as suggested by wild rumourmongers. In the case of Clontarf, the total value of all items, including agricultural produce and livestock as well as books and sacral vessels, amounted to £125 17s 7d. This rendered Clontarf the third most valuable of the Knights' preceptories in Ireland, after Clonaul and Kilclogan. For an order known everywhere as bankers and treasurers to kings, the three shillings in coinage in the Clontarf house represented a paltry sum.[20]

Meanwhile, the interrogation of the individual Knights in Dublin Castle, who were not subjected to torture as in France, did not elicit confessions, and a trial before 40 inquisitors, the vast majority of them clerics, took place in St Patrick's Cathedral in the first half of 1310. The witnesses called against the Irish Templars

Value of manor of Clontarf, 1308

170½ acres sown with wheat at 6s per acre

154½ acres sown with barley at 4s per acre

8 acres of oats at 4s per acre

8 acres of peas and beans at 4s per acre

42 cows each worth 6s

8 plough-horses each worth 2s

5 horses worth 6s each

40 pigs worth 12d each

156 sheep worth 10d each

4 cows and 2 steers each worth 20s

2 wagons worth 5s each

Total value of the income of the manor: £32 10s per annum

G. MacNiocaill, 'Documents relating to the suppression of the Templars in Ireland',

Analecta Hibernica 24 (1967), p. 214

gave vent to rumours and gossip, for the most part, with very little evidence being adduced of serious lapses. Perhaps in an effort to substantiate the charge that the Templars disrespected the Mass, allegations of a lack of decorum during the celebration of the Eucharist at Clontarf were aired. One of the inquisitors, Hugh de Lummour, a Dominican friar, claimed that, having often been at Clontarf preceptory, he witnessed William de Warecome, a Templar, turn his face to the ground at the consecration of the Mass, not caring to look at the elevated host. And William de Botiller weighed in by saying that, while assisting his brother in the celebration of Mass at Clontarf, he saw the Templars gazing at the ground during the consecration and failing to attend at the reading of the Gospel. He further alleged that, when he turned to exchange a kiss of peace with the brethren after the Agnus Dei, one of them refused the gesture, averring that the Templars did not care for peace. That the community at Clontarf was not particularly warlike is attested to by the presence in the inventory of the house of three swords, and nowhere else were weapons listed among the possessions.[21]

Despite the flimsiness and unreliability of the case against the Knights Templar in Ireland and elsewhere, the order was formally dissolved by the pope in

The trial of the Irish Templars, 1310

The only two witnesses who had anything definite to depose to were brothers Hugh de Lummour and William le Botiller. The former declared that he was often at Clontarf, and had seen a Templar, named William de Warecome, turn his face to the ground at the elevation of the sacrament, not caring to look at the Host. William le Botiller testified that one day he assisted his brother, who was celebrating Mass at Clontarf, and that, at the elevation of the Host, the Templars kept their gaze fixed on the ground, and paid no attention to the reading of the Gospel. Also, after the Agnus Dei, he wished to make the brethren the kiss of peace, whereupon one of their own clergy told him that the Templars did not care for peace.

Herbert Wood, 'The Templars in Ireland', *PRIA* 26C (1906–7), p. 354

1312 and its possessions granted to the Hospitallers. Among the 40 inquisitors who examined the Templars in Ireland were two people bearing the epithet 'Kilmaynan', Roger and Ralph. These were leading members of the Knights Hospitaller of St John of Jerusalem, whose Irish headquarters were at Kilmainham, to the west of Dublin. Roger, whose surname was Outlaw, became prior of the order in 1315, and it was under his headship that the Irish lands and houses of the Templars were finally vested in the possession of the Hospitallers. Thus one suspects that the ambitious Roger relished the task of proving the case against the Templars, as his own order, still very much in favour with the monarchy of England, was poised to benefit from their suppression. In the case of the manor of Clontarf, however, there was a hitch: on 26 December 1310 it had been granted by the crown in fee simple to Richard de Burgh, the earl of Ulster, who was father-in-law of the earl of Cornwall, the favourite of King Edward II and former lord lieutenant of Ireland. De Burgh apparently surrendered the estate to the crown, as by 1320 the Knights Hospitallers had got full proprietorial rights to Clontarf and the other former Templar preceptories in Ireland. The surviving Templars had been released from prison and were given a pension of two pence per day for the remainder of their lives.[22]

The legacy of the Knights Templar to the Clontarf area and its community has been an abiding one. Although part of a great international order, the Knights of the Clontarf commandery immersed themselves in the task of managing their locality and estate. They placed their stamp on the topography of the district through the organisation of a manor, with its mansion and church at the core, a village street as its spine, and productive fields and meadows delineated in the surrounding acres. Their consciousness of their overseas mission, as well as their entrepreneurial drive, led them to exploit Clontarf's maritime location through the port and anchorage. While asserting a sturdy independence through the secular administration of their manorial estate and the ecclesiastical management of the parish and rectory, the Knights maintained their ultimate loyalty to the English king as lord of Ireland and to the pope as head of the church. Their tenure as lords of Clontarf manor for a century and a half may be adjudged a success in terms of the development and management of an estate, the settlement of a village, and the farming and husbandry of the resources on land and at sea. The tide of royal approval and patronage turned in the early fourteenth century, however, particularly on the continent of Europe, and the Irish Templars, though guilty of no great corruption or turpitude, succumbed to the fate of their brother knights in other countries, forfeiting their properties if not their lives. Located in the verdant countryside close to the city of Dublin, their manor of Clontarf proved to be a very attractive acquisition for their bitter rivals, the Knights Hospitaller.

1 *Calendar of documents relating to Ireland* [hereafter *Cal. docs Ire.*], *1171-1251*, 13. The vill was called 'Clumtorf' in a reiteration of the grant in 1227 (*Cal. docs Ire., 1171-1251*, 225) and 'Clenmthorp' in one of 1286–7 (*Cal. docs Ire., 1285-92*, 329). That last reference was reproduced in the form of the original charter of Henry II in a court case relating to a County Waterford property in 1286–7 by the then master of the Templars.

2 Modern authorities do not attribute the church and parish of Clontarf to an era previous to the Norman settlement. Myles V. Ronan states that 'nothing is known of the origin of the [early seventeenth-century] church' of Clontarf: Myles V. Ronan (ed.), 'Royal visitation of Dublin, 1615', *Archivium Hibernicum* **8** (1941), 35. In their survey of the medieval churches of County Dublin, Fagan and Simms ('Villages in County Dublin: their origins and inheritance', 86) exclude Clontarf from the number of medieval manorial villages that had an Early Christian site, and Clontarf is not mentioned in an 1179 list of the churches of the Fine Gall region.

3 See Bradley, 'Some reflections on the problem of Scandinavian settlement'.

4 Mary Valante, 'Dublin's economic relations with hinterland and periphery in the later Viking age', in Seán Duffy (ed.), *Medieval Dublin I* (Dublin, 2000), 69–83.

5 Mac Ghiolla Phádraig, 'The Irish form of "Clontarf"', 127–8; *Cal. docs Ire., 1171-1251*, 13, 225; *1252-1284*, 368; *1285-92*, 329.

6 *Cal. docs Ire.,1171-1251*,13; *1285-1292*, 329. The exact date of the grant is uncertain, but it must have been made between 1172, when Henry II was in Avranches in Normandy, and 1177, when

a reference occurs in the Christ Church deeds to Matthew the Templar, betokening the establishment of the order in the Dublin region: *Calendar of Christ Church deeds*, 124.

7 For a discussion of relations between the Knights and the European monarchs see Helen Nicholson, *The Knights Templar: a new history* (Stroud, 2001), 160–80.

8 *Ibid.*, chapters 1 and 2, for the origins of the order; for the history of the Knights in Ireland see Herbert Wood, 'The Templars in Ireland', *PRIA* 26C (1906–7), 327–77.

9 For the international organisation see Nicholson, *Knights Templar*, 113–36, and for the Irish structure see Wood, 'Templars in Ireland', 332–4; for Walter, master of Cluntarf, see *Chartularies of St Mary's Abbey*, i, 173, 231.

10 Paul Ferguson (ed.), *The A to Z of Georgian Dublin: John Rocque's maps of the city in 1756 and the County in 1760* (Lympne Castle, 1998), 26; Murphy and Potterton (eds), *The Dublin region in the Middle Ages*, 133, 137, 146; Anon., 'Clontarf Castle, County of Dublin', *Irish Penny Journal* 1 (1840), 81–3; 'Clontarf Castle, Dublin', in Database of Irish Excavation Reports [www.excavations.ie/Pages/Details.php/Dublin 1715, 1994, accessed 4 February 2012].

11 Wood, 'Templars in Ireland', 334, 354; for the formation of parishes see Adrian Empey, 'The layperson in the parish, 1169–1536', in Raymond Gillespie and W.G. Neely (eds), *The laity and the Church of Ireland, 1000–2000: all sorts and conditions* (Dublin, 2002), 7–17; Murphy and Potterton (eds), *The Dublin region in the Middle Ages*, 209–63; Nicholson, *Knights Templar*, 168.

12 Nicholson, *Knights Templar*, 181–7; Murphy and Potterton (eds), *The Dublin region in the Middle Ages*, 75; J.S. Brewer and W. Bullen (eds), *Calendar of Carew Manuscripts* [hereafter *Cal. Carew MSS*] (6 vols, London, 1867–73), vi, 130; Newport B. White (ed.), *Extents of Irish monastic possessions, 1540–1541* (Dublin, 1943), 89; see also Thomas Phillips, 'Observations explanatory of a plan for a citadel at Dublin' (RIA Haliday MS Map no. 1: survey of the city of Dublin and part of the harbour, 1685).

13 Gearóid Mac Niocaill, 'Documents relating to the suppression of the Templars in Ireland', *Analecta Hibernica* 24 (1967), 188, 214–15; for the context see Murphy and Potterton (eds), *Dublin region in the Middle ages*, 287–324.

14 Mac Niocaill, 'Suppression of the Templars in Ireland', 188, 214–15; for the context see Murphy and Potterton (eds), *The Dublin region in the Middle Ages*, 326–45.

15 Philomena Connolly and Geoffrey Martin (eds), *The Dublin guild merchant roll, c. 1190–1265* (Dublin, 1992), 8, 29, 80, 104; White (ed.), *Extents of Irish monastic possessions, 1540–1541*, 89; Evelyn Lord, *The Knights Templar in Britain* (London, 2002), 119–21.

16 Wood, 'Templars in Ireland', 337, 353; Nicholson, *Knights Templar*, 113–36.

17 Wood, 'Templars in Ireland', 334, 354; Mac Niocaill, 'Suppression of the Templars in Ireland', 215; on religious associates see Nicholson, *Knights Templar*, 131–4.

18 Wood, 'Templars in Ireland', 334–6, 342; *Cal. docs Ire., 1285–1292*, 328–33; *Calendar of the justiciar rolls, Edward I*, 409.

19 Nicholson, *Knights Templar*, 196–226.

20 Lord, *Knights Templar in Britain*, 191–4; Mac Niocaill, 'Suppression of the Templars in Ireland', 188, 214–16, 224.

21 Wood, 'Templars in Ireland', 350–4; Mac Niocaill, 'Suppression of the Templars in Ireland', 215.

22 Nicholson, *Knights Templar*, 230; Wood, 'Templars in Ireland', 352–3, 358–60, 365; *Calendar of fine rolls, 1307-19*, 76; Eithne Massey, *Prior Roger Outlaw of Kilmainham, 1314-41* (Dublin, 2000), 21.

CHAPTER FOUR

Village and port: Clontarf under the Hospitallers, 1320–1540

Hospitality of the Knights

T HE MILITARY ORDER that took over the preceptory and manor of Clontarf as a going concern in 1320 bore many similarities to the one that it replaced. The Knights Hospitaller of St John had been founded in Jerusalem towards the end of the eleventh century and had as one of their original functions the care of the sick and the provision of hospitality to pilgrims. Later its role extended to defence of these same pilgrims as the order became more and more militaristic, and by the early fourteenth century the main aim of the Hospitaller knights was to do battle with the Moslem armies of Mediterranean Europe and Latin Syria. After the fall of Jerusalem in 1187, the order moved its headquarters to Acre, and in 1291, after the capture of Acre, to Limasol in Cyprus. They moved then to Rhodes in 1309 and finally to Malta in 1565. The head of the order was the grand master, and below him was a huge and highly structured organisation stretching from the Middle East to the western reaches of Europe. The order was divided into sections called 'langues', or tongues, according to the language of its members, the Irish priory coming under the English langue at Clerkenwell in London. The function of the western European langues was essentially to provide finance for the campaigns of the Knights in the east, through the payment of 'responsions' or annual sums due from each priory. In some countries, including Ireland, the Hospitallers' original task of the provision of hospitality had been transformed into the corrody or pension system, which provided long-term lodging to individuals in exchange for money, favours or service.[1]

Like their counterpart military order, the Hospitallers had been closely associated from the start with the settlement and expansion of the Anglo-Normans in Ireland. The order had eleven houses in all in the twelfth and thirteenth centuries, most of them situated in Leinster and Munster, and this number increased to seventeen with the acquisition of the Templars' houses and lands. Unlike the Templars, however, the Knights of St John of Jerusalem had a definite Irish headquarters, at Kilmainham. In the political sphere, the Hospitallers came to provide administrative expertise for the running of the lordship of Ireland, the priors and senior figures frequently filling some of the most important posts in the government, including the treasurership and chancellorship. In the localities, the Hospitallers fostered the development of farming and village communities on their manors, and, through their priests and chaplains, ran the parish churches associated with their houses. Profits from agricultural and other economic activities contributed to the payment of responsions for the crusading goals of the order in the Near East. The Hospitallers' obligation of hospitality, unique to them, was exercised through the 'frankhouses' or guesthouses in the towns and the corrody system in their preceptories at Kilmainham and elsewhere. The latter comprised a series of residentially based pensions for deserving dignitaries, as well as superannuated members of the order, who enjoyed board and lodgings in varying degrees of generosity. Through their extension of retirement facilities to some of the most prominent people in the late medieval lordship, the Hospitallers developed a strong and influential position in fourteenth-century Ireland.[2] [4.1]

Fig. 4.1—A member of the order of the Knights Hospitaller of St John of Jerusalem (James Ware, Whole works of Sir James Ware concerning Ireland *(Dublin, 1764)).*

For the Knights Hospitaller, the acquisition of the valuable manor of Clontarf on the north side of Dublin Bay offered important political and economic opportunities. Close to the seat of the colonial government, Clontarf preceptory could be used for an expanded corrodial system of maintenance. As a thriving agricultural entity, the manor promised a profitable income in the form of produce and rental of lands. Under the new management of the prior of Kilmainham, the hand of the Hospitallers may have come to rest more lightly than did that of the Templars on the manorial hinterland of Clontarf, most of which appeared to be farmed out to substantial gentry figures in the fourteenth and fifteenth centuries. The parish church retained its privilege of exemption from archiepiscopal supervision and could be looked to for revenues, and also as a means of ecclesiastical patronage. Importantly for a commercially attuned institution, the Hospital's ownership of the shoreline of Clontarf brought with it lucrative fishing rights as well as fees from vessels anchoring in the pool of Clontarf. Moreover, as Dublin's disadvantages as a trading port became more apparent in the late Middle Ages, the value of Clontarf pool and harbour as a place of safe anchorage within the bay was enhanced.[3]

As well as a source of income from the lands of the manor, the parish rectory and the cherished fishery and shipping rights, the Hospitallers used Clontarf as a place of patronage in the form of corrodies—that is, residential pensions granted to those who served the order. The most prestigious forms of corrody were those awarded to grandees and dignitaries, who were given special privileges such as dining at the prior's table, expensive robes and lodging for themselves, their servants and horses. While these more splendid forms of hospitality were laid on at Kilmainham, most of the Clontarf corrodians, to judge by the contracts of maintenance, were of a humbler category, being free servants and tradesmen of the brothers, with occupations such as janitor, butler, carpenter and cook. An exception was Cecilia, wife of Hugo de Nassingham, a clerk at Kilmainham, who from 1330 was entitled to claim annually from the stores at Clontarf dozens of pecks of wheat and oats and twelve cheeses. More conventional are the contracts for the support of Johannes Poytoun, William Geraud, Thomas Palfreyman and William Gay, respectively janitor, successive butlers and carpenter at the Clontarf preceptory, who in the 1330s and 1340s were granted dining rights at the table of the craft-workers there and an annual gift of robes and clothing, worth a mark (13s 4d) or ten shillings, appropriate to their stations. In addition, if they became too debilitated to attend the dining-hall, these retainers were entitled to be served a daily ration of bread and beer in their rooms, as well as adequate helpings of flesh meat and fish from the kitchen. Another serviceable corrodian, William de Ossyngham, was granted similar pension terms in 1348 in return for being custodian of the rabbit warrens of the Clontarf house of the Hospitallers, where Brother Herbert was then preceptor. The warrens were extensive, as attested to by the figure of over 300 rabbits being consumed by the Knights and their guests at a Christmas feast. Roger, the cook at Clontarf, and William, son of Nicholas de Kilmainham, held lands of the manorial estate.[4]

Hospitality at Clontarf, 1330

Hugo de Nassyngton, one of the priests of the Hospital at Kilmainham, had his commons and his robe as one of the brethren, and a groom to wait upon, but no horse. He was assigned a plot of ground outside the castle gate, on which to build a *camera* [chamber] for himself and Cecilia, his wife ... She was allotted a yearly allowance of 32 heaped pecks of wheat, 56 heaped pecks of oats and 12 cheeses from the dairy; and she was permitted to claim these either at Kilmainham or at the seaside preceptory of Clontarf.

Charles McNeill, 'The Hospitallers at Kilmainham and their guests', *JRSAI* 24 (1924), p. 27

For the Knights Hospitaller, the decades after the absorption of Clontarf and the other Templar properties into their network witnessed the strengthening of the Irish priorate within the international organisation. The high-profile career of Prior Roger Outlaw of Kilmainham, who also held the preceptorship of Clontarf, raised the standing of the order in Ireland, through his significant role in the government of the Irish lordship and his adept patronage of key figures through the corrodial system down to his death in 1341. Thereafter there may have been a period of economic and social decay, owing principally to the great cataclysm of the Black Death in the late 1340s. While we have no evidence concerning the death-toll in Clontarf, the plague must have affected the Dublin houses and estates of the Hospital very severely, inflicting as it did a huge rate of mortality of perhaps up to 14,000 on the city and its environs during the visitation. As a burgeoning port, Clontarf would have been particularly vulnerable to the spread of the virulent disease. It was a catastrophe for the whole of the Hospitaller Order, from which it may have recovered only very slowly. A series of English-born priors attempted to rule the Irish institution after 1350 in adverse circumstances, thus alienating the Knights who were born in Ireland of English roots. An opportunity for the assertion of a sharpened sense of Irish-English identity came during the Great Western Schism after 1377, which divided western Christendom into two factions, the followers of the Rome-based popes on one side and the adherents of the competing popes resident in Avignon on the other. Contrary to the policy of the English langue of the Hospital, which supported the French-based pope and his approved grand master, the Irish-born Knights gave their obedience to the Roman pope, who sustained an alternative grand master. After the healing of the split, the Irish priory established in 1410 the right to elect to its headship a person of Irish birth, and this position persisted as a rule until the end of the fifteenth century.[5]

Development of Clontarf port

The construction of a stone bridge over the Tolka in 1313, thanks to the benevolence of John Le Decer, a former mayor of Dublin and builder of many public utilities there, established a reliable artery of communication between the village of Clontarf and the neighbouring city. [4.2] The bridging of what had been 'a dangerous charge' of water allowed for agricultural and other produce to be conveyed with greater efficiency between the two locations. Contact by sea was

Fig. 4.2—*Modern bridge over the River Tolka on the site of the medieval bridge of 1313, which facilitated communication between Clontarf and Dublin city (Patrick Healy Collection, South County Dublin Libraries).*

also improved during the fourteenth and fifteenth centuries, as Clontarf harbour grew as a trading and fisheries station under the jurisdiction of the state and the Hospitallers. The Knights at Kilmainham had resorted to the law to defend their rights to fishing on the upper Liffey against the intrusion of the citizens of Dublin, and on acquiring Clontarf preceptory they were just as committed to protecting their fishing privileges at the estuary of the river, including the tithes of salmon.[6]

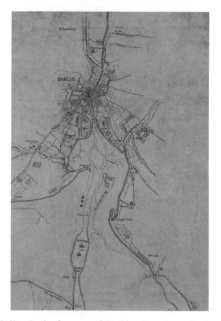

Fig. 4.3 — Thomas Phillips's draft map of Dublin Bay (1685), showing the spit of land at Clontarf Head, as well as Clontarf Island and Pool, all of which were features of the growth of the port of Clontarf (courtesy of the Royal Irish Academy).

The development of a harbour at Clontarf was aided not only by the local fishing industry but also by the proximity of the deep pool of Clontarf for the anchoring of ships unable to navigate the silted-up channels of the Liffey. [4.3] Alternatives to the port of Dublin city were sought by late medieval mariners and merchants, and Clontarf became an important member of a group of subsidiary ports, which also included Skerries, Malahide, Howth, Bullock, Dalkey and Wicklow. From the later fourteenth century the port of Clontarf appears to have come under the notional jurisdiction of the admiral of Ireland, whose office was largely honorific, but maritime matters were usually dealt with by the state court of chancery. These included the offence of exporting unlicensed goods and the evasion of customs tolls on imports. Another dimension to the ownership of these smaller ports was the claim of the municipal council of the city of Dublin to the customs revenue from the ports along the coastline from Skerries to Wicklow.

As the haven of Clontarf developed under these jurisdictions, the growth of trade and services no doubt contributed to the economic health of the area. In 1358–9 a royal licence was issued for the export of wheat from the ports of Dublin, Dalkey and Clontarf, notwithstanding an earlier ban on shipments of corn from Ireland. Local farmers were well placed to benefit, and transport and storage facilities were presumably in demand. Just over a decade later, the chancery court appointed searchers to examine cargoes in Clontarf and the other ports for amounts of grain in excess of the agreed export quota, the penalty being the arrest of offenders and the seizure of their ships and corn. Illegal imports of horses and other goods by Irish clerks, described as 'the king's enemies', were ordered to be seized by the sheriff of County Dublin in the port in 1378. Clontarf had become a place of embarkation and landing close to Dublin for state officials by the early 1400s, the departing lord lieutenant of Ireland, John Talbot, taking ship at Clontarf for England in 1416, for example. Further licensing of exports continued in the early fifteenth century, a grant being made in 1400 to Nicholas Finglas of Dublin, for instance, allowing him to ship 600 quarters of grain from Clontarf, Dublin, Howth or Baldoyle. It is not clear to what extent port facilities, such as a quay and jetty, had been developed at Clontarf. During the following decades, merchants from Clontarf were engaged in trade with Chester, though their cross-channel commerce was overshadowed by that from a number of north Dublin ports, including Howth and Malahide.[7]

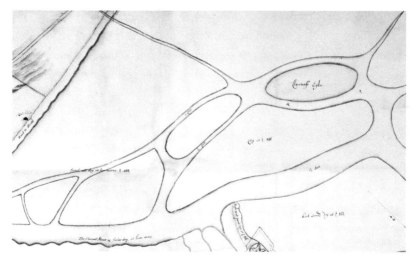

Fig. 4.4—Extract from Bernard de Gomme's map of Dublin (1673), showing Clontarf Island ('Clontarfe Eyle') (courtesy of the National Maritime Museum, Greenwich).

To judge by a statute of 1455, the inhabitants of Clontarf and its Fingal hinterland were under siege from the king's 'Irish enemies' and 'English rebels', i.e. the Gaelic clans and the Gaelicised English, who constantly raided the 'liege' or loyal people north of the Liffey. To prevent these attacks, a law was passed requiring that the fords along the river be suitably blocked and that barriers be built between the City Bridge and Clontarf Island, in the estuary of the River Tolka. [4.4] Yet the ethnic composition of the district may not have been homogeneous, as the openness of Clontarf to the sea and trading routes may have attracted settlers from a fairly wide catchment area. Certainly the bulk of the names mentioned in connection with the knightly orders are Norman. Templars at Clontarf included the knights Walter, Galfridius and Henricus, William de Warecombe and Robert de Pourbriggs, the chaplain, William de Botiller, and the more menial corrodians of the Hospitallers, William Geraud, William Gay, John Poytroun, Thomas Palfreyman and William de Ossyngham. Among the community of agricultural folk, fishers and traders it is likely that there was a fusion of ethnic strains. The earliest known merchants of Clontarf were Patricius Faber (who assumed as his surname his avocation as craftsman), and Rogerus, son of Ricardus Blund (whose father's blond hair may have given him his name). Interestingly, a Richard le Blount of Arklow petitioned for lands in Clontarf about 1320 in exchange for those he held in Killester and Raheny. Again, the composition of the fishing community is unknown, though among the names of salmon-takers at the Liffey estuary in 1473 were John Ullester and Denis Gaffney, both possibly of Gaelic origin. Not until the sixteenth century do we have definite evidence of a Gaelic element among the local population, when labourers employed in the quarrying of stone in the 1560s had names such as Rory Manchan, Donough O Schell, Art O Lennan and Connor O Bregane. They may have been recent migrants to the Dublin region from Gaelic territories, but the existence of an indigenous Irish population is confirmed in the findings of a survey of the mid-seventeenth century, when, albeit in the wake of great social upheaval, the proportion of those of English race to those of Irish on the manor of Clontarf was 57 to 43.[8]

Clontarf Hospitallers: the road to dissolution

For almost a century after 1410 the Irish Hospitallers were ruled by a series of Irish-born priors of English background, using to the full the privilege of electing natives conferred upon them at the chapter general of Aix.[9] Their ascendancy harmonised with the general self-reliance of the community, sometimes referred to as the Anglo-Irish, who were anxious to assert their capability of governing the lordship during a period of weakened English rule in the fifteenth century. It was in this setting that there evolved the concept and reality of the Pale, which was an enclave of the four eastern counties of Dublin, Kildare, Meath and Louth, wherein the population aspired to defend their English heritage of civic achievement and cultural expression against both Gaelic irruption and metropolitan interference. The interplay of institutional administration and national politics is perhaps reflected in the headship of the order of members of the leading aristocratic families—Butler, Fitzgerald and Talbot—during a 50-year period down to 1460. While not immune from the prevailing internal factionalism that was rife among these noble families, the priors were staunch in their withstanding of outside intrusion from all quarters—the church, the state and the international Hospital in Rhodes and England.[10]

The history of the preceptory of Clontarf in the fifteenth century mirrored this pattern of increasingly vexed relations between the Kilmainham priorate and outside sources of power. As successors to the Templars in holding the rectory of Clontarf, the Knights had the rights to the tithes of the parish and to the nomination of a curate to serve the parishioners. During one of several clashes between the diocese of Dublin and the Knights Hospitaller over ecclesiastical jurisdiction, the prior of Kilmainham had in 1367 cited the full temporal and spiritual powers that were vested in him by virtue of the exemption of the order's parishes, including Clontarf, from archiepiscopal visitation. The prior was successful in his case and the parish of Clontarf remained under the exclusive control of the Knights and their successors as holders of the rectory down to the Reformation and afterwards. That Clontarf was also reckoned a valuable secular prize within the Hospitallers' estates is attested by the appointment of a number of late medieval Irish priors as preceptors of the north Dublin house of the order. But the involvement of the priors in the political struggles of the mid-fifteenth century could be detrimental to the preceptory of Clontarf and other Hospitaller houses: in 1440, as a result of the kidnapping by the brothers of Prior Thomas Fitzgerald of the deputy lieutenant of Ireland, Clontarf and all of the other properties of the Hospitallers in Ireland were seized by the crown.[11]

Although apparently restored to its possessions soon afterwards, the order suffered dislocation in its organisation in the later fifteenth century owing to the political and economic imbroglio in which the priors were caught up. Because of the difficulties encountered in raising the Irish contribution to the order in Rhodes, the Irish Hospital leased out many of its estates, including Clontarf, to farmers for low rents. Thus in 1473 Robert Dowdall, the chief justice of the common bench, was mentioned as having held the farm of the manor of Clontarf from the Hospital for a number of years. Dowdall's son, Thomas, was also granted the farm of the manor in 1484 by the prior of Kilmainham, James Keating, who was also preceptor of Clontarf. Just over half a century later, at the time of the dissolution of the religious houses in 1540, the manor and rectory of Clontarf were on lease to Thomas Plunkett, a gentleman of the Pale, who also possessed lands in Killester and Coolock. Under this lease, Plunket would have had the right to nominate the curate to the parish church of Clontarf. It is probable that the Knights had chosen to ally themselves through these leases with members of the Pale gentry, who may have had contiguous properties in the vicinity of north Dublin. The most substantial neighbouring landlords to the manor of Clontarf in the later fifteenth century were the St Lawrences, barons of Howth, who had acquired the lands of Killester through marriage to the White family, from whom Thomas Plunket, a relative of the Howth family, held the latter estate.[12]

The contumacy of the Irish Hospitaller Order in the face of both crown and langue reached a climax during the priorate of James Keating, who was head of the Irish Knights from 1459 to 1494. A political ally of the ascendant Fitzgeralds of Kildare, Keating, who became preceptor of Clontarf, fell foul of the order in Rhodes during the 1460s and 1470s for failing to pay the Irish responsions and refusing to report to headquarters. He was removed as prior of Kilmainham in 1482 but was still apparently resident in Clontarf in that year. We know this because his English-born replacement, Marmaduke Lomley, recounted a frightening ordeal 'at a village called Clontarf, two miles asunder from the city of Dublin':

> 'Frere James [Keating] set on me with a number of people, a horseback and a foot, and there, violently putting hand on me, took me thither and kept me like a prisoner until the time that, by compulsion of dread in my life, I must have delivered as pleased him all manner of evidences, writings, bulls and letters which I brought with me into Ireland.'

Lomley enlisted the support of Archbishop Octavian of Armagh, but Keating refused to submit and was excommunicated in 1484. Eventually Lomley was again arrested at the behest of Keating and died in prison before the end of the 1480s.[13]

Keating's challenge to the state and Hospitaller authorities was seen by the new Tudor monarch, Henry VII, as part of a campaign of defiance by the colonial community which culminated in the crowning of the Yorkist pretender, Lambert Simnel, as king of England and Ireland in Christ Church Cathedral in Dublin in 1487. Having with difficulty secured a pardon for his part in that action, Keating again offended the king in the early 1490s by giving his backing to Perkin Warbeck, a

Confrontation at Clontarf, 1482

When I arrived at a village called Clontarfe, two miles asunder from the city of Dublin, Frere James [Keating] set on me with a number of people, a horseback and a foot, and there, violently putting hand on me, took me thither and kept me like a prisoner until the time that, by compulsion of dread in my life, I must have delivered as pleased him all manner of evidences, writings, bulls and letters which I brought with me into Ireland. And so, I being in a strange country, was so adread of my bodily death by the strength and inordinate disposition of the said Frere James that I durst not certify the Holy Father, your highness or the Lord Master of the premises [circumstances].

Marmaduke Lomley to King Henry VII (C. Litton Falkiner,
'The Hospital of St John of Jerusalem in Ireland', *PRIA* 26C (1906–7), pp 301–2)

second pretender to the throne. This time his removal was successfully achieved, and the monarch used the opportunity of the parliament held under Edward Poynings in 1494–5 to curb the autonomy of the Irish Hospitallers. Lamenting the alienation of the extensive properties of the order in Ireland by a succession of 'evil disposed priors' and their selling off of precious items and relics, including 'a piece of the holy cross', the legislators proceeded to pass a measure ensuring that in future all priors elected should be of English birth and be 'sad, wise and discreet'.[14]

From the 1490s until its dissolution in 1540 the Order of Hospitallers in Ireland, including its Clontarf preceptory, was under the charge of successive English-born priors, the most notable of whom was John Rawson, who succeeded to the position in 1514. Under his management the priory of Kilmainham was drawn into the mainstream of the Irish administration, Rawson serving in a number of state offices, including the treasurership and deputyship of Ireland. His successful service of King Henry VIII, however, gave rise to tensions with his superiors in Rhodes, who noted the comparative neglect of the spiritual welfare of the community of Hospitallers, membership of which had fallen to about a dozen by the 1530s, as well as the delay in the payment of responsions to the order.[15]

There is little evidence concerning Clontarf in the final decades of Hospitaller management. Evidently the manor and rectory were leased to laymen, who supervised the farming of the estates and were charged with appointing a curate to the parish. In 1540, when the order was dissolved, an enquiry into the properties at Clontarf found that Thomas Plunkett, a gentleman, held the lease for £26 13s 4d per annum. The main buildings of the preceptory comprised a hall, two towers, a kitchen and other farm buildings, as well as a dovecote. Of the 88 acres of demesne land, 80 were devoted to arable farming and the rest were pasture, meadow, underwood and scrub. Two designated farms, Busshells Farm and White Farm, contained 131½ acres, of which 114 were arable, and there were another 140 acres in various outfields. Besides the 360 acres of farmland, there were 24 wooded acres of the Priorswood at Coolock. The farming village comprised twenty cottages, for which the tenants each paid 4s per annum, contributed the service of a day's sowing of crops on the demesne and a present of a hen to the lord, each worth 3s 4d.[16]

The manorial lord was also entitled to a fee of 4d from every ship's captain putting in and casting anchor in Clontarf Pool off the shore. Evidence of naval activity in the nearby harbour may be gleaned from references to local mariners in contemporary chronicles and in the records of enquiries in the chancery court. A dramatic encounter in the port of Clontarf in 1514 between two Breton ships, probably commanded by pirates, and barques of Westchester and Dublin resulted in many deaths, including that of Thomas Beket the elder, who died of gunshot wounds. More routinely, in June 1526 Walter Kerby and Walter Fyan of Dublin were charged with conveying two workmen, John Dullard and William Doyn, overseas from Clontarf in the ship *Francis*, contrary to a law prohibiting exportation of labourers. In the same year Thomas Rochfort, a Dublin merchant, imported a cargo worth 40 marks at Clontarf without importing bows, as was

A naval battle at Clontarf, 1514

1514: Walter Pippard, mayor, the 5th year of King Henry VIII, Nicholas Hancoke and James Rerre bailiffs: This year 2 Breton ships fought with a bark of Westchester and with a bark of this city in the port of Clonetarffe and killed many. There was Thomas Beket the elder mortally wounded with a gun and so within a short space died. But the two ships went their way.

Alan J. Fletcher (ed.), 'The earliest extant recension of the Dublin Chronicle: an edition, with commentary', in J. Bradley, A.J. Fletcher and A. Simms (eds), *Dublin in the medieval world: studies in honour of Howard B. Clarke* (Dublin, 2009), p. 400

required by a law of 1473, and two years later merchants from Chester, Manchester, Westchester and Coventry who brought cargoes into Clontarf were fined for the same offence.[17]

In 1540 the preceptory of Clontarf was dissolved, and its possessions, along with those of the other Hospitaller houses, passed into the ownership of the crown. It was Prior John Rawson who was the agent for this major transformation in the landholding history of Clontarf that brought an end to the military orders' proprietorship. As Henry VIII asserted his power over church and state in Ireland in the 1530s, Rawson had proved to be a loyal servant. The king had determined to face down the challenge of the Fitzgeralds of Kildare to his plans for reforming the Irish administration and sent a large army to defeat the uprising of 'Silken' Thomas Fitzgerald, Lord Offaly, in 1534. Despite his previous attachment to the Geraldine party in Ireland, and notwithstanding the dangers to English-born officials in Dublin, Rawson took part in the defence of the city against the Kildare attackers and subsequently facilitated the arrest of the uncles of Thomas at Kilmainham. Rawson's loyalty to the crown ensured his acquiescence in the scheme to close all of the religious houses in the English parts of Ireland, but not before he had provided for the future of himself, his family and friends by contracting long leases of many Hospitaller estates on attractive terms. When the dissolution finally occurred, he wangled a huge pension of 500 marks (£332 13s 4d) from the crown. He also gained the title Viscount Clontarf and chose to spend his last years in retirement at the north Dublin preceptory, thus underscoring the prestige of the Clontarf holding. His greatest coup, perhaps, lay in his engineering of a grant of the entire manor, with all its economic and religious perquisites, to Matthew King, a royal servitor in Ireland and husband to Rawson's niece, Elizabeth. Thus the estates of the Knights at Clontarf passed to a close connection of the last prior, and they remained in the King family for over 100 years.[18]

As it passed from the proprietorship of a religious order to secular ownership in 1540, the manor of Clontarf had become a highly desirable possession over which several prominent landholders were to contend in the early modern period. A smooth transition was ensured through its passing from the last prior to his relative by marriage Matthew King. The Hospitaller Order to which Rawson belonged may have exercised a lightness of touch in the day-to-day running of the manor of Clontarf, preferring to draw income from gentry *rentiers* of the farms. But they did prize the house and preceptory for its accommodation for their mission of hospitality, and as a centre for their ecclesiastical and administrative role in late medieval Ireland. Clontarf under the Hospitallers continued to thrive as an agrarian economy. The 1540 survey revealed that up to 90% of the 359 acres in Clontarf consisted of arable land, with meadow and pasture making up the complement. The presence of a corn mill in Clontarf in the late Middle Ages also attests to the vitality of crop-growing in the locality. No doubt the buoyant demand of the nearby city markets was responsible for the maintenance of corn production. Under the jurisdiction of the Knights, who were very assertive in respect of their rights to river and sea fisheries, a prosperous fishing industry developed which supplied the fish shambles of Dublin city. The Knights, as an international order, would have favoured the growth of a port at Clontarf, especially in the opening of overseas communication but also for the attracting of fee-paying ships to the pool of Clontarf. Like the Templars, the Knights Hospitaller, through their religious, social and economic mission, drew Clontarf into the European cultural mainstream. Perhaps the most important feature of the immediate pre-Reformation period in terms of future developments was the emergence of a harbour for the shipping of goods and individuals to and from Britain and farther afield, with state and municipal officials taking a direct interest in the maritime affairs of Clontarf.

Report on possessions and value of the Clontarf preceptory of the Knights Hospitaller, 1540

On the site of this manor or preceptory, a hall, two towers, a kitchen and other houses, necessary for the farmers, and worth nothing above repairs. A dovecote: 3s 4d.

In divers fields around, 80 acres arable of the demesne lands: £4; 2 acres of meadow: 2s; 2 acres of hedged pasture: 2s; 2 acres of underwood: 2s; 2 acres of broom and heath: 7s.

Total for the demesne: £4 16s 4d.

In the manor, a messuage called Busshells Ferme, and 65 acres of arable, 3½ acres of meadow, 3 acres pasture: 71s 6d.
Another messuage called Whitefferme, and 49 acres of arable, 4 acres of meadow and 7 acres of pasture: 60s.
In divers fields around, 140 acres of arable and pasture: £7.

20 cottages: £4, and customs: 1 day sowing crops in the demesne: 3s 4d, and 1 hen: 3s 4d.

A wood called Pryorswoode at Cowlok containing 24 acres: 6s 8d.
Every skipper putting in and casting anchor at the bay called Clontarf Pool pays anchorage (4d.): 6s 8d.

Total for extern lands: £18 11s 6d.

Rectory of Clontarf

Tithes of sheaves, 9 couples: £6; altarages: 40s. A stipendiary priest celebrates, paid for by the farmer (of the tithes).

The manor and rectory are held by indenture for a term of years by Thomas Plunkett, gentleman, for £26 13s 4d, the lessee to find a curate and to repair the chancel and the cottages.

Total: £26 13s 4d.

Extents of Irish monastic possessions, 1540–1541, from manuscripts in the Public Record Office, London, ed. N.B. White (Dublin, 1943), p. 90

---

1 See Karl Borchardt, Nikolas Jaspert and Helen Nicholson (eds), *The Hospitallers, the Mediterranean and Europe: festschrift for Anthony Luttrell* (Aldershot, 2007); Gregory O'Malley, *The Knights Hospitaller of the English langue, 1460–1565* (Oxford, 2005).
2 C. Litton Falkiner, 'The Hospital of St John of Jerusalem in Ireland', *PRIA* 26C (1906–7), 275–317; O'Malley, *Knights Hospitaller*, 227–55.
3 Falkiner, 'Hospital of St John', 292.
4 Charles McNeill, 'The Hospitallers at Kilmainham and their guests', *JRSAI* 24 (1924), 15–30; Charles McNeill (ed.), *Registrum de Kilmainham, 1326–39* (Dublin, 1932), 9, 11, 26, 32, 44, 73, 84, 85, 93, 125; Massey, *Prior Roger Outlaw of Kilmainham*, 52.
5 Massey, *Prior Roger Outlaw of Kilmainham*, 42–56; Charles Tipton, 'The Irish Hospitallers during the Great Schism', *PRIA* 69C (1970), 33–43.
6 'The book of Howth', in *Cal. Carew MSS*, vi, 130; A.E.J. Went, 'Fisheries of the River Liffey:

notes on the corporation fishery up to the dissolution of the monasteries', *JRSAI* **83** (1953), 166–8; *Calendar of Christ Church deeds*, no. 304, pp 91–2.

7 Charles V. Smith, *Dalkey: society and economy in a small medieval town* (Dublin, 1996), 45–50; *Rotulorum patentium et clausorum cancellariae Hiberniae calendarium* [hereafter *Rot. pat. Hib.*], *Hen. II–Hen. VII* (London, 1828), 105, 209, 212, 213; Wendy R. Childs, 'Irish merchants and seamen in later medieval England', *Irish Historical Studies* [hereafter *IHS*] **32** (2000), 24.

8 *Statutes and ordinances and acts of parliament of Ireland: King John to Henry V* [hereafter *Stat. Ire., John–Hen. V*], ed. H.F. Berry (Dublin, 1907), ii, 314–15; *Chartul. St Mary's*, i, 173, 231; Connolly and Martin (eds), *Dublin guild merchant roll*, 8, 29, 80, 104; Wood, 'Templars in Ireland', 337, 350–4; McNeill (ed.), *Registrum de Kilmainham, 1326–39*, 9, 11, 26, 32, 44, 73, 84, 85, 93, 125; Phil Connolly, 'Irish material in the class of ancient petitions in the Public Record Office, London', *Analecta Hibernica* **34** (1987), 12; *Calendar of Christ Church deeds*, no. 304, p. 92; Raymond Gillespie (ed.), *The proctor's accounts of Peter Lewis, 1564–1565* (Dublin, 1996), 50–1; R.C. Simington (ed.), *Civil Survey, vol. vii: County of Dublin* (Dublin, 1945), 176.

9 Tipton, 'Schism', 42–3.

10 O'Malley, *Knights Hospitaller*, 231–2, 238–42; Art Cosgrove, *Late medieval Ireland, 1370–1541* (Dublin, 1981), 29–46.

11 Falkiner, 'Hospital of St John', 293–4; NLI, MS 4839, 'Notes from the archives of the Order of St John of Jerusalem at Valetta, 1350–1560', *s.a.* 1461, 1482, 1494; *Rot. pat. Hib., Hen. II–Hen. VII*, 262.

12 O'Malley, *Knights Hospitaller*, 236–7, 242n; White (ed.), *Extents of Irish monastic possessions*, 89; F.E. Ball, *Howth and its owners* (Dublin, 1917), 54; *Calendar of Christ Church deeds*, nos 1191, 1250, pp 239, 252; note that Patrick White, baron of the exchequer, who is referred to as a gentleman of Clontarf, was the father-in-law of Katherine, the natural daughter of the last prior of Kilmainham (and Viscount Clontarf), John Rawson: Mary Ann Lyons, 'John Rawson', in *Oxford Dictionary of National Biography* [hereafter *ODNB*] [http://www.oxforddnb.com/article/23199, viewed 20 April 2011].

13 O'Malley, *Knights Hospitaller*, 242–4; Mario Sughi (ed.), *Registrum Octaviani: the register of Octavian de Palatio, archbishop of Armagh, 1478–1513* (Dublin, 1999), no. 185, pp 185–6.

14 O'Malley, *Knights Hospitaller*, 246; Falkiner, 'Hospital of St John', 304.

15 O'Malley, *Knights Hospitaller*, 248–51.

16 White (ed.), *Extents of Irish monastic possessions*, 89.

17 Alan J. Fletcher, 'The earliest extant recension of the Dublin Chronicle', in J. Bradley, A.J. Fletcher and A. Simms (eds), *Dublin in the medieval world: studies in honour of Howard B. Clarke* (Dublin, 2009), 400; *Calendar of exchequer inquisitions, 1455–1699* [hereafter *Cal. exch. inq.*], ed. M.C. Griffith (Dublin, 1991), 15–16, 22.

18 O'Malley, *Knights Hospitaller*, 252, 254–5; Lyons, 'John Rawson'.

CHAPTER FIVE

Lords in contention: Clontarf and the growth of state power, 1540–1660

O N THE EVENING of 27 July 1534 a boat that was negotiating the shallow channel of the Liffey estuary along the northern shore of Dublin Bay fetched up on the sands near Clontarf, with disastrous consequences for the principal passenger. The archbishop of Dublin, John Alen, had decided that morning to flee to his native England to avoid the wrath of the rebellious Geraldines of Kildare, who seemed set to capture Dublin. Alen had fallen foul of the Fitzgerald family for opposing their control of political and religious patronage, and feared for his security if the city fell. Shipwrecked now with his servant, Bartholomew Fitzgerald, the archbishop made his way to Artane to seek refuge in the house of the local gentry family of Hollywood until the winds would suit for a voyage to England. Early the following morning, the rebel leader, Thomas Fitzgerald, appeared before the house with his entourage and summoned Alen before him. The archbishop knelt in his night attire, begging to be spared. Moved by mixed feelings of pity and vengeance, Fitzgerald gave the ambiguous order in Irish, 'Beir uaim an bodach', or 'Take this fellow out of my sight'. Fitzgerald's henchmen, John Teeling and Nicholas Wafer, perhaps deliberately misunderstanding the command, 'murdered the archbishop without further delay, brained and hacked him in gobbets'.[1]

Another Clontarf battle, or rather skirmish, a few months later presaged the full-scale military campaign to suppress the revolt of 'Silken' Thomas Fitzgerald. An advance party of the 2,300-strong royal army under William Skeffington, dispatched from London by Henry VIII, landed at Howth in mid-October 1534. The 80 spearmen under the command of two 'valiant and courageous gentlemen' named Hamerton, presumably brothers, were marching towards Dublin along the road to the city that passed through Clontarf. Lord Thomas gathered 200 horsemen and hastily rode around the city from Maynooth. Ambushing the English footmen at the bridge over the Tolka, Fitzgerald and his force attacked and defeated them. The English fighters had little chance in such an unequal contest and there

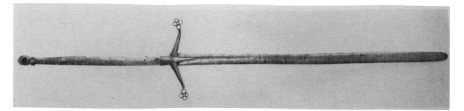

Fig. 5.1—A claymore sword of the sixteenth century which was in the possession of the owner of Clontarf Castle in 1947.

were several casualties, among them the Hamertons. Some harm was inflicted on the Geraldines, one Musgrave being slain and Thomas himself receiving a forehead wound. Buoyed by their victory, the insurgents hurried to Howth to drive off another detachment from England, and they also captured a ship from Brittany laden with horses for Skeffington's army. This successful resistance was short-lived, however, as within days the royal forces took over Dublin from its beleaguered defenders, and soon Skeffington accomplished the destruction of Thomas Fitzgerald and his allies. Within six months Maynooth Castle had fallen, and within a year Thomas and the leading rebels had surrendered and were prisoners of the king in the Tower of London.[2] [5.1]

The assassination of an archbishop and the defeat of an English army on the fringes of Clontarf in 1534 were forerunners to the impress of national events on the district, which eventually changed for ever its character as a detached manorial village. The seeds of these outside influences, which were sown even before the 1530s, began to come to fruition during the period of the Tudor and early Stuart monarchy, down to 1660. Clontarf was affected by renewed English engagement with Ireland through the general enforcement of both social and religious changes, and specifically in the expansion of Dublin as a real political capital of the new kingdom of Ireland. King Henry VIII's overthrow of the Fitzgerald rebellion was a prelude to a strengthening of royal power in Ireland through a programme of reform in state and church. In the ecclesiastical sphere, Henry dissolved the religious orders and secularised their lands, including those of the Knights Hospitaller. In the case of Clontarf, this meant that the entire manor with its perquisites was transferred into lay ownership under the patronage of the monarchs, who could grant it to favoured officers of the crown. Clontarf was a prize worth having, not only because of its rich natural resources but also because of its closeness to the city of Dublin. But the new proprietors had to battle to retain the traditional freedoms of the district from outside jurisdiction. The state was concerned with securing Clontarf as a northern gateway to

Dublin, as evidenced in the dramatic events of late 1641. And Dublin municipality asserted more and more control over the foreshore of Clontarf in order to meet the demands of city mariners and fishers. Accordingly, between the 1530s and the 1660s the history of Clontarf reflects the increasing tension between its status as a separate community on the one hand and an outlier of Dublin on the other.

Clontarf under lay rule

With the triumph of the royal campaign and the overthrow of the Kildare Geraldines, the way was open for Henry VIII and Thomas Cromwell, his chief minister, to enforce the sovereignty of the king in church and state. As part of the programme of attaining a more centralised regime in Ireland, the decision was taken to dissolve the monasteries and secularise their properties. This was a way of asserting Henry's supremacy over the Irish church and also of recouping some of the expenses involved in the recent war against the rebels. The Knights Hospitaller were among the richest orders in the country and their possessions were highly coveted. As the Knights were the proprietors not just of the church and parish but also of all the lands of Clontarf manor, the disbandment of the order meant a transfer of the whole district into lay hands. Although John Rawson was dubbed in 1538 the 'pecunious prior' of Kilmainham and deemed 'like to die', he was astute enough to anticipate the demise of his order in Ireland. Among the long-term leases made of properties belonging to the Hospitallers before the official closure were two of Clontarf property to Matthew and Elizabeth King in the summer of 1538. One was for the vill, lordship and rectory of Clontarf for 99 years, and the other (perhaps a confirmation of the first) was for the town and lordship, 30 acres of woodland at Coolock (the prior's wood) and the pool of Clontarf, as well as the church and parsonage, for the same length of time.[3]

The formal surrender of Clontarf and the other Hospitaller houses and lands to Henry VIII took place on 22 November 1540. Because of his long service and excellent connections, John Rawson was treated very favourably. He was granted a pension of 500 marks (£332 13s 4d), the highest granted to any prior or abbot at the time of the dissolution, and an additional annuity of 200 marks. In 1541 Rawson was awarded the title of Viscount Clontarf for life, with another annual fee of £10. It was reported to the king that he intended to make his abode at Clontarf. Rawson attended parliament as a peer in 1541 and continued to serve on the Irish council until his death, probably about 1543. When the former Knights' property at Clontarf was surveyed in 1540, it was found that the occupier was Thomas Plunkett, esquire, who rented the manor and rectory for £26 13s 4d per annum.

At its heart was the hall with two towers, where Rawson appears to have resided until his death, and encompassed within the estate were 383½ acres, including the demesne and also the prior's wood. The lord of the manor had rights to the tithes of the parish (in return for which a curate had to be supported), and to the fees of skippers anchoring in Clontarf Pool (a perquisite worth 6s 8d per annum).[4]

If the aged John Rawson presented a rather pathetic figure in the last years of his life, his longer-term triumph over adversity lay in ensuring continuity of ownership of the manor and rectory of Clontarf within his extended family. Matthew King, who had recently arrived from the north of England to serve the crown in Ireland when granted the lease of Clontarf manor in 1538, married John Rawson's niece Elizabeth (or Eleanor, as she appears in other records). He rose through the ranks of administrators of the army in mid-Tudor Ireland, occupying the positions of clerk of the check, muster-master and also constable of Dungarvan. Clontarf manor formed a solid base upon which to establish the position of the King family in Ireland through five generations, down to the upheavals of the 1640s and 1650s. When the lease of Clontarf for 99 years was confirmed to King in 1542, the grant included not only the town, lordship, rectory, woodland and pool of Clontarf but also the island lying to the west and the rights to fishing for the lord and inhabitants of Clontarf in the bay of Carlingford, without any payment of tithes or dues to the local vicar. That latter perquisite appears to have originated in the possession granted to the Knights Templar of the manor of Cooley and the advowson of the parish of Carlingford in the thirteenth century.[5]

The new era of lay ownership inevitably brought changes to the manorial community of Clontarf, but the effects of the transition were softened by the continuation of local gentry management of the estates for some decades after 1540. Matthew King does not appear to have settled in the district, having landholding and professional concerns which brought him to other parts of Ireland. Accordingly, the head tenants following Thomas Plunkett seem to have included such north County Dublin natives as Patrick White, Bartholomew Bathe and John Bathe, all of whom are described as 'of Clontarf'. White, who was baron of the exchequer and related to the St Lawrence family of Howth and Killester, consolidated his position in the area through the marriage of his son, Rowland, to Katherine Rawson, the natural daughter of Prior John. Perhaps it was this family that gave the name 'White farm' to one of the holdings, while one William White is mentioned as being a yeoman of Clontarf. By the later 1550s, Baron White 'of Clontarf' was contributing two archers on horseback from the district to general hostings against the enemies of the crown. This represented a break with the tradition whereby the manor of Clontarf under the Knights had been exempt from feudal levies. White may have

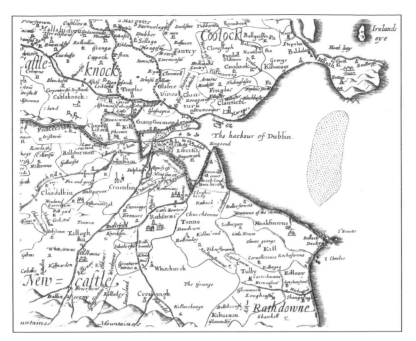

Fig. 5.2—Extract from William Petty's A general map of Ireland *(1685), showing the barony of Coolock with principal seats of gentry families with whom the King family associated.*

faced competition from another family with a neighbouring seat—the Bathes of Drumcondra—who were referred to as possessors of the farm called Clontarf by the 1570s. Bartholomew Bathe had had an interest in Clontarf prior to that of John Bathe, solicitor general, who petitioned in 1573 for an entail of the estate of 'his farm called Clontarf, part of the house of Kilmainham'.[6] [5.2]

That competition for the manor was engendered among the gentry families, who were also perhaps wary of a newcomer, is testimony to the agrarian and maritime productiveness of Clontarf, as well as to its ecclesiastical significance in the vicinity of Dublin. The 1540 monastic survey confirmed the productivity of 88 acres of demesne and of the balance of the estate of arable, meadow and pasturelands. Presumably farming life followed its wonted course under tenants-in-chief and sub-tenants, yielding for the lord a substantial annual rent of £26 13s 4d and a range of labour dues and services from the peasant folk. Most of the land was under cultivation and produced up to 90 couples of corn per annum. At some time before the mid-seventeenth century a windmill had been built at Clontarf, and a miller was resident in the district in 1641. In addition, there was extensive pastureland that in the late Middle Ages had supported large herds of sheep and cattle, as well as 100 pigs. Control of the rectory of the parish church also persisted, the lord or farmer garnering parochial tithes and paying a modest stipend to the curate, whom he appointed.[7]

The proprietors of Clontarf manor who were charged with protecting the maritime resources of the area against the irruptions of outsiders were successful to varying extents in the sixteenth and early seventeenth centuries. It was not until the 1620s that a sustained campaign was mounted by the civic council of Dublin to challenge the extensive fishing rights of the lord and community to the grounds off the shoreline of Clontarf. What little evidence survives for the activities of the Clontarf fishing fleet before then suggests that they were engaged in taking herring and salmon from the Liffey estuary and upriver, as well as from the banks along the northern shore of the bay, though there is no sign of their having exploited the Carlingford fishery. A dispute in 1577 between several fishermen from the coast north of Dublin, including Patrick Managhan of Clontarf, and the chapter of Christ Church Cathedral involved the rights to the tithes of fish, especially herrings, caught on the stretch of the Liffey between Chapelizod and the bar at the river-mouth.[8]

The fleet was based at the harbour at Clontarf, which benefited increasingly from the traffic of shipping through Clontarf Pool, the only deep-water anchorage for larger vessels within the northern inner bay of Dublin. As well as mulcting ships' captains for weighing anchor there, the lord of Clontarf manor apparently had the right to levy fishing vessels from outside the vicinity. The growth of general trade through the local harbour in the early modern period presumably generated customs revenue for the lord of Clontarf and also contributed to the economic well-being of the maritime community. Evidence that Clontarf was a busy port has been adduced already for the early sixteenth century, with passengers and cargoes being conveyed into Ireland and out to destinations in England, Wales, France and Brittany. From Piriac in the latter region, for example, came Gascony wine, brought into Clontarf on the *Laurans* in 1521.[9] In 1589 a mariner named John Browne of Clontarf was questioned by state officials on his return from an adventurous journey to La Rochelle during which he had been captured by a Spanish ship retreating as part of the Armada débâcle. Two ships' captains from Clontarf, named Tyrell, were engaged in aspects of cross-channel traffic in the 1560s: Patrick, who ferried home in his boat a cargo of slates for the reroofing of part of Christ Church Cathedral in 1565, and William, who was running a post-boat to Holyhead in 1568. The coastal village had its own merchant fleet in the early seventeenth century, the *Unicorne* of Clontarf, for example, importing wine in 1615, and the *Trinity*, which was owned by Christopher Browne, exporting a large consignment of hides and sheepskins as well as feathers, tallow, beef, bacon, tongues and herrings in 1622. The latter cargo, the property of Browne and the Dublin merchants Adam Talbot and James Nugent, was seized by the local community when the *Trinity* ran aground in Padstow Bay in Cornwall.[10]

The natural resources and raw materials of the foreshore at Clontarf, which became the subject of litigation in the eighteenth century between the landlord and the city council of Dublin, were attracting the attention of outsiders by the 1560s. John Challoner, an entrepreneurial alderman of Dublin, petitioned Sir William Cecil, Queen Elizabeth's chief minister, in 1563 for the right to exploit a lead mine which had been discovered close to the sea end of the village street of Clontarf. Nothing came of the scheme at this time and Challoner moved on to other projects, including the mining of alum on Lambay Island.[11] Clontarf stone was exploited on the city's behalf in a quarrying operation along the shore of the district in 1565. According to Donal T. Flood, the quarry, which yielded 'great broad black stone', was located between the road to the castle to the west and the area which became known as the Sheds to the east, but another possibility is a site to the east of the Tolka estuary. While the latter location would have avoided confrontation with the lord of the manor, as it lay within the city's franchises, the former is more likely, as

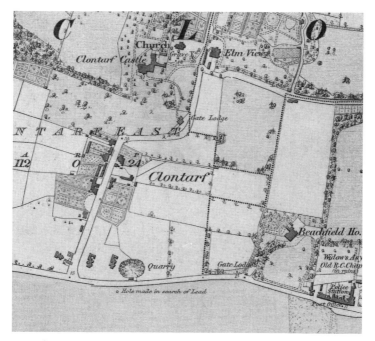

Fig. 5.3 — The position of the quarry on Clontarf shore, as shown on the Ordnance Survey map (1837–43).

there appears on the first Ordnance Survey map of 1843 a quarry just to the east of Castle Avenue. Also shown just offshore is the shaft of an old lead mine. It is likely that the vein of lead referred to by Challoner was discovered as a result of the intensive limestone quarrying operations in the 1560s. [5.3]

The stone was used in the reconstruction of Christ Church Cathedral, part of the nave of which had collapsed in 1564. The journal of the cathedral proctor or buildings manager, Peter Lewis, has survived and it provides information on the extraction of materials for the project from Clontarf in the face of many difficulties. Lewis had the stone transported to the city, where it was used in the strengthening of the foundations of the steeple. Some of the Clontarf stone also went into the erection of a new house for the dean of the cathedral on Oxmantown Green.[12] In order to quarry the stone for the building programme, Lewis supervised a party of five masons and up to thirteen labourers who worked on the site at Clontarf in early 1565. The masons, four of whom had Gaelic first names (Ferdorghe, Dermot, Brene and Melaghlyne), were forced to grapple with adverse conditions, as the quarry was partly affected by the tides, and the stones were covered by the sands. Working against the tide, they used pickaxes, crowbars and spades to uncover and cut the slabs. Because the stone was so hard, the masons' tools were constantly in need of repair by a blacksmith. While the masons cut the stone, the labouring men were busy baling water from the quarry with specially adapted vessels. Among the labourers' tasks was the bearing of the stones to a 'great heap' beside a jetty in specially constructed double-barrows. As wages for seven days of stonecutting at Clontarf quarry the masons received an average of 8d per day, the master mason, Henry, getting 10½d. They were also given an average allowance of six quarts of ale and fish caught locally. The labourers were paid at the rate of 7d a day, apparently without food and ale.[13]

As the transportation of the stone by land from Clontarf to the city would have been 'very chargeous and costly', Lewis decided to send the consignment by boat. The stones were loaded at a specially built pier by workers hired daily on the site at Clontarf and unloaded by them after a journey up the Liffey to Wood Quay. Thence the cargoes were wheeled in barrows to the cathedral. At least 26 journeys were needed to bring the full quantity. Lewis had to hire a boat at the cost of 3s 6d per day, which included a meal of meat for the boatmen. Labourers were hired to draw the stones on carts and barrows to the cathedral. For the community of Clontarf, the Christ Church project would have represented a big commercial opportunity. The smith who repaired the tools was from Clontarf, the local bakehouse supplied bread and presumably the labourers were local men also. The names of ten of the workmen have been preserved, and at least some of these are of Gaelic origin, including Rory Manchan (or Mangan), Donough O Schell (or O'Shiel), Art O Lennan and Conner O Bregane. Another person of Gaelic race was Philip O'Daly, a fisherman of Clontarf. This suggests that there was a significant Irish-speaking community in sixteenth-century Clontarf. The working party at the quarry was supplied by Clontarf clewers, or sailboats, with fish, including the

Quarrying stone at Clontarf, 1565

Account of Peter Lewis, proctor of Christ Church Cathedral

Monday, 23 January 1565

I took all my masons to the quarry of Clontarf upon the strand to draw home by boat, for carts were very chargeous and costly, and I took all my men, workmen with me.

Meat
Thomas Coyn, I paid him for a quarter of beef for my masons at 11 terstins the quarter macks, Irish money   3s 10½d

Ale
Also paid for 22 quarts of ale at 3 kynocks a quart for the masons at the quarry of Clontarf   2s 9½d

Tuesday, 24 January 1565

5 masons at the quarry of Clontarf

Ale   2s 9½d

Paid for the hire of 11 workmen, for the water came upon us every tide, and we lawe out water with bowls and skobes   6s 5d

Smith of Clontarf that we broke the points of 4 pickaxes and the points of 3 crows at both ends, the stones were so ill to break   12d

Raymond Gillespie (ed.), *The proctor's accounts of Peter Lewis, 1564–1565* (Dublin, 1996), p. 51

varieties of thornbacks (or ray) and cod. The boats and crews for transporting the stone probably came from Clontarf port, and a local merchant, Patrick Tyrell, was charged by Lewis to travel to Beaumaris in Wales to acquire a cargo of slates for Christ Church. Symbolically, on 17 May 1565 Peter Lewis arranged a ceremony for the completion of the restoration of the great foundations of the cathedral by the formal placing of Clontarf stone in the central area of the crypt. To mark the event, Lewis had the choristers of Christ Church bring a stone each to the foundations and then he beat them all so 'that they might bear in remembrance of the making of the work', and finally gave them a 'teston' or small coin.[14]

The ownership of Clontarf: the King family versus Fenton and Boyle

By the 1580s the lord of the manor of Clontarf was George King, grandson of the original grantee, Matthew, who had died in 1567, and son of John King and his wife, Mary Colley. John may have died prematurely, as his tenure at Clontarf scarcely appears in the records, while George was described as being '[proprietor] of Clontarf' by June 1585. George married twice, his first wife being Katherine, daughter of Alexander Clinton of County Louth, with whom he had three children, John, Elizabeth and Margaret. His second marriage was to Katherine Fitzwilliams, daughter of Michael Fitzwilliams of County Meath and niece of the lord of Merrion, Thomas Fitzwilliams. It is clear, then, that the King family had become integrated into the social milieu of the Englishry of eastern Ireland through propitious nuptial arrangements that included newly arrived planter stock such as the Colleys of Leix and the old colonial gentry of counties Louth, Meath and Dublin. The alliance with the Fitzwilliams family of Merrion brought the Clontarf Kings directly into the civic circle of prosperous patricians who dominated Dublin society. Yet, despite his seemingly secure position, George King was to become engulfed in a bitter feud over his ownership of Clontarf, the first of a number of such disputes that marked the history of the district down to the eighteenth century.[15]

During the climactic years of the Nine Years War (1594–1603), George King served as a captain in the royal army that was fighting against the Ulster confederate insurgents led by Hugh O'Neill, earl of Tyrone. He had charge of 100 foot-soldiers in 1599 on an expedition lasting seven weeks, and for this service he claimed and was granted expenses of £66 8s 2d on 9 December 1599. Early the following year he was charged with corruption and insubordinate behaviour, leading to his imprisonment for a brief period. The accusation was that, instead of bringing 500 troops into Munster as he was contracted to do, he brought only 333, and that he withdrew to Dublin, apparently without permission. The seriousness of his misconduct is questionable, given the laxity in general military discipline at the time and in view of the commendation that he received from the sergeant-major, Sir Oliver Lambert, that he was 'serving well'. There is a suspicion that King's misbehaviour, if any, was being magnified because his estate of Clontarf was coveted by a powerful official, Sir Geoffrey Fenton, the secretary or chief clerk of the Irish council of state. Fenton, who had a successful literary career as translator and Protestant polemicist in England, came to Ireland in 1580 and established himself as a leading councillor and policy-maker in government circles in Dublin, serving for two decades as secretary to the Irish council.[16]

In late 1599, presumably while King was still on active service, Fenton, complaining of losses sustained in his service of the crown, petitioned for a grant of the estate of Clontarf that might enable him to buy out the interest of the then proprietor, King, who held a long-term lease which had 36 years to run. In a request to Sir Robert Cecil the following month, Fenton mentions specifically the reversion of the lease of the house and lands of Clontarf, where he had recently rented a small farm from Lord Howth. He asked that Cecil procure royal assent to the grant of a lease, or else that he should block the claim of anyone else to the property. It is clear that Fenton was intent on settling himself in the Clontarf district, to which he was attracted because of its proximity to Dublin and its suitability for a country residence. Fenton's agent was despatched to London to sue for the lease and spent more than six weeks there, attempting to gain Cecil's assent.[17]

The discrediting of George King in the months subsequent to this petition may have been part of Secretary Fenton's campaign to attain his goal of the proprietorship of Clontarf. If so, he was brilliantly successful, for on 24 July 1600 Queen Elizabeth wrote from Greenwich, directing the lord deputy and the lord chancellor of Ireland to make over to Geoffrey Fenton a grant of 'the manor, preceptory or lordship of Clontarf' which had been leased to 'one King' 'for a great number of years yet to come'. Fenton's 'fidelity and sufficiency' over 22 years of service in Ireland, 'by which he has grown sickly', were cited by the queen as justification for the transfer of the property, for 'his better encouragement … in his old years'. The grant entitled Fenton to all the income from the estate, including the tithes and emoluments, in return for an annual rent of £20 sterling per annum. On 27 August 1600 there ensued a formal patent of the grant to Fenton of 'the manor, preceptory, lordship and town of Clontarf', including 30 acres of woodland, called 'the prior's wood', as well as the rectory with its tithe income. In addition to full rights to maritime activities along the shore, the proprietor's tenants who

Sir Geoffrey Fenton's grant of Clontarf from Queen Elizabeth, 1600

27 August 1600

Grant to Sir Geoffrey Fenton of the manor, preceptory and lordship of Clontarf, in the county of Dublin; 30 acres of wood at Coolock, otherwise called the Prior's wood; and the rectory, church, or chapel of Clontarf, tithes, great and small, alterares, oblations, obventions, as well spiritual as well as temporal, commons, pastures, woods, underwoods, islands, courts, waifs, strays, heriots, tolboll, waters, watercourses, weirs, fisheries, quays, creeks, sands, seashore, wrecks of the sea, with the custom called anchorage, lastage, flockage and all other customs, privileges and liberties; with liberty for the inhabitants of Clontarf, the tenants and servants of Sir Geoffrey, his heirs and assigns to fish with ships, picards and boats, nets and other engines, within the parish, liberties, limits, creeks and bay of Carlingford, without payment of tithes to the vicar or to the crown. To hold for ever, as of the castle of Dublin, in fee and common socage, and not in capite, or in socage in capite.

Calendar of the patent and close rolls of chancery in Ireland, 18th to 45th Elizabeth
(London, 1862), p. 570

were fishermen and sailors were entitled to fish in the bay of Carlingford, without having to pay tithes to the crown or the vicar of that parish. No mention was made of the rights of the family of King, who were the original grantees in the wake of the dissolution of the religious house of the Knights Hospitaller.[18]

Fenton's grant was bitterly resisted by King, who 'spake in a rude and high style' against him and stated that he would never acknowledge him as landlord of Clontarf. In his account of the contretemps written to Sir Robert Cecil on 12 December 1600, Fenton reported having taken an action of ejectment against the obstinate King. The latter's attempt to remove the case from the courts to adjudication before the council board failed, but Fenton felt at a disadvantage owing to the transfer of his own legal adviser (who was privy to the details of his case) to the side of King. Fearing that King would attempt to lobby Cecil directly, he begged the courtier to favour him, arguing that Clontarf was the recompense for his 22 years' service 'in this cursed land'. Claiming that King was 'a wicked malignant papist' who had dishonoured Cecil by his 'ill dealings', Fenton appealed as 'a faithful servitor' for his claim to be upheld. By raising the issue of religious affiliation, the secretary was deliberately pointing up a fault line between those newly arrived English who tended to eschew engagement with the existing communities in Tudor Ireland and those, like the Kings, who associated closely with the older English families and shared their recusant Catholicism.[19]

Despite this turbulent start to the Fenton proprietorship, the family appear to have settled down as landlords of Clontarf in the early years of the new century, with the Kings now relegated to the position of head tenants or 'farmers'. The Fentons' alliance in marriage with the richest of the recently arrived English planters, Richard Boyle, earl of Cork, not only boosted the family's prestige and fortunes but also impinged on Clontarf by bringing about another change of ownership. In 1603 Richard Boyle married, as his second wife, Katherine, daughter of Sir Geoffrey Fenton. In 1608 William Fenton, son and heir of Sir Geoffrey Fenton, who died that year, had his possession of the manor and perquisites of Clontarf confirmed by King James I. When William, now Boyle's brother-in-law, came to wed in December 1614, he chose as his partner Margaret Fitzgibbon, heiress of a large estate in Munster, whose wardship Boyle had bought for £1,000. In return for his investment in the wardship of Margaret, Boyle was allowed to purchase from Fenton the fee simple of the manor of Clontarf, which was thus valued at £1,000.[20]

Apparently, Clontarf was used by Richard Boyle as part of his manoeuvring to become the wealthiest and most successful of the colonial newcomers in late Tudor and early Stuart Ireland. Although he does not appear to have resided there, Boyle was for four years the landlord of the tenants of Clontarf. That Boyle may have harboured ambitions to further his vast Irish landholding interests by expanding into the north of County Dublin is suggested by his moves to purchase Donnycarney, which was 'near Clontarf', as he pointed out in a letter, but he appears not to have proceeded with the plan. Although he did not leave any permanent memorial in the area, there is impressive sculptural evidence in the form of the Boyle–Fenton monument in St Patrick's Cathedral, which the earl commissioned to commemorate his forebears. Into the huge tomb were transferred the remains of Robert Weston, Sir Geoffrey Fenton's father-in law and a former chancellor of Ireland, as well as those of Fenton himself and of his daughter, Katherine, Boyle's wife, who died in 1630. The four tiers of the monument contain in descending order the effigies of Weston, Fenton and his wife, Boyle and his wife Katherine with their sons, and the latter couple's daughters. It bodies forth in stone the genealogical roots of a new colonial dynasty.[21] [5.4]

During his period of ownership of Clontarf, Boyle drew fairly large sums of money from the estate, which he used to fund other financial transactions

Fig. 5.4 — The tomb of Richard Boyle, earl of Cork, in St Patrick's Cathedral, Dublin, incorporating on the third level the figures of Sir Geoffrey Fenton and his wife, the parents of Boyle's wife Katherine (courtesy of St Patrick's Cathedral, Dublin).

throughout Ireland, including the support of his brother-in-law, William Fenton. A lucrative source was the arrears of rent that had accumulated during the years after the Fentons took over the manor from George King in 1600 and were now being repaid through the agency of Sir John King. He was, like Richard Boyle, a highly ambitious official and landowner, who was probably related to the Clontarf Kings and who, like Matthew King, became muster-master and clerk of the check of the army in Ireland under King James I. It was Sir John who apparently managed Clontarf manor during the years of Boyle's proprietorship and it was also through him that an offer was made that brought the estate back under the control of the King family. The manor of Dungarvan in which the King family had retained a long-standing interest was in the heart of the bailiwick of Richard Boyle, and in 1617 Sir John King offered to him the fee farm of the manor of Dungarvan and a lease of the parsonage there for £4,000, in part payment of which George King of Clontarf might take over his old north Dublin estate. The offer was accepted, and in 1620 Richard Boyle, along with William Fenton, formally made over the manor and parsonage of Clontarf to George King and his heir, also named John, on condition that Boyle would receive £100 on top of the exchange value of £1,000 to reflect his profit on the investment.[22]

Richard Boyle, earl of Cork, purchases and sells Clontarf

Dec 1614

I purchased the fee simple of the manor of Clontarf in the County of Dublin of my brother Wm Fenton for one thousand pounds sterling, which 1000 li my brother, Wm Fenton, assigned me to pay the earl of Thomond for the wardship of his young wife.

The Lismore papers of Richard Boyle, earl of Cork, ed. A.B. Grosart (1886), vol. i, p. 57

Oct 1617

Sir John King sent me by Mr Archdeacon and Mr George King of Clontarffe an offer of the purchase of the fee farm of the manor and the lease of the parsonage of Dungarvan for 4000 li ster; so George King might have Clontarf in part payment which I accepted of in sort as the copy of my letter showeth ...

The Lismore papers of Richard Boyle, earl of Cork, ed. A.B. Grosart (1886), vol. i, p. 166

Mar 1618

Upon my lord deputy's and Sir John King's letter brought me by Rich Archdeacon I compounded with them and entered into covenants that upon Mr Edward Carie's passing to me the fee farm of the Castle and manor of Dungarvan for four thousand pounds English, whereof 2000 li to be paid by 19 May next and the other 2000 li the 28 November following, that I would pass to Mr Gerry King [sic] the fee simple of Clontarf (which cost me of my brother Fenton a thousand pounds ster: four years since) for 1250 li ster, whereof 500 li to be paid 9 May and the other 750 li the 28 Nov.

The Lismore papers of Richard Boyle, earl of Cork, ed. A.B. Grosart (1886), vol. i, pp 181–2

Feb 1620

I and Sir Wm Fenton conveyed to John King, son and heir to George King of Clontarf, the manor and patronage of Clontarf in the County of Dublin better cheap by one C li [£100] than I paid for it.

The Lismore papers of Richard Boyle, earl of Cork,
ed. A.B. Grosart (1886), vol. ii, p. 6

In spite of William Fenton's revival of his claims to Clontarf in the late 1630s, the Kings were now in control of the district, to be dislodged only by the huge upheavals caused by all-out warfare in Britain and Ireland in the middle years of the century. George King, now an elderly man, resumed his lordship of Clontarf. As part of the restored proprietorship, George appears to have been determined to exploit the burgeoning economy of Clontarf port, and in particular the fishing industry, and in doing so he incurred the wrath of the municipality of Dublin. The nub of the issue was control of the foreshore of Clontarf, beyond the Pool, over which the Kings had jurisdiction. Less certain were the rights to Clontarf Island, to the west of the Pool, and the Furlong (or 'foreland'), a region of sand and shingle stretching between Clontarf Head or Point and the island, which became a lucrative source of shellfish, particularly cockles. According to two city merchants, Edward Gough and James Sedgrave, in 1622 George King was claiming customs on catches of herring in the Tolka estuary, a sum of 3d per barrel being mulcted from 'free citizens' of Dublin in the early 1620s. In addition, he was extracting a barrel of salt from each ship as an anchorage fee in Clontarf Pool. Clearly a fish-processing operation was coming into being, probably at the site of the later Sheds at Clontarf Head, as suggested by the collecting of salt and also by a reference to 'making fish' at Clontarf in 1630.[23]

The many grievances being expressed about the extortionate practices of the owners of Clontarf initiated a long period of struggle between Dublin city council, representing the civic commercial interest, and the local proprietorship. The immediate response of the city authorities in the 1620s was twofold: firstly to test the title of the lords of the manor to the Island and Furlong of Clontarf, and secondly to shift the focus of inner bay fisheries to the southern shoreline at Ringsend. As to the first, the device used was to evoke a legal case by the granting of a lease of the Island and Furlong of Clontarf to successive recorders of Dublin— William Dongan, appropriately from a noted Dublin family of fish merchants, and, after his death in 1622, to Nathaniel Catelyn—for seven years at a peppercorn rent. In the event of the corporation's challenge being successful, longer leases of either 21 or 31 years were to follow for these men, the city's principal law officers. As Dongan failed to begin the proceedings, his successor was expected to do so, and it seems that a bill was eventually filed by Catelyn in 1630.[24]

It referred to the royal grant of liberties to Dublin in 1192 in which the boundaries of the city franchises were delineated, and these extended on the north side of the Liffey as far as the River Tolka. The city claimed, however, that before King John delimited the franchises of Dublin the two 'little pieces of land', the island of Clontarf and the foreland [furlong] of Clontarf, had been granted to the city to farm. Therefore they belonged to the city, being 'within the sea water marke near Clontarfe'. In their triennial riding of the franchises in 1603, during which the boundaries of the city's jurisdiction were ceremonially followed, the civic leaders *had* crossed the bridge over the Tolka and followed the highway to Clontarf, the official account noting that 'the old records say that the franchise stretcheth eastwards upon the north side of the channel as far as they might to the sea, and thence from the furlong to the island of Clontarf'. There is no record of a decision in the case, although, on the face of it, the corporation's claim to the title had a signal weakness in that the city charter of 1192 did not mention the east bank of the Tolka. Moreover, complete ownership of the foreshore of Clontarf appears to have been granted to Sir Geoffrey Fenton in 1600 as part of his lordship, the patent referring specifically to 'the pool and the island lying on the west side of the pool' and generally to 'islands, waters, watercourses, weirs, fisheries, quays, creeks, sands and seashore'.[25]

The other strategy adopted by the civic authorities to counter the monopoly of the lord of Clontarf over the northern shore was to shift the focus of herring fishing to the southern side of Dublin Bay. In 1621 the city council decided to negotiate with the lord of Merrion, Thomas Fitzwilliams, for the right to set up an alternative city fishery at Ringsend. This scheme would, it was hoped, 'draw the herring fishing and the access of merchants and fishers', 'for the utility of the common wealth'. In order to make Ringsend as 'convenient as Clontarf', the council decreed that new infrastructure be put in place. Thus, the carmen or porters of the city were to supply three days' labour for the construction of a new bank or furlong, being spurred on no doubt by the promise of access to the new facility, something that was denied them at Clontarf. Ships and boats putting in at Ringsend were expected to contribute to the work of shifting sand and stones and dropping ballast. A separate cooperage was to be established at Ringsend for the making of barrels for herring during the fishing season, and the city companies of bakers, butchers and cooks were authorised to trade in bread and meat there, paying a reasonable charge to the members of the consortium, the aforementioned Gough and Sedgrave and their associates. Tithes were to be levied on shiploads of fish, but at half the rate imposed across the bay in Clontarf.[26] It is not clear to what extent the proposed boycott of the Clontarf fishery affected the district in the short term, or indeed how successful the new operation was, but the fact that Clontarf had a noted fishing centre—called Herrington—by the end of the seventeenth century suggests that any impact was limited. [5.5]

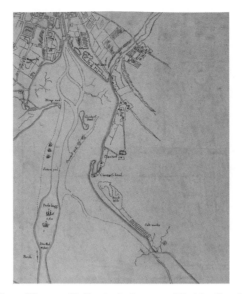

Fig. 5.5—Extract from Thomas Phillips's draft map of Dublin Bay (1685), showing the settlement at Clontarf Head, which became known as the Sheds of Clontarf (courtesy of the Royal Irish Academy).

The burning of Clontarf in 1641 and its aftermath

In 1631 George King died and the ownership of Clontarf skipped a generation, going to his grandson and namesake. This was unusual, as John, the son and heir of George senior and father of George junior, was still alive, though perhaps in poor health. He continued to derive an annuity from the estate as his son settled in as landlord. In that role, the younger George King, despite his family's comparatively recent arrival in Ireland, identified strongly with the older English gentry in the neighbourhood, including the Bathes of Drumcondra, the Hollywoods of Artane and the Fitzsimons of Raheny. [5.6] The Kings' marital ties with leading families of the Pale over the course of three generations had helped to consolidate their place in this Old English society. George's grandmother, Katharine, belonged to the Clinton family from County Louth, and his mother, Eleanor Finglas, who died in 1623, came from the branch of that Catholic family at Tobertown, near Dunleer, Co. Louth. One of George's aunts, Elizabeth, also married a man from that locality, Richard White of Richardstown, and his sister was wedded to Martin Scurlock of Rathcredan, Co. Dublin. George's own wife, Mary Talbot, was of a branch of that noble lineage seated at Belgard, and together they had a daughter, Jane, who wedded one James Aylmer. In view of this close social integration, it is hardly

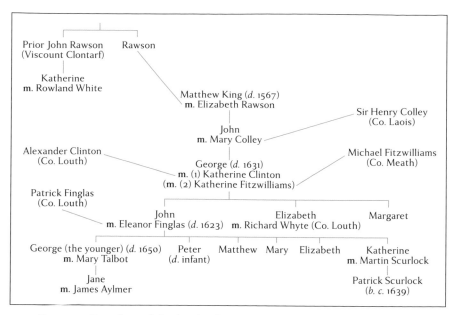

Fig. 5.6—Genealogy of the family of King of Clontarf, proprietors of Clontarf from 1540 to 1641.

surprising that George King subscribed to the political and cultural grievances of the Old English class which drove them into a rebellion that had fateful consequences for themselves and their followers.[27]

The events of late 1641 that affected Clontarf so adversely took place against a backdrop of the rising tensions between King Charles I and parliament in England that engulfed the neighbouring kingdom. These brought to the surface issues that had long festered among the inhabitants of Ireland, whether of newer or older English or of Gaelic origin, such as royal prerogative, religious toleration and titles to lands. Taking advantage of the breakdown of constitutional relations in England, the leaders of Gaelic Ulster rebelled in October 1641 in pursuance of the recovery of their estates from Protestant planters. Military activity spilled over into the Pale, destabilising the Old English, who were exercised by the question of toleration of their Catholic religion by the Protestant authorities, as well as by a general feeling of political alienation from the Irish government. On the part of the administration in Dublin, divided internally between supporters of the parliament and the king, the outbreak of insurrection in Ulster, accompanied by reports of the massacre of Protestants, occasioned a panic-stricken reaction which encompassed the Old English Catholics of the Pale within the sweep of its severe security measures. In response to an assembly of the gentry of the Pale, including George King, at Swords in early December 1641, the government issued a proclamation, ordering the named assembly participants to present themselves in Dublin on 18 December, on the promise of a safe conduct.[28]

Before that deadline expired, however, events centred on Clontarf led to an irreconcilable breach of trust between the two sides. Given its proximity to Dublin and already tainted by the rebellious stance of its owner, the seaside village came to be perceived by the Dublin Castle authorities by mid-December as a hotbed of subversive activity which had to be punished. The catalyst for the burning of Clontarf was the plundering of a ship owned by Philip Norrice of Liverpool which had run aground off the coast in a storm on 11 December. According to witnesses examined within subsequent weeks and months, fourteen rebels from Raheny, including one Fitzsimon, first raided the cargo, killing one man, a miller, who attempted to stop them, and sparing another only after he converted to Catholicism. A consignment of cloth belonging to a clothier of Dublin, Giles Dewhurst, worth over £200, was among the stolen goods. Another witness, a local man named David Powell, who was English, was later visited in his house by the rebels and ordered to leave because of his nationality. He had seen inhabitants of Clontarf, mostly fishermen, carrying away quantities of coal, salt, cheese and rope from the stricken ship to their houses. Yet another observer, an English Protestant gentleman named Edward Leech, who had with his family been expelled from Lambay Island by a force of rebels led by a Catholic priest, was a victim of robbers near the place of salting herrings at Clontarf on 14 December. His party of thirteen heard women who were picking cockles along the shore crying 'Siggy Sassinagh, siggy Sassinagh' ('There come English, there come English'). Leech also witnessed some inhabitants of Clontarf plundering coal from the stranded vessel. So terrified were the English refugees at the prospect of going through the 'town of Clantarfe' and by reports of 300 rebels in Prior's Wood near Artane that they stuck to the seaside and made their way to Dublin to inform the authorities of their ordeal.[29]

On the basis of these and other reports, the lords justices who headed the government prepared to make an example of Clontarf on account of the 'depredations' committed by its inhabitants and others in Dublin Bay. Categorising the coastal fishermen as 'all Irish and papists', they specifically identified 'divers of the inhabitants of Clontarf, Raheny and Kilbarrack' as self-declared rebels who were engaged in conspiracy against the state. The seriousness of the disaffection of the fishing community was perceived to lie in its control of the narrow channels along the shores of the bay through which ships could approach Dublin port. Thus the recent 'villainy' at Clontarf was seen as part of a campaign to deter

English ships from sailing to the capital, as were the personal attacks on English people and the robbery of their goods. There was also an attempt to link the activities of the predatory fishermen at Clontarf to the lord of the manor, George King, who was now targeted for his involvement in the political disaffection of the Pale gentry. If they needed an example of sectarianism on the part of some inhabitants of the area, the case of Randall Dimmock, a Protestant clergyman resident at Clontarf, would have provided it for the government leaders. Dimmock, who had had a long-standing dispute with George King over the non-payment of his clerical stipend as curate of Clontarf, was forced to abandon his home and flee to Dublin with his son Michael after his life had been threatened by rebels shortly before 15 December 1641.[30]

On that day, Sir Charles Coote, the sexagenarian governor of Dublin, was deputed to march the short distance from the city to Clontarf with 400 foot-soldiers and 100 horse. His orders were to punish the rebels by burning their houses and goods, but they had withdrawn from the district. Instead, Coote loosed his troops in the town to wreak havoc indiscriminately. In what became known as the 'burning of Clontarf', houses and property were torched and a

A clergyman's experience of the rebellion of 1641 in Clontarf

1 March 1642

Randall Dimmock, cleric, duly sworn and examined, deposes that he, [being] curate and minister of St Doulagh's, Portmarnock and Clontarf, for fifteen years, ... did live at Clontarf with his family before these grievous and woeful troubles began. Fleeing to Dublin to save his life, with his son, Michael Dimmock ... The town of Clontarf was burned and pillaged by the soldiers of Dublin. His house (although his household was there) lost all he had to the value of £30 sterling. His son who in the afternoon ... went down to know what was done found the house pillaged. Thinking to bring his people to Dublin, two rebel horsemen with twelve footmen beset him after the army had retired, took him prisoner to Swords, whereby he lost his horse to the value of £12. Being threatened to be hanged, a gallows was set up to hang him with another Dutch man, yet both escaped by God's providence.

TCD, 1641 Depositions Project, on-line transcript January 1970 [http://1641.tcd.ie/ deposition.php?depID<?php echo 809276r164?>] (accessed 24 July 2012)

massacre ensued, sixteen men and women and three infants being reported as killed. Special attention was given to Clontarf house or castle, the residence of George King. On the pretext that goods seized from the plundered ship had been brought there, the building and its contents were completely destroyed. Some prisoners were taken by Coote's men, but the members of the King family, including 'the young villain', George himself, escaped capture. As a sequel to the grim occurrences, Michael Dimmock, the son of the Protestant curate, returned to Clontarf in the afternoon of 15 December to inspect his house and found it pillaged. As he attempted to bring his household to safety, a party of fourteen rebels appeared and took him as a prisoner to Swords. Michael Dimmock was sentenced to be hanged and a gallows was erected, but he managed to escape.[31]

The burning of Clontarf, 1641

15 December 1641

Old Sir Charles Coote came out with a party [and] plundered and burned the town of Clontarf distant 2 miles from Dublin, belonging to George King, nominated in the Proclamation, and killed 16 of the townsmen and women and 3 suckling infants, which unexpected breach of the Proclamation (having deterred the gentlemen from waiting on the Lords Justices) forced many of them to betake themselves to their natural defence and others to abandon their houses. In the same week, 56 men, women and children of the village of Bulloch, being frightened at what was done at Clontarf, took boats and went to sea, to shun the fury of a party of soldiers come out of Dublin, under the command of Colonel Crafford, but being pursued by the soldiers in other boats, were overtaken and thrown overboard.

R.S., *A collection of some of the murthers and massacres committed on the Irish in Ireland since the 23rd of October 1641* (London, 1662), pp 8–9

Once again a bloody episode at Clontarf, albeit on a smaller scale than that of 1014, had ramifications far beyond the local. All expectations on the part of the lords justices that the Old English gentlemen, including George King, would be enticed to Dublin on 18 December on the promise of safe passage were now shattered. Their attempts to justify the burning of Clontarf served only to confirm the leading gentry of the Fingal region in their defiance of the Dublin government and their common cause with the Ulster insurgents. Rejecting an administration of 'notorious faith-breakers', they organised an 'army of the Pale' under the command of Lord Gormanston in early 1642. Significantly, it was in Gormanston's castle that George King and his wife had sought refuge for Christmas 1641 after the destruction of their house and property on 15 December. It is highly unlikely that George ever saw Clontarf again. His name figured on a list of those declared traitors in an official proclamation of 8 February 1642, the 590 acres of Clontarf manor being deemed to be forfeit to the government because of his outlawry and a reward of £400 being offered for his head. Later in 1642 the Irish Catholics of Gaelic and Old English background formed the Confederation of Kilkenny, King becoming a member. The confederates attempted to gain recognition for their position from the royal commander in Ireland, the duke of Ormond, in return for support for King Charles I in the British civil wars. A treaty was eventually concluded which afforded the confederates royal protection, but King Charles was captured and beheaded in 1649. George King, meanwhile, was appointed as royal customs master of Waterford by Ormond but died there in 1650, just after the capture of the city by Oliver Cromwell, who had come to Ireland on behalf of the English parliament to defeat the royalist forces.[32]

What of Clontarf after 1641? The shattered community lacked the leadership of a manorial lord for its recovery, with the attainder of George King as well as that of John, his father, who was also outlawed. Mary King, who survived her husband George, was among those who were granted lands in Connacht under the Cromwellian transplantation, receiving 155 acres. As the succession to the estate was thereby debarred to members of the King family, Clontarf attracted the envious interest of newcomers. For a time during the 1640s the district, and that of Artane, was in the custody of Charles Lambert, the military governor of Dublin in succession to Charles Coote. With the defeat of the royalist party, which Lambert supported, the property of Clontarf was granted on 14 August 1649 to John Blackwell, a soldier-official who was a strong supporter of Oliver Cromwell. Blackwell was an Adventurer, one of those who had advanced money in England for the suppression of the 1641 rebellion in return for a proportionate amount of forfeited land in Ireland. As a well-placed officer of parliament, he was positioned to choose the prime of Irish estates, including the 590 acres of Clontarf, Hollybrook and the island of Clontarf. As treasurer-at-wars in London during the early 1650s, it is unlikely that Blackwell would have spent time in Clontarf, and on 23 October 1656 he sold the manor on to Captain John Vernon, quartermaster of the Cromwellian army, thus beginning the long-standing association of that family with the district. Captain John did settle on his new estate and invested £2,000 in 'improvements', probably restoring the lands and buildings. He remained in 'quiet possession' of the manor until the restoration of King Charles II in 1660.[33]

Clontarf in the Civil Survey, 1654–6

Barony of Coolock

Parish of Clontarf

Geo King of Clontarf,	Clontarf	560 acres	meadow	012	By the jury
Irish papist			arable	448	£200. By
			pasture	100	us, £280

Observations

Proprietor: The proprietor (as the jury returns) deserted his house the first year of the rebellion and possessed the premises as his inheritance 1641.

Buildings: There is upon the premises a castle with a stone house slated (adjoining), a stone bawn, a dove house, an orchard with some fruit trees valued by the jury at £300, a windmill with several thatched houses, and a decayed church. An island called the Island of Clontarf.

Parish of Clontarf

Royalties: There is a fishing belonging to the premises.
              The tithes to the proprietor.

Bounds: Bounded on the east and south with the lands of Raheny and the sea; on the west and north with the lands of Donnycarney, Artaine, Killester and Skillinglass.

The total number of acres in the aforesaid parish is 560.

The Civil Survey, A.D. 1654–1656: Volume VII: County of Dublin,
ed. Robert C. Simington (Dublin, 1945), p. 176

After being in lay ownership for more than a century, the manor of Clontarf was surveyed by a jury of local inhabitants as part of the Civil Survey of the mid-1650s. The unit of survey was the barony, divided into parishes. In the barony of Coolock in north County Dublin, the parish of Clontarf (which was coterminous with the manor) was found to comprise 560 acres. Of these, 448 were arable, and the rest divided between 100 of pasture and twelve of meadow. The value placed on the manorial parish by the local jury was £200 per annum (though the survey commissioners reckoned it was worth £280). By comparison, the income for the entire estate in 1540 came to £26 13s 4d. The forfeiting proprietor, George King, described as an Irish papist, was reported to have deserted his residence in the first year of the rebellion of 1641. Included in the buildings listed were a castle and a slated stone house, a stone bawn or enclosure and a dovehouse. Along with an orchard of some fruit trees, the demesne premises were valued at £300. Nearby in the village were several thatched cottages, a windmill and a decayed church. Clontarf Island was also included as part of the manorial possessions, and a fishery was mentioned as belonging to the lord of the manor, who garnered the tithes of the parish. Not surprisingly, then, in view of its potential and location, Clontarf was an object of contention for vying proprietors after 1660, each intent on developing a country estate within a few miles of the burgeoning metropolis of Dublin.[34]

1 This account of the killing of Archbishop Alen is given by Richard Stanihurst, 'History of Henry VIII's reign', in L. Miller and E. Power (eds), *Holinshed's Irish Chronicle 1577* (Dublin, 1979), 268–9.

2 *Ibid.*, 276–7; *Letters and papers, foreign and domestic, of Henry VIII, 1509–47* [hereafter *L&P, Hen. VIII*] (London, 1862–1932), vii, 518; Laurence MacCorristine, *The revolt of Silken Thomas: a challenge to Henry VIII* (Dublin, 1987), 96–119.

3 For the background to the suppression of the monasteries see Brendan Bradshaw, *The dissolution of the religious orders in Ireland under Henry VIII* (Cambridge, 1974); Lyons, 'John Rawson'; *Cal. exch. inq.*, 90–1.

4 *Cal. exch. inq.*, 110–11; *L&P, Hen. VIII*, xvi, 1540–1, 13; Lyons, 'John Rawson'; White (ed.), *Extents of Irish monastic possessions*, 89.

5 *Cal. exch. inq.*, 90–1; John D'Alton, *The history of County Dublin* (Dublin, 1838), 44–6; Wood, 'Templars in Ireland', 375.

6 For King see, for example, *Cal. S.P. Ireland, 1566–7*, 17, 70–1, 201; *1571–5*, 137, 768; *Acts of the Privy Council in Ireland, 1556–71*, 13, 90, 91; *Cal. exch. inq.*, 148, 167; Ball, *Howth and its owners*, 54; Lyons, 'John Rawson'; for John Bathe's suit see *Cal. S.P. Ireland, 1571–5*, 455.

7 White (ed.), *Extents of Irish monastic possessions*, 89; *Civil Survey, County Dublin*, 176; TCD, MS 809, f. 214.

8 *Calendar of Christ Church deeds*, 120.

9 A.K. Longfield, *Anglo-Irish trade in the sixteenth century* (London, 1929), 128–9.

10 The Pool of Clontarf could take ships of up to 160 tons: *Calendar of material relating to Ireland from the high court of Admiralty examinations, 1536–1641*, ed. J.C. Appleby (Dublin, 1992), 116–17; *Cal. S.P. Ireland, 1588–9*, 121; Gillespie (ed.), *The proctor's accounts of Peter Lewis*, 82; *Cal. S.P. Ireland, 1568–71*, 37; Hugh Kearney, 'The Irish wine trade', *IHS* 9 (1954–5), 411; Maighréad Ní Mhurchadha, 'Contending neighbours: society in Fingal, 1603–1660' (unpublished Ph.D thesis, NUI Maynooth, 2002), 146–7.

11 *Cal. S.P. Ireland, 1509–73*, 225; Colm Lennon, *The lords of Dublin in the age of Reformation* (Dublin, 1989), 216, 237–8.

12 Donal T. Flood, 'Letter to the Editor', *DHR* 27 (1974), 72; Murphy and Potterton (eds), *The Dublin region in the Middle Ages*, 390; Gillespie (ed.), *Proctor's accounts of Peter Lewis*, 50–75, reference to Oxmantown house on p. 59.

13 Gillespie (ed.), *Proctor's accounts of Peter Lewis*, 50–80.

14 *Ibid.*, 66–78, 82, reference to choristers is on p. 75.

15 *Cal. S.P. Ireland, 1566–7*, 201; NLI, Genealogical Office [hereafter GO] MS 48, p. 37; D.B. Quinn (ed.), 'Calendar of Irish council book for 1581–86', *Analecta Hibernica* 24 (1967), 167.

16 NLI, MS 8068.

17 *Cal. S.P. Ireland, 1599–1600*, 214, 278, 375–6.

18 *Calendar of patent rolls, Ireland* [hereafter *Cal. pat. rolls, Ireland*], ii (1576–1603), 544–5, 570.

19 *Cal. S.P. Ireland, 1600–01*, 58; *1601–3*, 495.

20 For a biography of Richard Boyle see Nicholas Canny, *The upstart earl: a study of the mental and social world of Richard Boyle, first earl of Cork, 1566–1643* (Cambridge, 1982); D'Alton, *History of County Dublin*, 45–6; Michael McCarthy Morrogh, *The Munster plantation: English migration to southern Ireland, 1583–1641* (Oxford, 1986), 168–9; A.B. Grosart (ed.), *The Lismore papers of Richard Boyle, earl of Cork*, series 1, vol. i (London, 1866–8), 57.

21 Grosart (ed.), *Lismore papers*, i, 131; Amy Louise Harris, 'The funerary monuments of Richard Boyle, earl of Cork', *Church Monuments* 13 (1998), 81; Clodagh Tait, 'Colonising memory: manipulations of death, burial and commemoration in the career of Richard Boyle, first earl of Cork (1566–1643)', *PRIA* 101C (2001), 126–32.

22 Grosart (ed.), *Lismore papers*, i, 56, 57, 59, 100, 106, 131, 166, 181–2, 186, 204, 256; ii, 280.

23 D'Alton, *History of County Dublin*, 46; John de Courcy, *The Liffey in Dublin* (Dublin, 1996), 157, 169; Gilbert (ed.), *Ancient records*, iii, 132, 146–7; see TCD MS 809, f. 243, for a reference to a place of salting of herrings and cockle-gathering in 1644.

24 Gilbert (ed.), *Ancient records*, iii, 139–40, 177–8, 238–9.

25 *Ibid.*, i, 198; iii, 177–8; *Cal. pat. & close rolls*, i, 570; K.W. Nicholls (ed.), *Irish fiants of the Tudor sovereigns* (Dublin, 1993), iii, 363.

26 Gilbert (ed.), *Ancient records*, iii, 146–8.

27 Dublin, NLI, GO MS 48, 37; *Irish Memorials of the Dead* 11 (1907–9), 115, 155; *Cal. S.P. Ireland, 1669-70*, 447–8.

28 R. Steele (ed.), *A bibliography of royal proclamations of the Tudor and Stuart sovereigns, 1485–1714*, ii, 2 (Oxford, 1910), p. 358a.

29 TCD, 1641 Depositions Project, on-line transcript January 1970 [http://1641.tcd.ie/deposition. php?depID<?php echo 809273r161?>, accessed 24 June 2011; http://1641.tcd.ie/deposition. php?depID<?php echo 821231r157?>, accessed 24 June 2011; http://1641.tcd.ie/deposition. php?depID<?php echo 810244r274?>, accessed 24 June 2011; http://1641.tcd.ie/deposition. php?depID<?php echo 809276r164?>, accessed 24 June 2011].

30 *Calendar of the manuscripts of the marquess of Ormond*, ii (London, 1903), 39, 46; TCD, 1641 Depositions Project, on-line transcript January 1970 [http://1641.tcd.ie/deposition. php?depID<?php echo 809276r164?>, accessed 24 June 2011].

31 *Calendar of the manuscripts of the marquess of Ormond*, ii, 46; John Temple, *The Irish rebellion* (Dublin, 1713), 151–2; J.T. Gilbert (ed.), *A contemporary history of affairs in Ireland* (Dublin, 1879), i, 41–4; R.S., *A collection of some of the murthers and massacres committed on the Irish in Ireland since 23rd of October 1641* (London, 1662), 8–9; TCD, 1641 Depositions Project, on-line transcript January 1970 [http://1641.tcd.ie/deposition.php?depID<?php echo 809276r164?>, accessed 24 June 2011].

32 *Calendar of the manuscripts of the marquess of Ormond*, ii, 39, 46–8; Gilbert (ed.), *A contemporary history of affairs in Ireland*, i, 387, 393; ii, 237; TCD, 1641 Depositions Project, on-line transcript January 1970 [http://1641.tcd.ie/deposition.php?depID<?php echo 810209r246a?>, accessed 24 June 2011]; J.T. Gilbert (ed.), *A history of the Irish confederation* (7 vols, Dublin, 1882–91), iii, 3; *Cal. S.P. Ireland, 1660-2*, 372.

33 *Cal. S.P. Ireland, 1660-2*, 76, 433; *1669-70*, 447; Robert C. Simington (ed.), *The transplantation to Connacht 1654–1658* (Dublin, 1970), 33, 112; J.J.N. McGurk, 'Lambart, Charles, first earl of Cavan (*c.* 1600–1660)', *ODNB* [http://www.oxforddnb.com/view/article/15922, accessed 23 June 2011]; G.E. Aylmer, 'Blackwell, John (1624–1701)', *ODNB*, on-line edn, May 2008 [http://www.oxforddnb.com/view/article/37197, accessed 23 June 2011]; Dublin, Marsh's Library, MS Z I 1 13, no. 23, I, II; D'Alton, *County Dublin*, 46; *Calendar of state papers, domestic* [hereafter *Cal. S.P. dom.*], *1689-1702* (London, 1927–37), 201.

34 *Civil Survey, vol. vii: County of Dublin*, 176.

CHAPTER SIX

Consolidating the Vernon estate at Clontarf, 1660–1760

AFTER THE RESTORATION of the monarchy in 1660, Captain John Vernon's cousin, Colonel Edward Vernon, assumed ownership of the manor of Clontarf. From the start, he faced severe difficulties in establishing his proprietorship owing to a series of challenges from within and outside the family. Eventually his rights were vindicated and an unbroken period of Vernon lordship of Clontarf ensued, which lasted into the twentieth century. The family's contribution to the making of the estate and later suburb of Clontarf was enormous, but it was not achieved without a great struggle against natural and human forces that bore down upon the district. During the century under review in this chapter, the character of the early modern village of Clontarf was very much affected by the major engineering project that eventually reconfigured the greater Dublin Bay area. Not only did the work of reclamation and dredging of the northern foreshore have an impact on maritime and fishing activity in Clontarf but it also elicited expanded claims to the inner bay by the city council, bolstered by its new agencies such as the Ballast Office. The intensive legal battles between the Vernons and the municipality in the earlier eighteenth century over fishing and shoreline rights were part of what one legal historian has called the 'litigation topography' that summoned modern Dublin into being.

Vernon versus Vernon

In loyally serving Charles Stuart, son of the executed King Charles I, Edward Vernon, a royalist officer from Staffordshire, received lavish promises of rewards. He had been imprisoned by the Commonwealth government of Oliver Cromwell in 1655 but escaped to the Continent to join the Stuart court in exile. When Charles II landed at Dover in 1660 Edward was in the company, and later, as a 'gentleman of the privy chamber', he travelled to Ireland, where he received a grant of 'the manor and township of Clontarf, with Hollybrook and the island of Clontarf', on 26 October 1660.[1] Apart from the huge controversy caused within the Vernon family by his taking over as owner from his cousin, Captain John Vernon, Edward had to overcome two major legal barriers to the assertion of his lordship of Clontarf. One was that the Act of Settlement of 1662 specifically exempted all claims of title arising from the estate of John Blackwell, who, as a top Cromwellian officer, had been closely associated with the execution of Charles I in 1649. Blackwell's leasing of Clontarf to Captain John Vernon in 1656 thus also called into question the later transaction in 1660. Because Edward Vernon enjoyed the restored king's favour, however, a special clause was inserted into the Act of 1662 which stipulated that 'care was to be had of Colonel Edward Vernon, in the general saving of rights to exclude John Blackwell, as to any pretence to anything granted to the said Colonel Vernon'.[2] The other difficulty lay in the question of the innocence of the heirs of the outlawed George King of Clontarf.

Contested land titles arising from the upheavals of the 1640s and 1650s caused enormous complexities for landholding in Restoration Ireland. The claims of former Catholic landowners or their heirs conflicted directly with those of the Protestant adventurers who had received their lands under the Cromwellian settlement, and King Charles II struggled unsuccessfully to balance the two through a court of claims and other means. Clontarf may be taken as a microcosm of the island as a whole. Edward Vernon, a beneficiary of a grant to a Cromwellian adventurer, faced a strong challenge to his proprietorship of Clontarf from two branches of the ousted Catholic family of King. One was headed by Mary, the widow of the younger George, and their daughter Jane, who had married James Aylmer. The other was formed through the descent of John King, son of the older George (who had died in 1631), in the persons of John's daughters Katherine, Mary and Elizabeth, one of whom (probably Katherine) married a Martin Scurlock of Rathcredan, Co. Dublin, and had a son, Patrick Scurlock, who was born in 1639. The latter's claim to the estate of Clontarf appeared to lie in a provision of the senior George's will that if his grandson, the younger George, died without an heir the succession should pass to the heirs of his grand-daughters, daughters of John and sisters of the younger George. Wisely, the King family members appear to have made common cause in a joint claim against Edward Vernon put forward in the names of Jane Aylmer and Patrick Scurlock.

The Kings' case centred on the reversal of the outlawry of George King, who had been declared a traitor as a result of joining the rebellion in 1641. Under the terms of the treaty signed in 1649 with the confederate Catholics by the duke of Ormond on behalf of Charles I, those who adhered to the royal cause at that date but had been outlawed since 1641 were to have their attainders overturned and be considered innocent of rebellion. On that basis, in late 1661 Mary King, on behalf of her daughter Jane, applied for and was given permission to sue for a reversal of the outlawry of her father, as 'he died in the king's service … and was outlawed in his absence, though persons of his persuasion were not allowed to come to Dublin or appear in the king's courts'. It appears that a royal letter reversing the decree of outlawry was duly issued. Within the following year and a half, another claim to Clontarf was being made on behalf of Katherine King and Patrick Scurlock, the descendants of John King, arguing that Scurlock, who was two years old at the time of the rebellion, was an innocent Catholic and therefore entitled to inherit Clontarf through his great-grandfather. By the spring of 1663 the two wings of the family were combining in their claim against Colonel Edward Vernon.[3]

The colonel fought back strongly against the challenge of the Kings to his grant of October 1660. He enlisted the assistance of senior politicians in London and Dublin who were sympathetic to his case, and warned against similar influences being deployed on his opponents' side. Accusing Katherine King, whom he described as 'a professed nun', of presenting a forged deed to support the claim of her side of the family, he also asserted that the Kings had bribed officials of the court of claims with the sum of £40 to ensure a favourable hearing. As a counterbalance, Vernon adduced a copy of the proclamation of December 1641 which George King and other Pale gentlemen had flouted. Eventually, the elapsing of the deadline for the submission of new claims, including those of Katherine King and Patrick Scurlock, in 1663 was cited in Edward's favour. Perhaps most decisive of all in clinching his position as a loyal upholder of the restored Stuart establishment in Ireland, and hence a valued estate-holder, was his vital role in the suppression of a plot in March 1663 by Thomas Blood and his cadre of disgruntled Protestants to seize Dublin Castle and kidnap the duke of Ormond, the lord lieutenant. By mid-March 1663 King Charles II was indicating that the commissioners for claims should uphold Edward's case, and eventually Vernon's title to Clontarf was reconfirmed by a royal patent, entitling him to the full 593 acres, and the King claim was definitively dismissed.[4]

Much more tenacious as challengers to Edward Vernon's title were his cousin, Captain John, and the latter's son, also John, whose determined campaign to wrest Clontarf from the colonel's family continued into the eighteenth century. In the long-running litigation between the two branches of the Vernons, questions about the validity of granting Irish land to newcomers were less important than intra-family rivalry. Both Captain John and Colonel Edward belonged to a landed

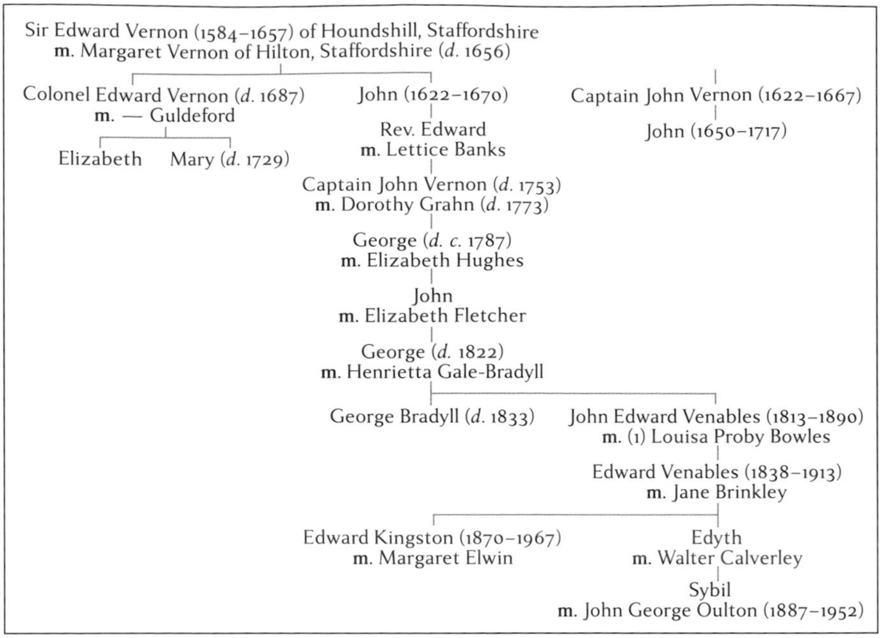

Sir Edward Vernon (1584–1657) of Houndshill, Staffordshire
m. Margaret Vernon of Hilton, Staffordshire (d. 1656)

Colonel Edward Vernon (d. 1687)   John (1622–1670)   Captain John Vernon (1622–1667)
m. — Guldeford   John (1650–1717)
                                          Rev. Edward
Elizabeth   Mary (d. 1729)   m. Lettice Banks

                                Captain John Vernon (d. 1753)
                                m. Dorothy Grahn (d. 1773)

                                    George (d. c. 1787)
                                    m. Elizabeth Hughes

                                         John
                                    m. Elizabeth Fletcher

                                    George (d. 1822)
                                m. Henrietta Gale-Bradyll

            George Bradyll (d. 1833)   John Edward Venables (1813–1890)
                                          m. (1) Louisa Proby Bowles

                                          Edward Venables (1838–1913)
                                          m. Jane Brinkley

    Edward Kingston (1870–1967)   Edyth
        m. Margaret Elwin   m. Walter Calverley

                                                 Sybil
                                    m. John George Oulton (1887–1952)

Fig. 6.1—Genealogy of the family of Vernon.

family based in the English midlands, the main branch having its seat at Haddon in Derbyshire. Edward, who was from Houndshill in Staffordshire, took the royalist side in the English civil wars, while his cousin John was a parliamentarian officer who had written an important treatise on cavalry tactics.[5] [6.1] Whereas John had benefited by the Cromwellian victory in his purchase of Clontarf in 1656, Edward was in the ascendant after the return of the king. Whatever the intention of the cousins at the time in the transferring of Clontarf from Captain John to Colonel Edward in late 1660, the exact nature of the arrangement gave rise to great acrimony in the succeeding decades.

The details were argued over during court battles from the 1660s onwards. According to his son's account, Captain John Vernon agreed in September 1660 to Edward's taking over the nominal proprietorship of the estate of Clontarf, which was to be held in trust for the captain and his heirs. To seal the bargain, a sum of £1,600 was to be paid and a purported deed of sale drawn up. According to his side of the family, Colonel Edward was the recipient of the manor from the king by a letter patent dated 26 November 1660, and he chose to disregard the gambit from his cousin in respect of a trusteeship. Edward's position as proprietor, validated by the clause in the Act of Settlement of 1662, was further strengthened by a renewal of the letters patent under the terms of the Act of Explanation of 1665.

After Captain John Vernon's death in 1667, his son John made several attempts to overturn the adjudications of the 1660s after he came of age. In 1674 and again in 1686 he filed bills in the court of chancery, seeking to have the alleged trust of 1660 upheld, but on both occasions his case was dismissed.[6]

Down to his death in 1687, Colonel Edward Vernon, moved by 'charity and compassion', had undertaken to make some payments to the family of John Vernon, because of arrears of rents of Clontarf that had arisen before 1660 and to compensate for some improvements made in the late 1650s. Such transfers were taken by the younger John Vernon as evidence of a legal obligation on the part of the colonel. Also deemed indicative of a guilty conscience was the evidence of one Charnell Wooley, a retainer of Edward Vernon, to the effect that the colonel was deeply troubled in his last years of life. Wooley had overheard Vernon suggest to his wife a plan to marry their elder daughter, Elizabeth, to John, as a way of settling the long-running dispute between the family branches, but she demurred, raising doubts about John's not being an Anglican. After Edward died, the Clontarf estate was settled on his two daughters, Elizabeth and Mary. In the event of their dying childless, the manor was to pass to Edward's brother, whose heir was a namesake, Edward Vernon, a clergyman in England. Elizabeth, who never married, died prematurely, and thus Mary Vernon inherited the Clontarf estate, though the lands there were apparently heavily mortgaged. Mary was sent to France during the Jacobite rebellion in the later 1680s to stay with relatives, and although she received pardon for outlawry and permission to return by an English act of parliament in 1703, the estate of Clontarf had been declared forfeit to King William III.[7]

This encouraged John Vernon to petition in 1699 for the setting up of a commission to enquire into the royal title to the estate. The king referred the case to the lords of the treasury in England, who in turn transferred it to the lords justices in Ireland. Although Mary Vernon was given possession of Clontarf once again, the lords justices appeared to leave open the possibility of a claim by John Vernon, if he could substantiate it. In 1705 he issued an appeal against previous dismissals of his case to the House of Lords. Both sides issued printed statements of their positions, rehearsing from their perspectives the history of the evidence for the title to the lands of Clontarf. While Mary Vernon's case was weakened by the loss of the deeds emanating from the acts of the 1660s and the lords seemed disposed to favour John Vernon as beneficiary of a trusteeship, the proceedings ended when parliament was prorogued. Two years later, John was granted two thirds of Upper and Lower Holly Brooks.[8] Eventually, Mary died childless about 1729, and the main Clontarf estate was taken over by a Captain John Vernon, son of Reverend Edward Vernon and grand-nephew of Colonel

The evidence of Charnell Wooley in the case of Colonel Edward Vernon of Clontarf versus Mr John Vernon, merchant of Dublin, 1686

Charnell Wooley of the city of London, gentleman, ... made oath that during the time of the suit in chancery concerning the estate in Clontarf and the Holly Brooks, Colonel Vernon, with whom this deponent then lived, [came] to London where his wife was then resident, and the next morning being in bed with her, told her in the said deponent's hearing (he being bid to withdraw which he accordingly did into a back closet but could hear what was said) that he, Col. Vernon, was advised by his friends to propose a marriage to the aforesaid John Vernon between him and his daughter, Betty, and desired to know her opinion in it ... To which his lady replied that she was too young as yet to be offered in the matrimony but besides she told him that she had formerly acquainted him that she had designed to make a match for her, to a friend of her own, ... a much more agreeable man for a husband for her than Mr Vernon could be, he being of the same persuasion in religion as she was brought up in, and Mr Vernon being of different principles ... To which Col Vernon made answer that what he had offered to her was not so much from his own inclination, as he found John Vernon to be of a turbulent spirit, and would give him great disturbance in his possession of Clontarf, but that this marriage would cement all differences and he might keep the possession of the estate during his life and settle the remainder upon him and his daughter, Betty ... He then further told her that, the estate [was] the young man's father's, that although he had obtained a grant from him of the estate in his own name without giving him any consideration for it, only the promise of protecting it from being made a forfeiture to the king, and that therefore he thought himself obliged in his conscience, the father being dead, to make such provision for this since that he (Col. Vernon) might in some measure discharge himself of what he had undertaken by way of promise to the father.

Dublin, Marsh's Library, MS Z 1 1 13, 'Case of John Vernon', p. 6

Edward. The ramifications of the Vernon versus Vernon dispute rumbled on until the early 1740s, but by the middle of the eighteenth century the landlordship of Clontarf through the Vernon line was settled, with Captain John Vernon, the then proprietor, bequeathing the manor in 1753 to his son George, who in turn passed it on to his heir, John, about 1785. But the struggle for this later smooth intergenerational transmission of Clontarf had been hard fought, during its course engaging the attention of successive monarchs of England and Ireland, the lord lieutenant, the duke of Ormond, and the duchess, his wife, the lords justices and lord chancellors of Ireland, and the Houses of Lords in England and Ireland.[9]

The Vernon estate takes shape

Notwithstanding the uncertainty over the exact proprietorship after 1660, the Vernons were to impress their stamp very firmly on Clontarf immediately after their arrival in the neighbourhood. Indeed, successive owners became notorious for their tenacity in defending the integrity of their manor against individual or corporate intruders. The total extent of the Vernon estate was 590 acres, including the island of Clontarf off the south-western shore and the designated unit of Holly Brook or Upper Holly Brook.[10] Bounded by the sea to the south, the manor had as its perimeters to the west and north the road from Dublin to Baldoyle (now the Howth Road), and to the east the Raheny River (as the southern stretch of the Santry River is called), which flowed into the sea at present-day Watermill Road. By far the most prominent of the neighbouring landlords were the St Lawrences of Howth, occupying the contiguous lands of Killester and Raheny as well as a narrow strip stretching to the coast in eastern Clontarf, and among the other nearby seats of gentry families were Donnycarney and Artane. Access to the city was via Ballybough Bridge over the Tolka and along the strand road, which led eventually to Howth. The traveller John Dunton described his walking sometimes from Dublin 'along the strand at Clontarf, which when the tide is in, is very pleasant'. It was within the rough triangle of terrain thus formed that the Vernons developed their country estate by the mid-eighteenth century, with its town and fishing village and other topographical features, and also attempted to control the uses and amenities of the shoreline.[11]

John Dunton's impressions of Clontarf, 1699

Sometimes I walk along the strand, up to Clontarf, which, when the tide is in, is very pleasant.

John Dunton, *The Dublin scuffle* (Dublin, 2000 edition), p. 209

Clontarf in the 1660s was still a town in recovery after the devastating raid of December 1641. A 'census' carried out for Ireland in 1659 found that there were 79 taxpayers in Clontarf, of whom 45 were English and Protestant and 34 were Irish. Another national survey about the same time, this one of the number of houses and hearths for a new hearth tax, revealed that there was one dwelling with eleven hearths in Clontarf (the castle), another with five (possibly the stone house mentioned in the Civil Survey of Clontarf) and 29 houses with one or two hearths (perhaps the 'several thatcht houses' of the Civil Survey). These findings show that Clontarf had a higher proportion of good-quality housing than any other parish in the Fingal area of north County Dublin. At the heart of the town was the manor-house or castle of Clontarf, which had been the main target of Coote's attack with fire in 1641, the damage to the building and the immediate environs being very severe. When John Vernon took over from John Blackwell in 1656, he is said to have expended over £2,000 on 'improvements' to the estate, including presumably the repair of the house. The refurbishment continued after the Restoration, as in 1665 it was reported that a dispute arose over the conduct of an apprentice mason who was doing work on Clontarf House.[12]

As well as supervising the rebuilding of the manor-house, the Vernons oversaw the construction of a new church on the site of the old one, which had been described as 'decayed' in the Civil Survey. Thus was restored to the area a significant symbol of its identity as a parish community after a hiatus of several decades, and the position of Clontarf parish was consolidated by the uniting to it of the Anglican parish of Killester in 1686. Also boosting the status of Clontarf under the new owners was a royal grant of a new manor court in 1675. Contrary to the trend elsewhere, which saw the widespread disappearance of feudal institutions after 1660, King Charles II chose to enhance the jurisdiction of the manor and its traditional privileges. As well as the manor court, the landlord was given power to lay out a private deer-park of 300 acres, and also the right to hold two fairs annually, one on 10 April and the other on 6 October.[13]

The earliest maps of the district of Clontarf, dating from the second half of the seventeenth century, show us topographical features that were being marked for the first time or are known previously only from literary sources. The various map-makers had different purposes in their surveying of the land and sea. In the case of the Down Survey and maps of the mid-1650s, the cartographer was concerned to show the lands forfeited in the rebellion of 1641 and not then occupied by Protestant settlers. Clontarf is thus not detailed in the map of the barony of Coolock, but the island and a windmill are depicted. Sir Bernard de Gomme, a military engineer, came to Dublin in 1673 with his colleague Thomas Phillips to

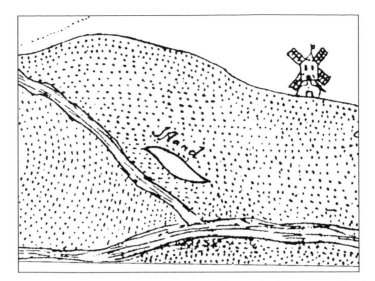

Fig. 6.2—Extract from Down Survey map (1656–8), showing a windmill on the coast of Clontarf.

report on the possibility of building a major fortress near the coast. As well as a map of the city and suburbs of Dublin, de Gomme produced a map of Dublin harbour, dated 1673, which shows some details of the Clontarf coastline. Phillips returned to Dublin in 1685 and delineated the bay and its maritime features in a number of draft maps. The following year, Captain Grenville Collins, a navy hydrographer, mapped the Irish coast as part of a major survey, and his depiction of Dublin Bay included several landward features along the Clontarf shoreline.[14]

The first representation from actuality of a feature of the area is seen in the Down Survey map of 1654, which shows 'Clantaff Island' and the 'Island' in maps of the baronies of Rathdown and Coolock respectively. [6.2] Mentioned in records of the previous two centuries, we now see the island as an elongated lozenge shape, lying in an east–west position in the estuary of the River Tolka, off the south-west coast of Clontarf manor. De Gomme, Phillips and Collins each indicate the island in more or less the same position, though with variations on the shape. No habitation is shown on the island, but plans were afoot from 1666 onwards to establish a quarantine area or 'pest-houses' there for the containment of passengers and goods from places overseas that were infected with plague. A sum of £85 was set aside by the civic council for the construction of two pest-houses on the island by 1682, and 45 years later the 'plague-house' on Clontarf Island was to be walled around at great public expense.[15] There is no reference to the reaction of the Vernons to this use of the island. The windmill that appears on the Down Survey maps does not feature in the work of the cartographers of the 1670s and 1680s. It was located along the shoreline of Clontarf to the west of the promontory later known as Clontarf Head. A millpond is shown on a map by Phillips as located to the east of present-day Castle Avenue, but the site is relatively distant from a possible watermill at the mouth of the Raheny River.

Thomas Phillips's maps of 1685 give us the first real indications of how the core nucleation and the peripheries of the manor of Clontarf were configured. [6.3] At the centre was the manor-house or castle, represented by a shape containing jutting-out wings to the south, probably the towers. This orientation would correspond to the details in the first drawing of the castle by Gabriel Beranger just under 100 years later. Facing the house is a road running south to the coast, lined by a number of houses, which were represented by square blocks, and this was the spine of the town in the 1680s. To the west of the castle is an oval-shaped area of woodland, named 'Clantarff Wood' in one of the maps, perhaps a remnant of what was once called 'prior's wood'. This is referred to by a visitor, John Dunton, in the last years of the century as 'a fine grove called Clontarf Wood', and as a

Fig. 6.3—Extract from Thomas Phillips's draft map of Dublin Bay (1685), showing the castle ('The House') and the oval-shaped Clontarf Wood at the north of the main street of Clontarf (courtesy of the Royal Irish Academy).

location for duels and romantic trysts. The embryonic road system is suggested by the continuation of the avenue at right angles to its junction with the castle close and its subsequent northwards turn, prefiguring the later route of Castle Avenue. The vestiges of another eastward-tending roadway are also traced, suggesting the later Seafield Road. Phillips's maps do not signify the church building, but in the delineation by Grenville Collins, in which several substantial buildings appear, most of them surrounded by trees, the church may be marked in close proximity to the castle.[16]

To the east of the core town of Clontarf are depicted for the first time at the shore the herring sheds, which we know to have existed at least since the early seventeenth century. Called the 'fish house' by Phillips and located at the eastward-pointing headland dubbed by him 'Clantarff Head', this feature appears as a small settlement named 'Herringtowne' on the map by Grenville Collins.[17] Destined to become a substantial settlement in its own right, Herrington, or 'Herronstown' as it later became, was the hub of the thriving fishing industry at Clontarf. Also indicated by Phillips, to the east of the 'fish house' along the coast towards the Nanniken River were brick kilns and saltworks, suggesting manufacture and production for local and urban uses. To the west of the central town and east of the road to Baldoyle some settlement is shown in Collins's map. One of the buildings was probably a house connected to the unit of land named Hollybrook or Holly Brook, which begins to appear in the records of the area from 1649. Depicted beside a small stream, possibly the River Wad, the residence is ringed by trees. The first cartographic entry of the designation 'Holly Brook' may be that on a map of the Wide Streets Commissioners of 1704, showing the district of Donnycarney.[18]

Changes in Dublin Bay affect Clontarf

The topography of coastal Clontarf, along which these landward developments took place under Vernon proprietorship, was significantly altered by major engineering works from the early eighteenth century onwards. In response to the perennial problems caused by restricted access for shipping into and out of the port of Dublin, these projects aimed at deepening the channel of the Liffey to allow vessels of greater draught to approach the quays of the city, and also to break up the sand bar that blocked the mouth of the harbour. Inevitably, the radical reconfiguration of Dublin Bay had consequences for existing pools, anchorages and fisheries along the northern and southern shorelines, including that of Clontarf. While its subsidiary agency, the Ballast Office, carried out its task of maritime improvement, the parent body of Dublin municipal council had ambitious plans for the economic development of the inner bay at the estuaries of the Tolka and Dodder rivers. As well as unwittingly affecting currents and flows in the waters off the coast through the work of the Ballast Office, the council's plans for land reclamation and exploitation of marine wealth had a more direct and immediate impact on the Clontarf area, raising once again issues about the ownership of the foreshore and the accessibility of the district to citizens and travellers. Faced as they were by encroachment on land and diminution at sea, the Vernons, as the new owners of Clontarf, donned the mantle of defenders of the district against the metropolis.

As with the topography of the land, the marine features off Clontarf were charted for the first time in the later seventeenth century, some of them with great scientific accuracy. The naturalist Gerald Boate, writing about 1650, pinpointed only two places within the inner bay at which it was not possible to walk dry-foot about ships at anchor, one of these being the Pool of Clontarf and the other the Poolbeg, both of which had 9–10ft of water at low water.[19] Clontarf Pool, a creek in the lee of Clontarf Island, continued to provide shelter for larger vessels visiting Dublin port, a fee of fifteen pence per boat being payable to the landlords of Clontarf.[20] In his map of 1673, de Gomme recorded a sounding of 3ft at low water just east of the oval-shaped 'Clontarf Eyle'. In Thomas Phillips's map of the city and bay in 1685, this erstwhile assistant of de Gomme gave a depth of 4ft for a channel just east of Clontarf Island,

---

Clontarf Pool as an anchorage in Dublin Bay, 1652

Dublin haven hath a Bar in the mouth, upon which at high flood and spring-tide there is fifteen and eighteen feet of water, but at the ebb and neap-tide but six. With an ordinary tide you cannot go to the Key of Dublin with a Ship that draws five feet of water, but with a spring-tide you may go up with ships that draw seven and eight feet ... This haven almost all over falleth dry with the ebb ... so as you may go dry-foot round about the ships which lie at anchor there, except in two places: one at the North-side, between Dublin and the Bar, and the other at the South-side ... In these two little creeks (whereof the one is called the Pool of Clontarf, and the other Poolebeg) it never falleth dry, but the ships that ride at anchor remain ever afloat, because at low water, you have nine or ten feet there.

Gerald Boate, *Ireland's naturall history* (London, 1652), pp 25–6

---

though no sounding is given for Clontarf Pool itself, and a draught of 11ft for Poolbeg. Phillips also indicated a buoy at the bar at the harbour mouth (which had a depth of 6ft at low tide). In the following year, 1686, Captain Grenville Collins sketched Clontarf 'Poole' as a narrow creek off the promontory (which, though unnamed, is Clontarf Head) with a low-water depth of just under 4ft. He also showed the bar between the South and North Bull sandbanks, the latter, extending from Howth along the inner shore to the Tolka, as being 'all dry' at low tide.

Dublin City Council began seriously to address the question of how to deepen the channel of the Liffey with the setting up of the Ballast Office in 1707. Petitions preliminary to its establishment had stressed the problem of great quantities of loose sand being carried into Clontarf Pool, among others, with the effect of the loss of 2ft of its depth in recent years.[21] By way of alleviation, the Ballast Board undertook the building of a wall on the north side of the channel by means of kishes or baskets filled with stones. This wall, backed by the infilling of gravel and shingle from 'Clontarf Bar', stretched from present-day Butt Bridge almost to Clontarf Island (equivalent to the modern Point Depot). In contrast, a wall on the south side was constructed by the driving of piles into the seabed east of Ringsend and continuing it on the South Bull by the sinking of wooden frames with stones. Making the Liffey estuary 'more commodious' to accommodate larger ships was of limited value unless the blockage at the harbour mouth could be removed. A scheme for dissolving the sand bar was presented by Captain John Perry to the

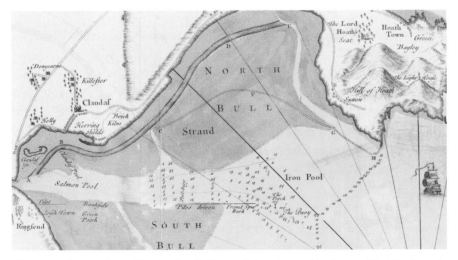

Fig. 6.4—Extract from Charles Price's Chart of the city and harbour of Dublin (1730), showing the marine canal proposed by Captain Perry. Note the coastal features, including Holly[brook], herring sheds ('shelds') and brick kilns (courtesy of Trinity College Library).

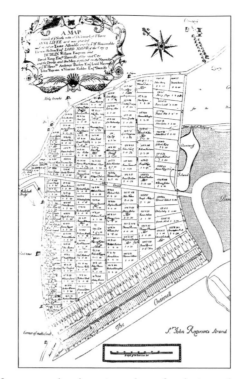

Fig. 6.5—Map of a proposed reclamation scheme for the inner bay of Dublin, which would have taken in the area between Ballybough bridge and Clontarf Island, and a new Tolka canal and eastern Clontarf, 1717.

Ballast Office about 1720, involving, among other elements, the construction of a ship's canal along the shore at Clontarf from Sutton Creek.[22] While this proposal, which was illustrated on a map of 1730 published by Charles Price, never became a reality, there is little doubt that the channelling of the Liffey ultimately affected the shoreline of Clontarf and its island and pool. [6.4]

In 1717 Dublin City Council endorsed an elaborate plan for the reclamation of much of the northern shore of Dublin Bay from Ballybough to Clontarf, in order to capitalise on the walling-in of the channel of the Liffey. In addition to the already-forming wedge of land contained within the arms of the north and east walls, the grand scheme (which was carefully mapped) envisioned another, completely new reclamation. [6.5] This roughly triangular wedge of 77 acres was to stretch across from the outlet of the Tolka River at Ballybough Bridge in an easterly direction along a new canal to opposite the east wall or quay, and northerly in a direction just to the west of Clontarf House or Castle, meeting the shore at a point between present-day St Lawrence Road and Castle Avenue. The northern and southern reclamations, separated by the new 80ft-wide canal to bear the Tolka to the inner bay, were to be divided into 134 lots, or allotments for development, to be drawn for by civic worthies.

Plan of Dublin City Council for the reclamation of the north inner bay as far as Clontarf, 1717

We, the committee [for taking in and setting out in lots and surveying the strand between Mabbotts mills and the sheds of Clontarf], have surveyed the Strand, and are of opinion that the Strand on the north side of Ballybough [Tolka] river, from the highest ground on the north end of Clontarf Island to the next angle on the west side of Clontarf house, on the road, containing seventy seven acres, be divided with the Strand on the south side of Ballybough river, containing in all four hundred forty one acres; that the Ballybough river be carried on the south end of Clontarf Island in a straight line from the first angle on the east side of Ballybough Bridge in a new canal, the same canal to be eighty foot wide; that the front lots of the channel be divided into eighty eight lots, and the lots to the rear into forty four lots, which make one hundred thirty two lots, and that all the rest of the ground be divided into one hundred thirty four lots, two whereof to be reserved to the city, seventy seven on the south side and ninety two on the north side of the canal, for such public use as shall be thought necessary; that that part of the Strand undivided be reserved in common for raising of stones, for carrying on the whole work and improving the same, and accordingly there is a map drawn, which is hereunto annexed.

That a quay be continued from the northeast corner of the 132 lots to Clontarf Island, and from thence to the shore on the angle on the west of Clontarf house, be built at public charge.

That the road or strand leading from the Abbotts wall towards Ballybough Bridge, from thence to Clontarf, be all eighty foot wide, and that the key fronting the channel and also the key continued to Clontarf Island, and from thence to the angle on the road to the west of Clontarf house, be all sixty foot wide.

That the little river at Hollybrook be carried to the sea at public expense.

Calendar of ancient records of Dublin, vol. vii, pp 30–3

The topographical and administrative implications raised by this plan for the district of Clontarf were considerable. By land and sea there would be changes: the existing strand road from Ballybough along the coast to the castle would be driven inland, while a new approach route would be opened along the eastern quay, envisaged as being 60ft wide. This new road would, moreover, absorb some of Clontarf Island along its south- and north-western perimeter, rendering the rest of the island an extension of the land. The effects of the reclamation on Clontarf Pool were not adverted to, the area appearing on the periphery of the map. Significantly, the expanse of foreshore still surviving to the east of the new land was designated as a quarry 'in common for the work', corresponding to the site of the quarry shown later on the Ordnance Survey map of 1843. The proposed conveying of the Holly Brook (or Wad River) to the sea at public expense raised questions about rights of ownership in the western part of the manor. The developed lots would bring dozens of new proprietors close to the heart of the town of Clontarf, thus threatening the interests of the Vernon landlords. Essentially, the civic council was engaged in an attempt to assert municipal control over a newly reclaimed area of the inner bay of Dublin, planning for its economic and social development and the exploitation of its coastal resources, over which local claims were traditionally made.[23]

The reluctance of the Vernons to cooperate with the plans of the Ballast Office and the civic assembly for widening the channel, let alone for reclaiming the land north of the Tolka outflow, soon became evident. There was an early indication of this in 1710, when the Ballast Office reported that 'persons interested in the ground on the north side of the channel' would not contribute to the expenses of the project.[24] Nor was John Vernon prepared to work with Sir John Rogerson, the developer of the southern quay wall, in supplying stones from the shore at Clontarf in 1716.[25] Such recalcitrance is of a piece with the Vernons' extreme territoriality as far as Clontarf manor was concerned. Successive owners, first Mary and then Edward and Captain John, either jointly or solely after 1729, drew up meticulously detailed deeds for the leasing of property in Clontarf to noble and gentry folk, such as Sir Thomas Southwell, who leased a house in the early 1700s, and Paul Hale and his brothers, who acquired 29 acres at Blackbush in 1747.[26] Subsequent sub-leasing for the building up of the community at the Sheds from the 1740s bore the stamp of the careful leasing policies of the Vernons.[27] Both Mary and Captain John controlled the development of manufacture at Clontarf. Mary had promoted the production of salt from the sea by laying salt-pipes on the strand to the east of the Sheds, and the Salt House was leased by her and John jointly in 1729 to Thomas Eaton and William Christison. Similarly, the brickfields, between the Sheds and the saltworks, were overseen by John Vernon, who leased them to William Goodrick before 1730.[28] Charitable patronage was also tightly controlled by the family: when the royal charter school at Clontarf was proposed, land for the project was leased along the coast from Captain John Vernon.[29]

It is not surprising, then, in view of this tight proprietorial control, that the Vernons engaged in a series of legal battles with the civic authority over rights to the maritime area of Clontarf, particularly during John Vernon's lordship of the manor after 1729. He staked out his ground formally in 1731 during the triennial riding of the franchises of the city by the lord mayor and his civic entourage. Confronting the mounted party at Ballybough Bridge on the Tolka, John made a formal speech of protest against any proposed incursion along the north strand road by the coast of Clontarf as far as Raheny mill. In the face of the city's 'pretended' claim to incorporate this route within the city's franchises since the seventeenth century, John Vernon cited the exemption of Clontarf from the city of Dublin since the time of King John's charter and the grant of the manor to the Knights Templar.

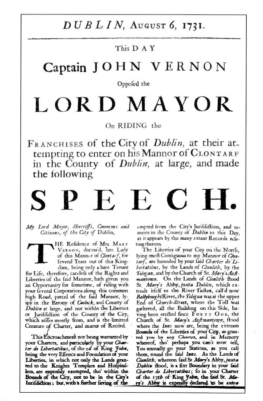

Fig. 6.6—Printed version of Sir John Vernon's speech of 1731, condemning the city's intrusion on the manor of Clontarf during the riding of the franchises.

Acknowledging that Mary Vernon might have been lax in challenging civic claims to the shoreline, being merely a tenant-for-life in succession to her father and not fully possessed of the manor, he nevertheless took his stand against the forceful incursion of the 'swelling city' into his estate. The contention between the city and the owners of Clontarf over the rights to the Furlong and island has been referred to in the previous chapter. As early as 1603, in the municipal riding of the franchises, the civic party had included a passage from the Furlong to the island, ridden at low tide. In 1720, however, the municipal ceremony of the riding of the franchises had included in its regular circuit the road by the Sheds (or 'Shades') of Clontarf (and on out to the watermill at the outflow of the Fox Stream), a deliberate landward intrusion on the presumed liberties of the manor.[30] Now, to mark his determination in withstanding the city's claim, John Vernon had his speech of protest printed by George Faulkner in Dublin later in 1731.[31] [6.6]

The immediate context for this skirmish was the mounting tension between the municipality and the proprietor of Clontarf over rights to the foreshore implied in the conflicting claims to the liberties of the area. When he succeeded Mary Vernon as owner of Clontarf, John Vernon offered to enter into negotiations with the Dublin civic assembly to resolve 'whatever disputes have happened in law or equity' between him and the municipality.[32] There had been recent conflict over the perennial issue of the rights to seizure of goods cast up on the shore at Clontarf as a result of shipwrecks and storms within the bay. Flotsam in the form of wooden piles from the engineering works on the South Bull, uprooted in a tempest, fetched up on the shore of Clontarf, whose owner refused initially to relinquish them.[33] Another dispute occurred over the right to quarry stone on the north strand. In about 1722 the city had granted to William Maple a plot of three and a half acres on the north strand off Clontarf, probably that shown on the map of 1717, for the quarrying of stone and for the taking away of sand and gravel. Vernon and his agents had in 1729 quarried stones from Maple's plot with a view to 'finishing several large buildings and improvements on the estate of Clontarf'. Maple obtained an injunction and the case went to a hearing at the bar of the House of Lords in 1730, no record of a decision having been found.[34]

A major focus for the disputed rights emerged in the form of Crab Lough (or Crablake Water), an area of the strand to the east of the Sheds of Clontarf that was rich in shellfish. In an evident testing of the rights to ownership in 1718, the city had granted part of Crab Lough to Alderman Humphrey French for 61 years at an annual rent of £70 to lay down oyster-beds and farm the produce. He was to bestow 10,000 oysters each year on the lord mayor and 2,000 on each of the sheriffs, as well as allowing one day per annum for the mayor and citizens to come and eat oysters on the strand.[35] On becoming lord of the manor, John Vernon responded to this provocation by encroaching on French's oyster-beds, taking off his oysters and burning them.[36] The matter went to court, the civic assembly obtaining an injunction against Vernon's entry into French's patch. Vernon appealed the injunction and pursued his case against a decision of the court of chancery in Ireland to the House of Lords in England. During the course of the hearings, which continued until 1734, Vernon mentioned an area of the strand called Quire's Island, where he laid down oysters and on which Mary Vernon had salt-pipes installed below the high-water mark for the use of the saltworks. He admitted to having had four tumbrels of French's oysters roasted and eaten. Ultimately both sides could claim victory, as Vernon was successful in having the injunction lifted but part of the strand was to be preserved for the city's use.[37] The legal confrontation continued, however, into the nineteenth century with, in one case, George Vernon being awarded a shilling in 1814 in acknowledgement of his right of fishery on the strand near part of the North Lotts. In 1820, correspondence in the records of the Ballast Board suggests that Dublin Corporation was then acquiring the Vernon rights to the North Bull, and in 1823 it was recorded that the North Bull fishery had been let by the city to William Campbell for an annual rent of £35.[38]

In the short term, the indeterminate outcome in 1734 paved the way for further disputes about the foreshore between the Vernons, the city and the

Leasing of Crabb Lough by Dublin City Council, 1718

Alderman Humphrey French is to have leave and licence for a lease for sixty-one years to lay down and take up oysters on that part of the Strand commonly called Crabb Lough, bounded to the north east by the road below **the shades of Clontarf**, to the east by a channel running by the North Bull, to the south by the Poolbeg, to the southwest by Clontarf Pool, and to the west by the Beech or Furlong of Clontarf, containing 195 acres or thereabouts, at a yearly rent of £70, and duties of 10,000 large oysters yearly to the Lord Mayor of the city of Dublin, and 2,000 large oysters to each sheriff ... with liberty for the Lord Mayor, Sheriffs, aldermen, commons and their ladies to go and eat oysters at the said bed for one day each year.

Calendar of ancient records of Dublin, vol. vii, pp 66–7;
J.W. de Courcy, *The Liffey in Dublin* (Dublin, 1996), p. 290

customs officers of the revenue commissioners, who were based at the Sheds.
John Vernon salvaged part of the cargo of a sloop from Cornwall that was wrecked
on the North Bull in April 1737 and appears to have been left in possession by the
revenue officials. Nine years later, when a consignment of tobacco was washed
ashore at Clontarf, John Vernon seized twelve barrels or hogsheads and withheld
them from the customs officers. Despite requests to hand over the hogsheads
or else pay the duty chargeable, Vernon announced his intention of selling the
tobacco at a public auction. Legal proceedings were initiated but the outcome
is unclear.[39]

When Captain John Vernon died in 1753, the succession to Clontarf of his heir,
George, was the first not to be seriously disputed in several generations. The
elder son of the marriage of John Vernon and Dorothy Grahn, George inherited a
coherent and productive district circumscribed by defined boundaries.[40] This was
eloquently attested to in the map of the district by John Rocque that appeared in
his *An actual survey of the county of Dublin*, published in 1760.

1 *Cal. S.P. Ireland, 1660-2*, 60, 71, 366.

2 L.J. Arnold, *The restoration land settlement in County Dublin, 1660-1688: a history of the administration of the acts of settlement and explanation* (Dublin, 1993), 48.

3 *Cal. S.P. Ireland, 1660-2*, 372, 478, 685-6; *ibid., 1663-5*, 39, 170; *ibid., 1625-1670, with addenda*, 447-50; Arnold, *Restoration land settlement*, 82-3.

4 *Cal. S.P. Ireland, 1663-5*, 37, 39, 95, 170, 171, 447-50.

5 See *Burke's Landed Gentry of Ireland* (London, 1912), 197-8, though note that Captain John is erroneously identified as a son of Sir Edward Vernon of Houndshill (d. 1657) and hence a brother of Colonel Edward: they were in fact cousins (Dublin, Marsh's Library, MS Z I 1 13, 'Case of John Vernon', p. 1).

6 Dublin, Marsh's Library, MS Z I 1 13, 'Case of John Vernon', pp 1-5.

7 *Ibid.*, 'Case of John Vernon', p. 6; 'Case of Mary Vernon', pp 1-5.

8 Josiah Browne (ed.), *Reports of cases upon appeals and writs of error in the high court of parliament, 1701-1779*, vol. iv (London, 1781), 383-96.

9 *Cal. S.P. dom., 1689-1702*, 201-2.

10 The first reference to Holly Brook as a distinctive element within the manor of Clontarf occurs in the grant to John Blackwell in 1649.

11 John Dunton, *The Dublin scuffle* (Dublin, 2000), 209.

12 Seamus Pender (ed.), *A census of Ireland circa 1659 with supplementary material from the poll money ordinances (1660-1661)* (Dublin, 1939), 382-92; *Historical Manuscripts Commission, ninth report* (London, 1883-4), 130; 'Hearth money roll for County Dublin, 1664' (second part),

Journal of the County Kildare Archaeological Society 11 (1930–3), 386–44.

13 *Cal. S.P. Ireland, 1675-6*, 155.

14 Note also a map of the east coast of Ireland, including in Dublin Bay a few landward features such as 'Ballibough', 'Clantarf', with a symbol for a town, and 'Kilbaach' on the north side, in John Seller, *The English pilot, first book, describing the coasts of ... Ireland* (London, 1690), between pp 12 and 13.

15 Gilbert (ed.), *Ancient records*, iv, 379.

16 John Dunton, 'Letter No. 5'.

17 'Harogscom' appears at this location on William Petty's 1685 map, *Hibernia delineatio*.

18 WSC, C1/S1/130.

19 Gerald Boate, *Ireland's naturall history* (London, 1652), 25–6: even at that depth the sea off Clontarf could be treacherous, as the stranding of Archbishop Alen's boat in 1534 shows.

20 John Perry, *An answer to objections against the making of a bason, with reasons for the bettering of the harbour of Dublin* (Dublin, 1721), 19.

21 Charles Haliday, *The Scandinavian kingdom of Dublin* (Dublin, 1881), 245–6; Flood, 'The birth of the Bull Island', 149.

22 John Perry, *The description of a method humbly proposed for the making of a better depth coming over the barr of Dublin, and also for making a bason within the harbour* (Dublin, 1721).

23 Niamh Moore, *Dublin docklands reinvented: the post-industrial regeneration of a European city quarter* (Dublin, 2008), 16–25; de Courcy, *The Liffey in Dublin*, 80–1, 169–79, 268–70; Niall McCullough, *Dublin, an urban city: the plan of the city* (Dublin, 2007), 50.

24 Haliday, *Scandinavian kingdom*, 233n.

25 Gilbert (ed.), *Ancient records*, vii, 5–7.

26 Maighréad Ní Mhurchadha, 'Clontarf' (unpublished paper), 18; Joan Ussher Sharkey, *St Anne's: the story of a Guinness estate* (Dublin, 2002), 9.

27 Ní Mhurchadha, 'Clontarf', 34.

28 *Ibid.*, 8–10.

29 Bernardine Ruddy, 'The royal charter school, Clontarf', *DHR* 57 (2004), 69.

30 G. Lennox Barrow, 'The franchises of Dublin', *DHR* 36 (1983), 79–80.

31 *Speech of John Vernon opposing the lord mayor on the riding of the franchises of Dublin at their attempting to enter his mannor of Clontarf, 6 August 1731* (Dublin, 1731).

32 Gilbert (ed.), *Ancient records*, vii, 481.

33 *Ibid.*, 435, 445.

34 *John Vernon, Esq., appellant; William Maple, merchant, respondent. The appellant's case* (London, 1730).

35 Gilbert (ed.), *Ancient records*, vii, 66–7.

36 *Ibid.*, 439–40; Brown (ed.), *Reports of cases upon appeals and writs of error in the high court of parliament from the year 1701 to the year 1779*, iv, 129.

37 Brown (ed.), *Reports of cases upon appeals and writs of error*, iv, 128–39; Gilbert (ed.), *Ancient records*, viii, 82–3, 153–4, 156.

38 De Courcy, *The Liffey in Dublin*, 408.

39 Ní Mhurchadha, 'Clontarf', 35, 38–41.

40 John Vernon's death was reported in *Faulkner's Dublin Journal*, 28 July 1753.

CHAPTER SEVEN

Castle and Sheds: Clontarf in a changing landscape, 1760–1837

T HE CLONTARF THAT John Rocque depicted in 1760 was entering its final 60 or 70 years as a detached country village before the advent of suburbanisation during the Victorian period. As well as attesting the settled nature of the Vernons' manor, the map foreshadows the later evolution of roadways and avenues in the line of field boundaries and country lanes. Out to sea, the details of Clontarf's coastal topography are clearly delineated, but the newly developing South Wall adumbrates changes in tidal flows and the marine morphology of Dublin Bay.

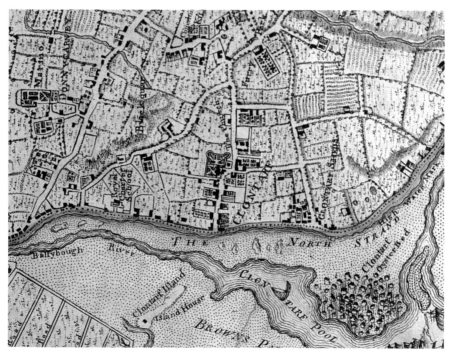

Fig. 7.1—Extract from John Rocque's An actual survey of the county of Dublin *(1760), showing the Clontarf area (courtesy of the Royal Irish Academy).*

While not overwhelming the rurality of the terrain, the number of substantial seats of gentry and professional residents continued to increase. Visiting commentators and artists during this phase bear testimony to the vibrancy of aristocratic life centred on the castle, and the growth of a culture of leisure in late eighteenth-century Clontarf. They also show the reality of the workaday world of the fishing community with its hub at the port opposite Clontarf Sheds about 1800. For a time the fishing industry of Clontarf supported a thriving maritime economy, but its rapid decline by the 1830s marked a profound social transformation in the district. A contributory cause was the construction in 1820–3 of the North or Bull Wall from Clontarf shoreline as a counterpart to the southern one, for the deepening of the entry to the harbour of Dublin. While dooming the local fisheries to extinction, the Wall promoted the growth of the North Bull Island, which became a major focus of recreation and tourism from the mid-nineteenth century. [7.1]

John Rocque's Clontarf, 1760

Rocque's survey of the county of Dublin includes all of the villages and rural areas of the county, with roads, buildings and natural aspects such as rivers, parks, gardens, woods and maritime features. It represents the first really detailed survey of the county. The exact reasons for the great cartographer's coming to Dublin in 1754 and his extended stay until 1760 are unknown, but he obviously reckoned that there was a market for Irish maps. The city and county maps in particular were a triumph of Rocque's work as surveyor, cartographer and engraver. They show a wonderfully detailed, house-by-house representation of the city, suburbs and satellite villages. Comparisons between his maps and those of the Ordnance Survey some 70 years later attest the value and accuracy of the earlier cartography. In this depiction of the houses, buildings, roads, fields and gardens of the neighbourhood, as well as its maritime features, the Vernon manor of Clontarf displays aspects of the rational and enlightened estate-planning of the 'age of improvement'. A series of other illustrations and maps over the following decades, however, reflects the changing face of Clontarf as it began very slowly to be transformed from manorial enclave to suburb of Dublin.[1]

There is a reminder of a lost battle on the Vernons' part in the form of the dotted line running along the coast road from Ballybough to Black Bush. This line, representing the border of the municipality's franchises, reflects the city's jurisdiction over the entire marine expanse off Clontarf. Disputes continued to flare between the Vernons and the corporation over rights to fisheries and other resources down to the twentieth century. Within the roughly triangular shape formed by the shoreline and the inland road through Killester, turning towards the sea at Raheny, the spine of the district is the avenue from the sea by the castle to 'Raheny Road', along which there are about twenty residences, described as mostly 'well-built houses', with gardens. Included among these may be a house called the 'Tavern of Clontarf', at the seafront end of the castle avenue, which had gardens, stables and a paddock. Running eastwards at right angles to the avenue were two roads, which met the parallel arterial route of the avenue, later called after the Vernons, and which were fronted by some properties with gardens. The many fields of the manor contain a mixture of pasture and arable, as well as landscaped gardens. Particularly intense cultivation of lands, for example, is seen to the north-east of what was later the junction of Vernon and Mount Prospect Avenues (and part of the future St Anne's). Also prominent is the residence of the Southwell family opposite the castle, called Yew Park or Elm View, nestling in the corner of Castle Avenue and Seafield Road and described as a 'fine seat with beautiful gardens'. Further along to the east of Castle Avenue, on an avenue that came to bear the name of the house, is Verville, with its buildings and gardens, which had been built and laid out only a couple of years before the map.

At the hub of this town of Clontarf was the Vernon mansion, referred to contemporaneously as 'the castle'. Facing south, the central building was flanked by two substantial wings, and to the west and the north were depicted enclosed formal gardens, the latter containing two circular corner-towers within its perimeter walls. Abutting the wall north of the building was the church, enclosed in its small churchyard. The enclosure with a rectangular building symbol further to the north on Castle Avenue that seems to bear the ascription 'The church' is a misplacement. No contemporary drawing or description has been found of the church building, which seems to have been modest enough architecturally. As the Anglican parish church, it served the Church of Ireland community of the Clontarf district until the new building was opened on Seafield Road in 1866. John Rocque does not depict any Roman Catholic chapel in Clontarf at this time, the nearest one being located in Coolock, which catered for a union of eight parishes on the north side.

In the segment of Clontarf to the west of the castle avenue there were just over a dozen properties, the most significant of which was the Royal Charter School close to the shore. It had been built only a dozen years or so when it was depicted on this map, and its architectural design attracted the interest of artists. Also shown, but not named, was Hollybrook, the seat of a Mr Stephens in 1786, a substantial residence with a garden, on the south side of the inland road to

Raheny. Superimposed lightly over the field boundary markings were lines that possibly represented the denominations of Upper and Lower Holly Brooks.[2] The other named gentry seat on the map is Furry Park House, which was built in 1730 for the banker Joseph Fade. It had impressive gardens, according to Rocque's map. To the north-east, off the road to Howth, is another property, Sybil Hill, which had been built in the 1730s and later became part of St Anne's estate.

The other major nucleation within the district was on or close to the shore at Clontarf Sheds, where seventeen properties are represented—mostly small and, unlike the tidily ordered housing along the castle avenue, fairly scattered in their dispersal. This settlement is at the southern end of the artery between the coastline and the interior that became Vernon Avenue. Just opposite the most easterly-built houses at the Sheds, on the sea side of the road, were two small structures, which could be sheds or a wharf or jetty associated with the fishing industry. The Sheds (or Shades) figured as an identifiable village entity in late seventeenth-century maps, centred on the fishing port and Pool of Clontarf. By the middle of the eighteenth century a 'colony' of mostly small dwellings had been established at a place called the Green at the Sheds for families engaged in fishing and maritime activities on plots sub-leased for periods of 31 years.

Fig. 7.2 — Beachfield House, one of the large mansions shown on John Rocque's map of 1760 (courtesy of the Clontarf Historical Society).

Rocque's map clearly showed this cluster. Apart from the settlement at Clontarf Sheds, there is a large residence to the west of 'Vernon Avenue' which may be the newly built Beachfield House, shown with a garden. Apart from that, there was only one other residence with garden on this avenue, corresponding in location to what became the convent house of the Dominican nuns. [7.2]

There is very little habitation in the eastern part of Clontarf, as delineated by Rocque. In a directory entry of 1786, over twenty years after Rocque's map, there is mention of four residences to the east of the Sheds: Winton Lodge, belonging to Mr Seaton, Black Bush, Bay View (the seat of Mr Gardiner) and the seat of Colonel Eustace (opposite the beginning of the North Bull).[3] Drawn in on the map in a fairly detailed way are small oval shapes, one of which could be Crab Lake, but there could perhaps be an attempt to illustrate sepulchral mounds near Conquer Hill, which were sketched in conjunction with the Ordnance Survey of the district in the 1830s.[4] Of the salt-water pipes and brickfields for which this shoreline was noted in the earlier eighteenth century there is little sign, though the symbols to the east of the Sheds could be an attempt to reflect residual activity in production of salt and making of bricks. Inland from these seaside properties, the only substantial residence seems to be located on the Greenlanes (or Mount Prospect Avenue West). At the extreme eastern point of the manor is Black Bush at the ruined Water Mill, the limit of the city's franchises. Off the shore is a stone wharf. An indication of the beginnings of the future St Anne's estate is a property approached by an entry from the seafront. About fifteen years before the map was drawn, the first lease of St Anne's land by the Vernon estate was drawn up in favour of Paul Hale and his brothers, and it contained the right to use 'the wharf or quay facing the premises'. On this tract of land, close to the Nanniken River, was built Thornhill House, the forerunner of the Guinness mansion of St Anne's of the nineteenth century.

As to the coastal features of Clontarf, the high-water mark of the tide on the north side of Dublin Bay is shown as lapping the coastal road from Ballybough to Sutton and Howth. The expanse of sand off Clontarf left uncovered at low water is termed 'the North Strand' as far as Dollymount, which contained, opposite the shore to the east of the Sheds, Clontarf oyster-beds, which are drawn in great detail. Retaining its depth at low tide and fed by the Tolka or Ballybough River, the narrow Clontarf Pool, stretching offshore from opposite the castle avenue to the Sheds, contains the Rocquian symbol of a small vessel, perhaps a fishing boat. Projecting in a north-easterly direction from just off the newly formed north lotts to the south of the channel formed by the Tolka is the thin shape of Clontarf Island, which is depicted as having a house at its southern end. There is no sign of permanently dry land opposite the Clontarf coastline. The North Bull is depicted as a sandbank overswept by the water and divided from the mainland by a narrow creek called the 'Raheny Lake'.

Clontarf Castle as the focus for aristocratic society

Now firmly ensconced as county gentry and retaining their pretensions to manorial lordship, the Vernons presided over the district from their seat at Clontarf Castle. Described in 1787 as 'a fine edifice', containing 'noble rooms' and adjoining a 'very pleasant garden and demesne',[5] the castle was depicted in Gabriel Beranger's watercolour of 1772 as a substantial but plain building, having a central three-bayed section with two storeys of Gothic windows and main door. It was flanked by turreted towers to the west and east: the latter had a central buttress containing a large Gothic-style window on the first floor, with smaller ones above and below, where there was also a bow-shaped projection, and the former had varying-sized Gothic-style windows flush with the façade. Above the turrets on each side could be seen the tops of older, possibly medieval towers. To the west of the building there was a glimpse of some of the formally planted garden, and in the foreground two gentlemen admire the castle.[6] [7.3]

Fig. 7.3—Gabriel Beranger, 'Clontarf Castle', before 1812
(courtesy of the National Library of Ireland).

*Fig. 7.4 — Thomas Snagg, 'View of Clontarf Castle', 1805
(private collection, image courtesy of Whyte's).*

In an oil painting of the castle and its surroundings of 1805 the artist, Thomas Snagg, shows castellated walls in the garden, with higher walls around the demesne pierced by a couple of gateways. The architectural details match those in Beranger's sketch. Looking south-east beyond the rural countryside of the district, there is a great sweep of landscape of the shore and the bay, including the South Wall. The 'lilliputian' houses depicted along the seafront have been described by Dr Peter Harbison as 'fanciful', as the Clontarf shoreline at that time was mostly slob land. [7.4] A romantic perspective of the castle was presented in a painting ascribed to the English painter J.M.W. Turner, who, apparently working from a sketch drawn perhaps about 1817 by Maria Sophie Vernon, depicted the architectural features with more depth and afforded a pastoral view of the surroundings, with mature trees in the foreground and to the sides of the castle. To the west, castellated walls and arches are shown, perhaps as part of the garden, while to the east the lines of the church can be seen. In all three pictures there are fashionably dressed figures disporting themselves, either on foot or in carriages.[7]

To judge by these paintings of Clontarf, the castle was a social hub for gentlemen and women of that part of the county of Dublin and beyond. A visiting writer mentions the 'great variety of beautiful seats' in the area in 1791.[8] Several wealthy individuals of the gentry and civic patrician classes had leased lands and properties from the Vernons during the course of the eighteenth century, including Thomas Southwell, later Baron Southwell, who was an MP and commissioner of the revenue, and whose mansion was located opposite Clontarf Castle. Up to a dozen large houses with gardens attached appear on Rocque's map of Clontarf, many along the length of the castle avenue, and three giving off the Raheny/Howth road—Hollybrook, Furry Park and Sybil Hill. Winton Lodge, Bayview and Black Bush are listed in a directory of 1786, along with the names of Mr Seaton, Mr Gardiner (the occupiers of the first two mentioned) and Colonel Eustace, who was seated opposite the North Bull.[9] The owners of some of these properties signed a decree in 1775 against those who carried out depredations to the environment in Clontarf through stealing hay, grass, fruit and fowl, cutting hedges and trees or stripping gates of locks and iron. (Such misdemeanours were not unprecedented in Clontarf: in 1751 two men were shot after stealing flowers and fruit trees from a garden there).[10] Among the signatories were Thomas, second Viscount Southwell, George and Edward Vernon, Anthony Weekes and H. Gleadow Newcomen. Members of these landowning families were named in an act of 1788, along with several others, as responsible for supervising and implementing the tolling of the roads to Raheny and Howth, to the north and south of Clontarf. The purpose was to raise revenue for the maintenance and repairing of the highways. The act specifically rescinded another forbidding

Fig. 7.5—*Extract from John Taylor's* Map of the environs of Dublin *(1816), depicting the Black Quarry to the west of Howth Road, and the lead mine at the bottom of Castle Avenue (courtesy of Trinity College, Dublin).*

the erection of toll-gates or turnpikes on the road from Ballybough Bridge to the Sheds of Clontarf by the Strand. Among the specific concerns in respect of the road along the strand from Ballybough was the inadequacy of the sea wall in preventing flooding. A petition of the residents to parliament in 1789 requested money for the building up of the rampier wall from the Black Quarry lane (leading to the Hollybrooks) to Cold Harbour, at the east end of the Sheds. The Black Quarry, as shown in maps of the area drawn by John Taylor in 1816 and by William Duncan in 1821, occupied a large area on the north side of the road to Howth, opposite the Holly Brook or Hollybrook Park in the former.[11] [7.5]

Artistic representations indicate also the growth of a culture of leisure in eighteenth-century Clontarf. The Vernons' formal tree-lined gardens suggest the fashionable promenading grounds of central Dublin, such as the Rotunda and St Stephen's Green. The gardens of Clontarf were evidently well maintained, that planted originally by the tallow-chandler Joseph Rathborne being described as 'in good order and well cropped'. Pierre Rieusset, a Huguenot émigré who leased a house called the 'Tavern of Clontarf' at the seafront end of the castle avenue, had gardens, stables and a paddock. This house apparently had a room convenient for dancing, where ladies and gentlemen could dine and dance during the season, the subscription being a guinea per annum. The *Annual Register* noted in 1761

Fig. 7.6—The Casino at Marino, built about 1775 by Sir William Chambers for the earl of Charlemont, whose estate was immediately to the west of that of the Vernons at Clontarf.

Fig. 7.7—William Ashford (1746-1824), 'The Royal Charter School, Clontarf, County Dublin', Irish, eighteenth century, 1794. Oil on canvas, 69cm x 126cm. Photo © National Gallery of Ireland NGI 577 (courtesy of the National Gallery of Ireland).

Fig. 7.8—Francis Jukes, 'Royal Charter School on the Strand', 1785 (courtesy of the Board of the British Library).

that 'Clontarf [is] crowded in the season for sea-bathing, and ... surrounded with numerous villas of the nobility and citizens whom the beauties of Dublin Bay attract to the coast'. Clontarf became the principal venue for musical recitals on the north side of Dublin. The castle provided an élite cultural milieu in the form of musical recitals. In 1742 George Frideric Handel had stayed for two months at the home of the Vernons, where the chatelaine, Dorothy Grahn, originally from Hanover, was a friend of his, for whom he composed *Forest music*. Later in the century, the famous instrument-maker Ferdinand Weber attended the castle on a number of occasions to tune and rewire a harp.[12]

The Vernons and their fellow grandees aspired to architectural distinction in their patronage of domestic and charitable buildings. While Lord Charlemont's neo-classical temple, the Casino, built by Sir William Chambers in the 1770s on the neighbouring estate at Marino, was universally recognised as an architectural gem,[13] the design of the Royal Charter School on the shoreline of west Clontarf also elicited the interest of artists. [7.6] On ten acres of land owned by John Vernon and leased to a Mr McCausland, the school was erected according to the plan of Arthur Jones Nevill in the late 1740s. The school, one of almost 50 'charter schools' under the control of the Incorporated Society for Promoting English Protestant Working Schools in Ireland in the eighteenth century, aimed at educating destitute Catholic boys and girls in an Anglican milieu to become productive workers through practical and academic instruction. At Clontarf, where the school became single-sex, cotton- and linen-weaving were among the industrial activities undertaken by up to 100 boys. The building, in the Palladian style, had a fine portico with steps on either side and was crowned by a cupola. There are at least four illustrations of the Charter School dating from the later eighteenth century. The most lyrical is that by William Ashford of 1794, in which the building provides the foreground to a splendid view of Dublin Bay from the shoreline. The road along the Strand is traversed by carriages passing in opposite directions, the width of the thoroughfare having been extended under Vernon supervision within the previous few years. [7.7] Three other drawings concentrate on the building itself, from the front and rear, the latter view showing the extensive nature of the suite of buildings, including residences, schools and workshops, to which an infirmary for all ill pupils of Irish charter schools was added in the mid-1790s.[14] [7.8]

The attraction of artists such as Ashford, Snagg and Turner to the beauty of the Clontarf landscape attests to the opening out of the district beyond the manorial world which the Vernons and their predecessor lords had bestridden since the Middle Ages. True enough, the owners of Clontarf Castle continued to set the tone in terms of social ascendancy and cultural patronage, and they dominated their area as landlords and lessors. In addition, through their control of tolls the Vernons could determine the development of roads and other aspects of local infrastructure and administration. The stability of the Church of Ireland parish, aided by the successive incumbencies of four members of the Ussher family from 1680 to 1811, no doubt bolstered the Vernon lordship of the district. Yet certain trends in the local economy and topography around the turn of the eighteenth century presaged a major transformation in their role and the status of their neighbourhood during the Victorian era. These may be encapsulated in the history of the coastal stretch that included the Sheds.

Coastal change and the Sheds of Clontarf

Illustrations and descriptions of the Sheds of Clontarf afford us a view not only of a countervailing pole of habitation to that of the castle but also of a popular cultural and social milieu very different to that of the privileged élite. The Sheds of Clontarf was the designation of the seaside village that contained many plots leased for short terms. One of these small plots adjoined the stable and wall of the substantial house of the revenue officers. The later proliferation of cabins and

*Fig. 7.9—Print of Francis Wheatley, 'A view of Dublin bay and the Sheds of Clontarf',
1785 (courtesy of the Board of the British Library).*

thatched cottages was facilitated by this short-term sub-leasing. Rocque's map of 1760 had shown this cluster cartographically at the seaward end of later Vernon Avenue, but the first depiction of the neighbourhood occurs in Francis Wheatley's 1785 drawing, 'The sheds of Clontarf'. [7.9] From his eastern vantage point there are evident two terraces of single-storey cottages, one of them having thatched roofs and the other consisting of more substantially built housing. In the foreground, overlooking the harbour is a tall, dormered building with long narrow windows, flanked by pillars, possibly leading into a yard. This could be the Fish House, or else the revenue establishment at the port. At least one fishing vessel lies at anchor just offshore, while further west along the coast a rowing boat appears to be unloading some passengers. Two figures in workaday attire are engaged in conversation by a loaded cart at the shore. In the middle ground there are some figures on the village street, while counterpointed in the background some larger houses and villas front the shoreline in the direction of the castle avenue.

Christmas Weekes's philanthropy at Clontarf, 1786

The Sheds and the town of Clontarf and the adjoining neighbourhood have been lately most essentially benefited by the acquisition of a supply of fresh water, from the ingenuity and labours of Mr Christmas Weekes, a gentleman residing at the Sheds, and possessing no small share of public spirit. He has had conveyed, at his own private expense, a stream of excellent water through his grounds to the Sheds; where both the inhabitants and the shipping near that coast are now amply supplied gratis, with this necessary article of life. To render this of general utility, he has built an aqueduct, extending near half a mile, to the public road, opposite his own house; from whence it is continued across the road to a large reservoir, which is built on the beach, and enclosed, and furnished with valves to carry off the overflowing of water. This reservoir supplies two pumps, at a convenient distance for the use of the public. To one of those pumps, which is constructed on the principles of a fountain, is affixed a machinery which conveys the water along a commodious wharf, extending several hundred feet towards the sea; and at the end of the wharf there are tackle and hooks to sling water-casks for the use of the shipping, and a leather tube and brass cocks to fill them, which is done with singular ease and expedition.

The post-chaise companion: or traveller's directory through Ireland (Dublin, 1786), pp 308–9

There is no sign in Wheatley's drawing of the improvements at the harbour installed by Christmas Weekes by 1786. This resident of the Sheds had built an aqueduct conveying fresh water across his land and the sea road to the beach, where he had constructed a reservoir. From this, a pumping system provided water for the local village consumption, and also for vessels visiting Clontarf Pool and Dublin port. The latter utility worked by conveying the water-supply from the reservoir along a wharf extending 'several hundred feet' into the sea, at the end of which pipes and brass cocks allowed sailors from boats to fill their casks. Weekes also oversaw the erection of breakwaters on the shore, parallel to the wharf, to prevent sand and gravel being cast onto the embankment of the beach. Much praised for his disinterested and patriotic philanthropy, Weekes (who reckoned the cost of the works at £3,000) shunned public acknowledgement, being, it was said, more comfortable in his library. He did, however, accept nomination to membership of the Dublin Society on 29 March 1787, the grand jury of County Dublin presented an address of thanks for his munificence in supplying both the inhabitants and visiting shipping with water supplies, and the freedom of

The village and Sheds at Clontarf, 1787

The Castle at the upper end of the town is the seat of John Vernon, Esq. It is a fine edifice, and contains noble rooms. The gardens and demesne are also very pleasant. Near this Castle is the church of Clontarf; opposite to which is the beautiful seat of Lady Southwell.

The Sheds as they are called, derive their name from fishing stages having been formerly erected there for the purposes of drying and curing fish. At that time we may suppose that, like other places where fishing stages are erected, the buildings near them were poor and mean, serving only as temporary accommodations for the poor fishermen that occasionally resorted to them; but the village that now bears the name of the Sheds of Clontarf has a far different appearance, containing a large number of handsome and well built houses. This place is much frequented by the citizens of Dublin at all times of the year, but particularly in the bathing season, it being excellently well situated for that purpose, and having very convenient little edifices, in the form of small houses, with proper apartments in them.

Richard Lewis, *The Dublin guide, or a description of the city of Dublin* (Dublin, 1787), pp 110–11 the city of Dublin was conferred on him. Weekes played a part in rescuing the crews of ships driven onto the North Bull in the spring and autumn of 1787, not just through the safe refuge of his wharf but also by personally taking care of shipwrecked sailors and passengers in his home.[15]

Richard Lewis, a visitor to Clontarf in 1787, described the village at the Sheds as containing 'a large number of handsome and well-built houses' and 'very convenient little edifices in the form of small houses, with proper apartments in them', for bathers, with whom the place was popular.[16] Reference was made to the Sheds as providing the only bathing place convenient to the north side of Dublin in 1789.[17] Four-wheeled bathing machines are pictured at Clontarf for the first time in an engraving by John Laporte in 1796. [7.10] Also shown is a short wooden jetty, which is probably Weekes's wharf, and a few fishing boats drawn up on the sands. In his map of the harbour drawn in 1803, Captain William Bligh depicted Weekes's wharf at the Sheds, but within twenty years the wharf, with its seats for the recreation of promenaders, was said to have been allowed to decay, along with other works, following the departure of Weekes from the area. Indeed, an elegiac commentary of 1818 suggests the decline of the Sheds as a fishing village, though the whitewashed houses on the picturesque promontory and the neat villas in

Fig. 7.10—John Laporte, 'Dublin bay from the Sheds of Clontarf', c. 1795, showing Weekes's wharf, as well as bathing machines (courtesy of the Board of the British Library).

the green lanes running inland were presented in an attractive light, and seven or eight fishing yawls were still operating at Clontarf in that year.[18] A definite sense of anteriority is conveyed, however, by the statement that 'Clontarf was a celebrated fishing town, and this part was called the Sheds'.[19] This is confirmed in D'Alton's statement in 1838 that 'the Sheds of Clontarf have long since vanished with the good days of the fishermen', the substandard cottages and cabins of the 200 families having been cleared to make way for the new Roman Catholic church of St John the Baptist in the earlier 1830s.[20]

The Vernon landlords may have welcomed the opportunity to get rid of the poor dwellings and to rehouse the maritime community at the Sheds, but the decline of the fishing industry in the north inner bay had serious implications for their economic position. At their most productive, the fisheries off Clontarf were highly lucrative for lords and fishers alike, producing shellfish such as mussels, oysters, cockles and lobsters, and fish species such as herring, whiting, mackerel and turbot. Topographical changes caused by the great engineering works of the Ballast Office in the eighteenth century, as reflected, for example, in the shrinkage of Clontarf Island and the loss of depth in Clontarf Pool, were compounded once the decision was taken to proceed with the construction of the Bull Wall, or Great North Wall, in 1819.[21] The reduction in the stocks of herrings and oysters in the inner bay may have made the issue of ownership of fishing-grounds academic, as symbolised in the award of a shilling to George Vernon in 1814 in acknowledgement of his right of fishery on the strand near part of the North Lotts. In 1820 the corporation set about acquiring the Vernon rights to the North Bull, and three years later it was recorded that the fishery there had been let by the city to William Campbell for an annual rent of £35.[22]

Nor did the landward natural resources of the district provide an alternative to compensate for the loss of the fisheries. Quarrying of stone along the Strand appears to have benefited mainly the engineering works in the greater bay area under the auspices of the Ballast Office, though some local extraction of pebbles and stones continued.[23] The salt- and brick-making enterprises along the eastern shoreline of Clontarf may have wound down by the 1750s, but an alternative resource was tapped from about the same time. This was the lead mine which had originally been recorded in the Tudor period, when its exploitation was briefly mooted. Colonel Edward Vernon had been careful to secure a grant of the mine from Charles II in 1661,[24] but it was not until 1756 that the vein of metal reaching out towards the sea between the castle avenue and the Sheds was properly mined. A shaft topped by a tower was dug from the shore to a depth of 30ft, and thence the vein was followed in a northerly direction. The lead was a blend of

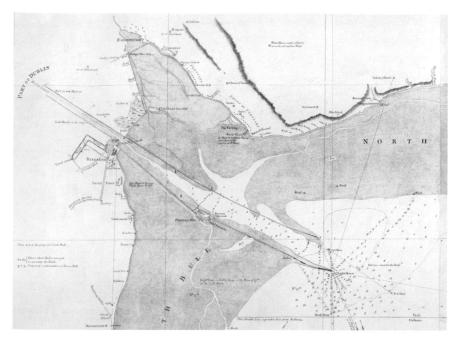

Fig. 7.11—Chart of Dublin Bay, drawn by Captain William Bligh (1803), showing the suggested line of a new north wall, almost parallel to the south wall (courtesy of Trinity College, Dublin).

galena and antimony, and the mine appears to have been producing tons of ore by the early nineteenth century, though the small quantities of silver found were not worth assaying. But the enterprise was not a success in the long term, and by 1818 was already languishing: the sides of the shaft gave way owing to insufficient timbering, and incursions of the sea made it impracticable to continue mining the seam. By the early twentieth century all that remained, according to F.W.R. Knowles, were the abandoned shafts, one in a field along the seafront and the other on the foreshore topped by the tall stone tower with walls 'about twenty feet thick'. Knowles stated that when the promenade was being developed in the 1950s the dredgers filled in the shaft, cut the tower down to sea-wall height and made it the base of the circular shelter beside Clontarf Baths.[25]

The most decisive event in the marine history of Clontarf before the construction of the promenade was the building of the wooden bridge across Crablake Water and the stone causeway, later termed the Bull Wall, between 1819 and 1823. The building of the great South Wall, as well as continual dredging, had already contributed to the deepening of the channel of the Liffey by 3–4ft, but the problem of the bar at the harbour mouth persisted. As a remedy, the newly constituted port of Dublin authority or Ballast Board (which replaced the Ballast Office in 1786) proposed to build a second wall, this one from the coast at Clontarf, near Clontarf Head, to the edge of the North Bull.[26] After 1800, various plans continued to be discussed under the auspices of the newly created Directors General of Inland Navigation. Even the project for a canal parallel to the Clontarf shoreline was revived by one Thomas Rogers.[27] By far the most influential voice was that of Captain William Bligh, who was commissioned by the Admiralty to undertake a survey of Dublin Bay in 1800. [7.11] A highly skilled maritime cartographer even before his notoriety as commander of the *Bounty*, Bligh spent the winter of 1800–1 examining the sandbanks, tides and currents in the bay and sounding its depths before producing a most detailed chart. Dismissing the notion of a canal, he proposed instead a wall from the north side which would have the effect of funnelling the tidal flow to scour the channel of sand and mud. Bligh's suggested wall was not the one that was eventually built at the North Bull, but his analysis provoked debate among marine experts.[28]

Eventually, under the advice of Captain Daniel Corneille, the original 1786 proposal was adopted in about 1804 for a wall running from near Seafield Road. It

Fig. 7.12 — Extract from William Duncan's Maps of the county of Dublin *(1821), showing the newly built wall extending from Cold Harbour at Dollymount (courtesy of Trinity College, Dublin).*

was Francis Giles, an English engineer, who produced the final report upon which the project went ahead. Under his supervision the Bull Bridge was erected in 1819 to connect the Great North Wall or Bull Wall with the shore. The wall itself is of stone, extending 2.7km to the North Bull lighthouse, and 25m wide at the base and 7m in height for 1.7km of its length. The remaining kilometre is overswept by the sea at half-tide. The total cost of the project, which was completed by 1824, was £95,000. The wall was successful in helping, through the concentrated power of the tide, to scour out mud and sand from the channel, which was deepened by 20ft in some areas. The bar was eventually pushed seawards by 500m.[29] [7.12]

Another great, though unintended, effect of the building of the wall was the accelerated growth of the tiny sandy island on the North Bull. Captain Bligh had noted on his chart a dry bank of about 350m by 150m just to the east of Crablake Water, near the west end of the present island, and Captain Giles showed it as having grown about tenfold in length by 1819. Gradually, after the construction of the bridge and wall, the island increased in width as well as in length, extending north-eastwards for 2.56km according to the 1837 Ordnance Survey map. It eventually attained a length of almost 5km, reaching into Sutton Creek, and a

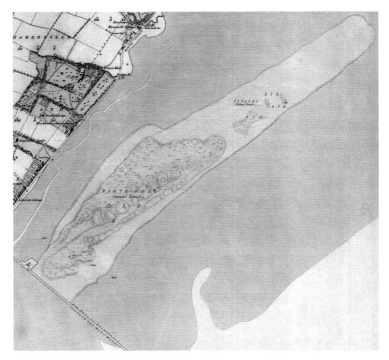

Fig. 7.13—Extract from the Ordnance Survey map of 1837–43, showing the growth of the Bull Island, comprising separate sandbanks which later merged into one.

breadth of 0.75km at its widest point. On its seaward side the sweep of Dollymount Strand fringed Dublin Bay, while to the landward an area of intertidal marshes and flats developed. The island became a focal point for the visitors and day-trippers who came to Clontarf for sea-bathing and other forms of aquatic and sporting activity, such as sailing, rowing, shooting and golf. It also became an important bird and wildlife sanctuary.[30] [7.13]

In 1822 the proprietor of Clontarf Castle, George Vernon, grandson of his namesake and predecessor who had taken over in 1753, died. After the death of his elder brother, also George, in 1833, John Edward Venables Vernon, who was born in 1813, succeeded as owner of the estate and lived until 1890. During his adulthood he witnessed a major transformation in the district over which his family presided. In 1822 William Drummond wrote of the 'pleasing and romantic appearance' of the village of Clontarf, its church, castle and many of the houses being 'embosomed in trees', and the neighbouring countryside intersected by roads appropriately named 'the Green Lanes' because of their 'verdant and umbrageous foliage'.[31] Yet the external world pressed more insistently upon the district. The lure of sea-bathing brought increasingly large crowds of visitors to the shoreline. The city of Dublin continued to press its ownership claims to the foreshore, and the spreading of surburbs into the hinterland of the city threatened to absorb former neighbouring villages within its sprawl through housing and transportation links. True to the tradition of his ancestors, Vernon attempted to uphold the autonomy of the old manorial area in the face of this expansion, standing out against development, but the ineluctable progress of municipal and state government systems, suburbanisation and tourism could not be halted.

Clontarf—a popular bathing resort, 1822

During the bathing season, the shores are greatly frequented, and the scene is full of animation. Vehicles of all descriptions, from the curricle of the peer to the jingle of the plebeian, are seen passing rapidly along the road; and numerous groups of bathers are enjoying the refreshing coolness of the waves. Few cities, indeed, are more happily circumstanced than Dublin, with respect to the health and recreation of their inhabitants, or more disposed to avail themselves of the pleasure and advantage, which the vicinity of an inviting bay presents.

William Drummond, *Clontarf: a poem* (Dublin, 1822), preface, p. vii

1 John Rocque, *An actual survey of the county of Dublin, 1760* (Dublin, 1760); see also John Montague, 'John Rocque and *The exact survey of Dublin*', in Colm Lennon and John Montague (eds), *John Rocque's Dublin: a guide to the Georgian city* (Dublin, 2010), xi–xxiv.

2 These are more clearly evident on a 1765 version of the map, edited by Bernard Scalé.

3 *The post-chaise companion: or traveller's directory through Ireland* (Dublin, 1786), 307–9.

4 O'Gorman, 'On the site of the battle of Clontarf', 169–70.

5 Lewis, *The Dublin guide*, 110.

6 See Peter Harbison, *Beranger's rambles in Ireland* (Dublin, 2004); there is an illustration of the castle as depicted before its restoration in the late 1830s in P. Dixon Hardy, 'A day's ramble on the north side of the city', *Dublin Penny Journal* 2 (1834), 273–5.

7 Peter Harbison, 'Note on Thomas Snagg (1746–1812), *View of Clontarf Castle, 1805*', in *Whyte's catalogue of Irish and British art*, 12 March 2012 (Dublin, 2012), 35.

8 Bowden, *A tour through Ireland*, 80.

9 *Post-chaise companion*, 307–9; see also Matthew Sleater, *Introductory essay to a new system of civil and ecclesiastical topography and itinerary of counties of Ireland* (Dublin, 1806), 16.

10 *Faulkner's Dublin Journal*, 20 August 1751.

11 *Resolution by inhabitants on depredations committed in Clontarf* (Dublin, 1775); 'Act for … the roads leading to Dublin through Raheny and Clontarf, 1788' and 'Petition of landholders and inhabitants of Clontarf, 1789', in *Journal of the House of Commons of Ireland* (Dublin, 1788, 1789).

12 *Daily Courant*, 9 May 1747; Ní Murchadha, 'Clontarf', 7; *Faulkner's Dublin Journal*, 12 March 1729, 13 and 31 May 1740; *Annual Register, 1761* (London, 1762), 99; W.H. Grattan Flood, 'Fishamble Street Music Hall, Dublin, from 1741 to 1777', *Sammelbände der Internationale Musicgesellschaft* 14 (1912), 53; Jenny Nex and Lance Whitehead, 'A copy of Ferdinand Weber's account book', *Royal Musical Association Research Chronicle* 35 (2000), 125, 129, 139; Brian Boydell, 'Venues for music in eighteenth-century Dublin', *DHR* 29 (1975), 33.

13 See de Latocnaye, *Promenade d'un français dans l'Irlande* (Dublin, 1797), 319: 'le Temple … est sans contradict un modèle brilliant d'architecture'.

14 *A sermon preached at Christ Church, Dublin, on 20th day of March 1747 by Michael Cox, bishop of Ossory, before the Incorporated Society for Promoting English Protestant Working Schools in Ireland* (Dublin, 1748); Kenneth Milne, *The Irish Charter Schools, 1730–1830* (Dublin, 1997); Ruddy, 'The Royal Charter School'.

15 *Post-chaise companion*, 307–9; www.rds.ie/cat_historic_member_detail.jsp?itemID=1097586, accessed 18 August 2012; www.clontarfonline.com/hphphp4. jpg; / hphphp7. jpg; hphphp8.jpg, accessed 16 August 2012.

16 Lewis, *The Dublin guide*, 111.

17 *House of Commons Journal* (1789), 269.

18 Robert Fraser, *Review of the domestic fisheries of Great Britain and Ireland* (Edinburgh, 1818), 9.

19 J. Warburton, J. Whitelaw and R. Walsh, *History of the city of Dublin* (2 vols, London, 1818), ii, 1251–2.

20 D'Alton, *History of County Dublin*, 52.

21 Warburton *et al.*, *Dublin*, ii, 1249, 1251–2; Flood, 'The birth of the Bull Island', 150; *A general history of Ireland in its antient and modern state* (Dublin, 1781), i, 258.

22 De Courcy, *The Liffey in Dublin*, 414; commercial trawling of the seas off Dublin began with the setting up of the Dublin Fishery Company in 1818: J.L.H. Hughes, 'The Dublin Fishery Company, 1818–1830', *DHR* 12 (1951), 34–46.

23 Flood, 'The birth of the Bull Island', 150.

24 *Cal. S.P. Ireland, 1660-2*, 432.

25 Warburton *et al.*, *Dublin*, ii, 1250; F.W.R. Knowles, *Old Clontarf* (Dublin, *c.* 1970), 12–13: I am grateful to an anonymous reviewer who supplied many helpful references for this and other aspects of the text.

26 Flood, 'The birth of the Bull Island', 151.

27 Thomas Rogers, *Observations on a road or safe anchorage at Ireland's Eye* (Dublin, 1800).

28 Gerald J. Daly, 'Captain William Bligh in Dublin, 1800–1801', *DHR* 44 (1991), 30–3.

29 De Courcy, *The Liffey in Dublin*, 53; Flood, 'The birth of the Bull Island', 152.

30 See W. Jeffrey *et al.* (eds), *North Bull Island, Dublin Bay: a modern coastal natural history* (Dublin, 1977).

31 Drummond, *Clontarf: a poem*, preface, pp v–vi.

CHAPTER EIGHT

Resort and township:
Victorian Clontarf, 1837–1901

I N THE MID-1830S the Vernon family embarked on a major refurbishment of their
ancient mansion at Clontarf. The old Norman structure that had been repaired
many times in the previous six centuries was showing signs of decrepitude. Two
illustrations, from 1834 and 1840, demonstrate the dramatic make-over that the
building received in line with the designs of the distinguished Irish architect
William Vitruvius Morrison. While the earlier picture shows the south-facing
façade flanked by castellated wings, familiar from previous depictions, the later is
of a medieval and Tudor pastiche, with soaring gables, towers and battlements. [8.1]

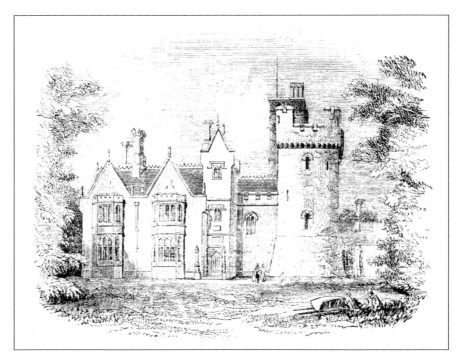

Fig. 8.1—Drawing of the recently restored Clontarf Castle in 1840 (Irish Penny Journal).

Gone is the overwhelmingly ecclesiastical look, appropriate to the monastic past, and instead there is evident a self-consciously antiquarian style. As an extensive programme of rebuilding was necessitated owing to the discovery of sunken foundations, the only part of the old structure retained was the 70ft-high tower, incorporated within a massive Norman-style keep. The main entrance retained its central position, set in a narrow but lofty tower. Twin gables decorated with family crests capped the western end of the building, each of which contained two-storey oriel or bay windows. Thus the newly rebuilt castle bodied forth the three styles of construction—Norman (the keep), fourteenth-century (the tower) and Elizabethan (the manor-house). A low extension from the eastern side of the great tower, containing the servants' quarters and small bedrooms, obscured the old church building seen in the 1834 view. Inside the new castle building, according to the 1840 account, was a profusion of Tudor and Gothic features and ornamentation, including dark oak panelling, stained glass windows and a huge dark marble fireplace at the centre of the reception area.[1]

In 1837, as the Vernon residence in the heart of Clontarf was being refashioned as a neo-Gothic castle, Queen Victoria ascended the British throne. While the 'new' mansion house harked back to a manorial and baronial past, the young queen's accession heralded an era of rapid change that was to transform her dominions in general and Clontarf in particular. For much of the 64-year span of her reign the district continued to be noted for its rurality and greenery, but suburban development eventually transformed the nature of the village and its environs. This chapter examines how social, economic and cultural forces brought about the transformation of Clontarf in the Victorian period from fishing and estate village into a dormitory suburb. Political and social changes profoundly affected the pattern of urban life in Dublin, with the inner city becoming less hospitable as a place of residence for the middle class and gentry. The migration to new suburbs to the south and north of Dublin, especially along the maritime fringe, resulted in the settlement of thousands of newcomers in the erstwhile satellite villages of Blackrock, Sandymount, Kingstown and, rather later, Clontarf. The Vernon landlords had played a major role in attempting to halt the extension of the nearby, louring municipality, whether in terms of its boundaries on land or at sea or its engineering works in the bay. Their concentration and that of their fellow landowners in the mid- to later nineteenth century was on mitigating the effects on Clontarf of the flight to the suburbs and the resort of seaside excursionists.

The crucial issues that divided opinion in the mid-nineteenth century were not only whether Clontarf was to be preserved as a green *rus in urbe* or to become a residential suburb but also how best to manage its maritime tourism.

Suburbanisation relied particularly heavily on advances in transportation by rail, tramway and omnibus, facilitating commuters who lived at a distance of some miles from city workplaces. The advent of the railway to the district was an early cause of tension between landowners and entrepreneurs over their perspectives on the future of Clontarf, owing to its potentiality for bringing atmospheric and visual pollution as well as day-trippers. There were also alternative visions of the broader development of landscape. While the big landowners consolidated their estates, piecemeal building of housing and roadways took place almost everywhere in Clontarf from the 1850s, necessitating the installation of facilities such as sewage, lighting and paving for an expanding population. Apart from questions of environmental protection, those of the control and cost of development bulked large in public discourse. There is no doubt that the paternalistic model of private patronage helped the evolution of a distinctive cultural milieu in Victorian Clontarf, through its associational life, recreational areas and community and parish institutions. For addressing the serious social and economic problems caused by the decline of fishing and agriculture, as well as infrastructural deficiencies, however, private philanthropy and the weak county grand jury system were inadequate.[2]

Victorian Clontarf: county gentry or suburban developers?

Dating from the beginning of this period are two sources, Lewis's *Topographical dictionary* (1837) and the first Ordnance Survey map (1843), which provide complementary depictions of the district before its intensive development. In the former, Clontarf, environed by 'very richly wooded and finely cultivated' country, is described as 'formerly a fishing village of some importance'. Although John D'Alton stated in 1838 that the Sheds 'have long since vanished with the good days of the fishermen', Lewis mentions that the wooden buildings, 'formerly used for the purpose of curing fish', are still to be seen along the shoreline, and Clontarf Sheds are clearly shown at the southernmost point of the district on the map. While the evocative place-name was retained, the demise of intensive fishing at Clontarf did occasion topographical change. As was mentioned in the previous chapter, when the Roman Catholic church of St John the Baptist was being constructed in the 1830s, the parish priest, Father James Callanan, undertook with the landlord, J.E.V. Vernon, to clear the 200 families living in mud cabins on the site of the new building and to erect cottages for them on a plot set back from the shore. The new settlement, named Snugborough, does not appear on the early Ordnance Survey map but it remained in existence at least until the

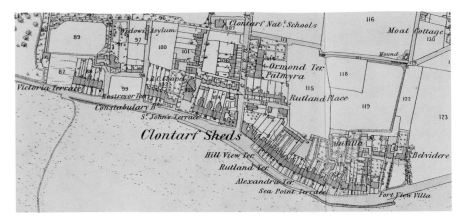

Fig. 8.2—Extract from Ordnance Survey map of 1868, showing the area around the new St John's Roman Catholic church, including the rehoused fishing community and early seafront terraces (courtesy of Trinity College, Dublin).

1860s, when living conditions in the cabins were being described as insanitary, squalid and filthy. Once again the Vernon landlords were under pressure to rase 'wretched hovels' and 'rookeries'.[3] [8.2]

According to Lewis, the village of Clontarf was now 'much frequented for sea-bathing by visitors from the north of Dublin'. Evidence for this form of recreation is gleaned from the attachment of the name 'bathing island' to Clontarf Island, while the recent conversion by John Brierly of the former Royal Charter School, now Kingscourt House, into hot and cold sea-water baths reflected the demand for comfortable bathing. The character of the architecture of the village was being affected by the resort of visitors, Lewis referring to 'neat lodging-houses' as well as villas and cottages, and the map displaying a ribbon of seaside building. D'Alton again strikes an elegiac note, referring to coastal houses and villas as being for the accommodation of bathers 'in the better days of this suburb'.[4] The building of the wooden bridge across Crablake Water and the stone causeway, later termed the Bull Wall, helped to promote the growth of the Bull Island as a recreational centre after the 1820s.[5]

The 1843 map shows that while settlement in the area had become slightly denser in the decades since John Rocque's depiction in 1760, the network of roads had not yet greatly developed. Within the arms of the Raheny Road running north-east and the southerly coast road to Dollymount and Howth, the two main north–south routes, later called Castle Avenue and Vernon Avenue, are joined by the bisecting routes Seafield (or Sea View) and Verville. [8.3] Seafield continued eastwards to meet the seafront near the wooden bridge, while Green Lane

Fig. 8.3—Extract from Ordnance Survey map of 1868, showing the heartland of the
Vernon estate, known as the 'Green Lanes', with some of the mansions and properties of
the leading landowners (courtesy of Trinity College, Dublin).

Fig. 8.4—Seapark House in 1911, one of the large mansions in the Green Lanes of
Clontarf (courtesy of the Clontarf Historical Society).

(later Mount Prospect Avenue) is also delineated, though as yet irresolute in its eventual course to the coast. [8.4] The seafront was an artery of communication from Marino Crescent to Dollymount, continuing thence along the shoreline fringe of the burgeoning St Anne's estate, and beyond to Kilbarrack and Howth. Notable coastal development had taken place in the area now called Dollymount, to the east of the wooden bridge and causeway. As well as a route which later became Strandville Avenue East, other vestigial ways which became roads may be divined, but they had not become thoroughfares by the late 1830s.[6] Lewis lists 27 substantial detached residences with their owners' names, most of which are shown on the 1843 map, a significant clustering occurring along the length of what became Vernon Avenue. While the western and central areas of Clontarf were fairly well inhabited, the section between eastern Vernon Avenue and Dollymount had comparatively fewer houses. In general, the larger habitations of the prominent householders were well spaced out, but some connecting lanes presaged the opening out of more permanent ways of communication.[7]

Also clearly discernible in the 1830s sources are a number of social and religious institutions, mostly established under the patronage of the Vernons and other philanthropic families. At least three schools operated in the area by the mid-1830s. J.E.V. Vernon had recently given a schoolhouse rent-free on Seafield Road for an Anglican parochial school which was supported by subscription. A resident of Clontarf, Michael Keary, had donated £500 for the education of Catholic children, and also £200 for the erection of a schoolroom. The school, catering for 100 pupils, was located in the old Catholic chapel on the west side of Vernon Avenue, near the seafront, and drew upon charity sermon income. A third school was privately run by James Keily in the large mansion, Baymount House, which he owned at Dollymount. Also situated in the cluster of buildings ranging along Vernon Avenue near the sea was an almshouse for twelve widows, who were supported by charity sermons and Sunday collections. Meanwhile, a Loan Fund Society had been established in 1833 for lending money at 5% to 'industrious poor' people within the parishes of Clontarf and Killester. The site for the new Roman Catholic church of St John the Baptist on the seafront at Vernon Avenue had been given by J.E.V. Vernon, and Michael Keary had donated £1,000 for its construction. Vernon was later to provide the site on Seafield Road for a new Church of Ireland parish church to replace the old one on Castle Avenue.[8]

The topographical and social details of the district, as revealed by the sources in the late 1830s, suggest its potential for suburban growth but also countervailing tendencies. With a population of 3,314, according to Lewis, Clontarf was a substantial community, though *Thom's Directory* lists only about

150 premises in 1839. Impermanent buildings, including cabins, accommodated a large number of poor families. Of the residents mentioned, almost half (44%) were men and women of gentry standing associated with specific houses, normally substantial detached villa-style edifices. A fifth of the inhabitants listed in *Thom's Directory* belonged to the professions, including barristers, a surgeon and a senior clergyman. Significantly, in view of the lure of the district as a seaside resort, almost 30% were engaged in the provision of services for visitors, including lodgings, jaunting cars, taverns and groceries. Only a small number of trades were listed, comprising 6% of the named residents, though these included builders and a carpenter. Overall, there was little in about 1840 to prefigure Clontarf's rapid growth from the 1860s, as landed and leisure interests appeared to hold sway.

Indeed, the middle decades of the century witnessed the consolidation of much of the district as a great landed estate under new nobility, in concert with two long-established landlords. Centred on St Anne's mansion in the eastern lands of Clontarf, the estate of Benjamin Lee Guinness and his son, Arthur, Lord Ardilaun, took shape through propitious leases from J.E.V. Vernon and the earl of Howth, who was proprietor of Raheny and Killester. Through the acquisition of existing estate houses and lodges with attached lands, the Guinness family built up a 500-acre estate in Clontarf and Raheny by the 1880s, thus precluding any suburban development over a vast tract. Instead, St Anne's estate was laid out in beautifully landscaped gardens and tree-lined walks, focused on St Anne's mansion, built in 1838 by Benjamin Lee Guinness and incorporating part of Thornhill, an older house on the site. Satellite estate houses, including Bedford Lodge and nearby Baymount Castle at Blackbush, Sybil Hill and Maryville on the Howth Road perimeter, as well as other cottages and lodges at Raheny, all previously occupied residences, were absorbed by the Guinnesses. Lord Ardilaun patronised the Church of Ireland at Raheny by sponsoring the construction of a new church for the parish, but his protectiveness of the landscape was symbolised by his building of a tunnel for pedestrians along a right of way from north to south underneath his splendid new avenue from St Anne's mansion to Sybil Hill. He also negotiated the possession of most of the North Bull Island through leases from Vernon and Howth, selectively conserving walking, bathing and sporting rights.[9]

The clash between progress and conservatism in Victorian Clontarf was epitomised in controversies over the advent of the Dublin and Drogheda railway, which passed along the western boundary. The promoters of the railway in Dublin and Drogheda and along the coastline pointed to the success of the service between Dublin and Kingstown, adjacent to which the land was occupied with 'villas and enclosures'. The incorporation of the Dublin and Drogheda Railway

Company in 1836, with the support of Daniel O'Connell, took place against the backdrop of strong opposition to the proposed route of the line. A deviation along the shoreline of Clontarf through the Sheds was preferred by John E.V. Vernon, who was unwilling to let the railway run through or even beside his estate, as was the earl of Charlemont, who took issue with a more westerly route through his Marino lands. Objections were also raised to the planned route through the Clontarf oyster-beds. When work on the main line from Amiens Street and the Royal Canal was eventually commenced, Vernon continued to object to its passage through the west of his estate and demanded £25,000 in compensation. Also recalcitrant was the Admiralty, whose approval was needed for the building of the embankment bringing the railway across the Tolka estuary to Clontarf. Disputes took place over the purchase of stone from the company's quarry for the building of the protective wall along the Clontarf Road by the Board of Works, and also contentious was the building of the railway bridge over the Howth Road. This thoroughfare was administered by the Malahide Turnpike Trust, who feared for their future with the construction of the railway. Early appointments of contractors and engineers by the company were less than auspicious, and it was not until the arrival of John MacNeill as engineer in succession to the ineffectual George Halpin that work on the Clontarf stretch of the line forged ahead.[10]

Fig. 8.5 — Sir John MacNeill's railway bridge over Howth Road, 1843, with the railway station building of 1897 on the right.

Fig. 8.6—'View of Dublin from the railway bridge at Holybrook', c. 1850, showing the new Dublin–Drogheda railway (© Science and Society Picture Library).

Two of MacNeill's engineering feats span the two principal roadways bounding Clontarf. His two-arched stone skew bridge over the Clontarf Road still forms an iconic entrance into the suburb. Both arches are now used for road traffic, though originally only the northern one was so open, the other being built over the sea wall. The second bridge, that over the Howth Road, was of cast iron, though with special insulation to assuage the objections of the residents of Hollybrook Park, who feared the noisiness of the passing trains. [8.5] Also overridden were the complaints of John Vernon, who eventually was awarded sixpence as compensation for his interest in the strand at Clontarf. By 1844 the line was ready for locomotives, and the first train ran from Dublin to Drogheda through Clontarf on 18 March. On 13 April the lord lieutenant, Earl de Grey, knighted John MacNeill on the occasion of the laying of the foundation stone of Amiens Street station and the running of the first regular passenger train. [8.6] Although the railway went on to achieve success as it extended into Ulster, there was a sting in the tail for the service at Clontarf. A station was opened there at the inception of the line but it closed in the 1850s owing to under-use. The service of a local station was not resumed until 1898.[11]

The closure of the railway station may have reflected the slowness of suburban development at Clontarf by the mid-century. Ribbon development there in the years before 1850 was only a prelude, however, to a more general migration from the 1860s onwards, mainly from the municipal area of Dublin. Wealthy and professional people were abandoning the inner city areas to poorer residents, not only attracted by the perceived wholesomeness of suburban, and especially coastal, living but also, less positively, repelled by the political and administrative upheavals in the wake of the Municipal Corporations Act of 1840. Reform of the city's government to incorporate the Roman Catholic majority resulted in politico-religious tensions within the corporation, which in turn gave momentum to the exodus of many Protestants from the municipal area. Indeed, the events surrounding the abandoned monster meeting at Clontarf, which was to have been part of O'Connell's Repeal campaign in 1843, were a reflection of the serious divisions between nationalists and those who upheld the Union. Located outside the municipal boundary now formed by the Royal and Grand Canals, the older, mostly seaside villages of Dublin within easy reach of the metropolis, such as Kingstown, Dalkey, Blackrock, Sandymount and Clontarf, offered asylum.

A variable rate of development was evident in these and the other new suburbs, including also Rathmines, Drumcondra and Kilmainham, with Clontarf being one of the latest to attain suburban status. The reluctance of the principal landlord family, the Vernons, to countenance substantial settlement in the latter district has been identified as a crucial factor in this slow growth. But, as elsewhere in the Dublin region, there were other general influences prevailing to retard suburban growth, including the lack of an effective system of local government. As an alternative to the antiquated county grand jury system, which was inadequate to the demands of new suburban-dwellers with their needs for water, lighting, paving, sanitation and transport, urban townships were established in many new suburbs, the first of a series being founded in Kingstown in 1834. These bodies were run by commissioners, comprising the wealthiest in the districts, who took on responsibility for improvements in water-supply, lighting, road-building and maintenance and transport through the revenues generated by the payment of local rates.[12]

Clontarf was among the last of the townships to be established, in 1869, its slowness to develop as a suburb being reflected in the premature opening and subsequent closure of the railway station. But transportation was not the major issue: a successful omnibus service was in place from Nelson Pillar in the city centre to Clontarf by 1860. Among other factors cited for its 'retrogradation' as 'a slow suburb'[13] were environmental ones. Approaching Clontarf from the inner city meant traversing a zone of docklands and industries before a malodorous and miasmal slob land, stretching from Annesley Bridge to the new railway embankment, was encountered. Allowance for a tidal scouring of the Fairview shoreline had been made by the piercing of the embankment by an arch between Clontarf and the East Wall Road, as well as the leaving of the seaward arch of the skew bridge for the flowing of the tide, but to little avail. Not only was the swamp offensive to the eye and the nose but it also presented a significant health risk, forming as it did a receptacle for city waste. The problem of the slob land elicited some ingenious suggestions for its solution during the decades down to the early twentieth century, before the eventual completion of Fairview Park. First proposed in 1859 as a 'people's park', it was envisaged as a space for the youth of 'working-men's abodes' to enjoy 'manly games such as cricket and football', and the gentry and middle class a summer evening's 'promenade or drive'. An alternative, abortive scheme was for the construction of a broad sea wall up to half the height of the arches of the railway bridge at Clontarf Road to create a tidal scour for

Poor state of Clontarf as a suburb, 1859

While the southern suburbs of Dublin are rapidly spreading and becoming populous, there is if possible a retrograde movement in the northern. Why such should be we know not, unless it may be a lack of encouragement by the lords of the soil, which deters capitalists and others from embarking on building projects ... Our remarks are peculiarly applicable to Clontarf, a locality replete with historic and natural interest, combining proximity to and easy access from the metropolis with the beautiful scenery, an expansive shore offering facility for the healthy luxury of sea-bathing, and a succession of beautiful avenues thoroughly sheltered from every kind of blast and forming a continuous shady grove.

Some of the lodgings along the road are in a most dilapidated state, others roofless, and again others patched up each spring, and exhibiting a painful shift to make them commonly tenantable as 'lodging' for those who are compelled during the summer months to seek fresh air even in these tottering structures.

Among the first and most desirable improvements to be effected is the reclamation of the waste space between Annesley and Ballybough bridges: at present it is palpably objectionable, both to the optical and nasal organs.

Dublin Builder, 1 July 1859

'a fresh and pleasant little lake'. This was to be used for boat races in summer and skating in winter. But as long as the threat of an overspill of city effluent loomed over the seashore at Clontarf, the future for residential settlement was uncertain. The crumbling sea wall, barely maintained by the barony of Coolock, was insufficient to keep flooding at bay. Nevertheless, a review of the street directories for the 1850s reveals that terraces of modern housing were being built along the seafront, accounting for half of the residences listed in Clontarf, while Castle Avenue and Vernon Avenue formed the most populous north–south axes.[14]

By the early 1860s the lack of progress in suburban development at Clontarf was becoming a source of media comment, unfavourable comparisons being made with its southside maritime counterparts such as Blackrock and Kingstown. The newly founded periodical for the building industry, *Dublin Builder*, whose proprietor, J.J. Lyons, was an architect with vested interests in building in the area, conducted a coruscating campaign in the early 1860s against 'the lords of the soil', J.E.V. Vernon and Lord Howth, for their impeding of progress. But the most immediate problem to be addressed was the many 'tottering structures'— ruinous cabins and 'wretched hovels'—along the shore, interspersing the new villas. Dilapidated bathing cabins were among the worst offenders and many calls were made for their replacement with 'decenter' accommodation. The journal's editor was all the more regretful of this suburban retardation of Clontarf because

Fig. 8.7—Oliver Matthew Latham, 'Beached boats at Clontarf, Dublin', Irish, nineteenth century. Graphite on watercolour paper, 15.3cm x 26.4cm. Photo © National Gallery of Ireland NGI 2497 (courtesy of the National Gallery of Ireland).

of the outstanding attractions of the locality, with 'its expansive shoreline, beautiful avenues and shady groves'. His campaign began to bear fruit with the announcement in successive numbers of the journal in 1862 and 1863 of the rasing of the ruinous dwellings with thatched roofs at or near the Sheds that marred a view 'unrivalled in the three kingdoms in its beauty'.[15] [8.7]

Clontarf looking up! 1862

With pleasure proportionate to the pain previously experienced in noticing the neglected state of the favourite—and by nature favoured—suburb, do we now find ourselves in a position to announce that at last the good genius of progress has visited the locality, razing the wretched hovels that disfigured the main road, and rearing in their stead domestic structures of a suitable character. The ruins at the town side of the police barrack have disappeared, and in their stead a couple of plain but neat dwelling-houses occupy their places. Further on, next Rutland Terrace, a plot for a single house has been taken by a gentleman who has more or less a business interest in the prosperity of Clontarf, and immediately adjoining, the proprietor of a well-known extensive furniture and upholstery establishment in this city is about to commence another dwelling-house and three cottages, of somewhat uncommon design and character.

Dublin Builder, 1 May 1862

The less-than-encouraging attitude of the great landlords, most notably the Vernon estate which owned most of Clontarf, was regarded by the *Builder* as the biggest hindrance to the development of the area. Would-be property developers in the early 1860s complained of comparatively short leases of 150 years for seafront houses, and excessive ground rents of 4s 6d per foot. They also baulked at restrictions on the class of housing to be built, claiming that too many expensive embellishments, such as bow-fronted windows, were being insisted upon by the landlord, making for residences too costly for modest renters. Moreover, the lack of sewerage facilities and boundary walls bespoke the lack of proper planning by the Vernon estate. Building materials such as calp and brick clay, even though in abundance in the soil at Clontarf and Killester, were not being extracted in adequate quantities from local quarries. Instead, stone and clay were being transported into the district by canal and road transport at exorbitant rates.[16]

By the early to mid-1860s, much of the reluctance of the landowners was being overcome and suburban development in Clontarf began to gather momentum. Individual resident-proprietors built mansions on larger sites along the inland avenues: Sir John Bradstreet's villa, Castilla, was erected at the intersection of Seafield and Vernon Avenue by 1859, and Blackheath House was built on Castle Avenue for Gibson Black, a wine merchant, in the 1870s. More common, however, were the entrepreneurial developers who built substantial houses for rents of from £30–£40 per annum upwards. These speculative builders employed architects who had a commitment to suburban development and significant experience of designing town housing elsewhere, such as J.J. Lyons and Edward Carson. Most of the new dwellings were arranged in terraces, many along the seafront. Among the early examples of such development were a terrace of five houses built near to St John's Roman Catholic church, one funded by a Mr Kenny of Earl Street from the design of John Bourke, and the other four financed by George Tickell, whose architect was J.J. Lyons. These dwellings were red-brick-fronted, with oriel windows and 'neat capping cornices'. Those on the eastern and western wings were two-storey over basement, the middle ones being one-storey. All were planned 'commodiously' inside. Another terrace in close proximity on a site secured by Tickell to the west, named after Queen Victoria, was of twelve houses designed by Lyons. These were being advertised by the developer in 1865 as being for rent at £40–£55 per annum to respectable tenants or permanent residents, located in the 'most healthy location in Dublin', with the 'bus passing the doors every thirty minutes.[17]

George Tickell was the archetypical suburban developer in Clontarf for almost four decades. Owner of a large furniture and upholstery establishment in Mary Street, he became a successful auctioneer, with later business interests in mining and newspapers, becoming proprietor of the *Evening Mail*. His first major acquisition in Clontarf was Baymount, which he purchased after the fire of 1851 from the Loreto sisters. He then took on Merchamps, or Mercamp, which he commissioned Lyons in 1862 to divide into two spacious dwellings, one letting on to Seafield Road through a gateway and gatelodge. There followed his ventures into speculative building, and so successful were they that Tickell had property rated at £1,421 at the end of his life in 1892. His property portfolio, rated at £2,097, in Dublin city included some tenement housing in the Gardiner Street district. His estate was valued at £72,492. As well as presiding over building projects, Tickell was active in local and municipal politics. Despite opposing the erection of Clontarf township in 1869, he served as a dedicated commissioner from then until his death. He was also elected to Dublin Corporation and to the Poor Law

Union of North Dublin on a number of occasions, holding pronounced unionist and anti-Home Rule views. His service of the Clontarf community extended to the vestry of St John's parish, and he was an enthusiastic supporter of sporting clubs in the area, including the sailing, rugby, tennis and riflery associations. A tragedy occurred in the family when George and his wife, Adelaide, suffered the loss of their son, Robert, through suicide on a train journey from London in 1888.[18]

A fairly patchy pattern of suburban growth was manifested in Clontarf in the decades down to 1900. Castle Avenue may have been still at the heart of the district but only in the sense of reflecting the traditional gentry settlement on large plots of an acre and more, the older mansions such as Clontarf Castle and Yew Park being complemented by large residences with names such as Tivoli, Everton, Danesfort and Hughenden. The terraced housing at the south-western side of the avenue, including Walpole Terrace, was of a superior quality. The seafront from Clontarf to Dollymount was filled in progressively by terraces of villas and lodges, some of them consisting only of two or three units, such as Ardilaun Terrace and Belgrove Villas. Others were longer, including the aforementioned Victoria Terrace and also Vernon Parade, both of which eventually stretched to contain twelve residences. The old fishing core retained its name of Clontarf Sheds and it saw the growth of small developments of cottages, such as the short-lived denominations of Clontarf Green, Ingham's Row, St Mary's Terrace and

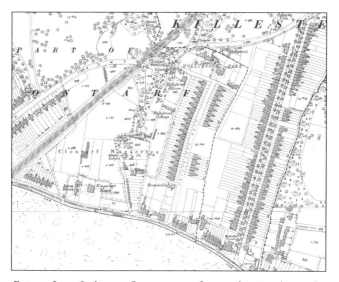

Fig. 8.8—Extract from Ordnance Survey map of 1907, showing the newly completed St Lawrence Road, the developing Hollybrook Road, the new Methodist church and the Town Hall (courtesy of the National Library of Ireland).

Fig. 8.9—Photograph of St Lawrence Road, early twentieth century (© Irish Historical Picture Company).

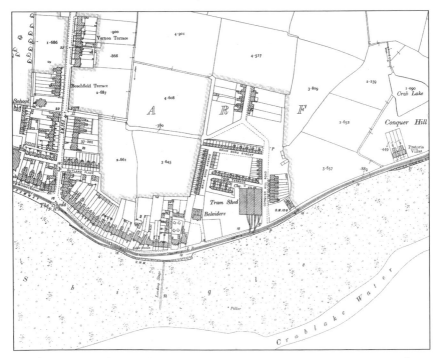

Fig. 8.10—Extract from Ordnance Survey map of 1907, showing the Conquer Hill area and the Tram Shed (courtesy of the National Library of Ireland).

Snugborough Cottages, which were absorbed into Vernon Avenue and its network of roads. Perhaps the best model for suburban settlement may be drawn from St Lawrence Road. [8.8] Opened up from 1870 on land owned by the earl of Howth, the avenue was developed in several smaller terraces of four to five villas, each of which bore distinct names such as Aloysius Terrace, Laird Terrace, Hope Terrace and St Patrick's. By the time it was numbered consecutively for the first time in 1898 it had become the most populated thoroughfare in the neighbourhood. [8.9] Slower to develop by 1900 were the Vernon project of Haddon Road and the Hollybrook Park/Road development. Interspersed with some of the fine villas and lodges along the Strand, not yet definitely termed Clontarf Road, were clusters of small cottages, such as Mooney's Lane, Byrne's Cottages and the Dublin United Tramways Company dwellings at the newly designated Conquer Hill.[19] [8.10]

Seaside and recreational activities in Clontarf

Besides the seigneurial and entrepreneurial interests, a third sector with a vital stake in the growth of Victorian Clontarf was the recreational, including the seaside industry and sporting associations. Optimistic commentators on the environmental development of Clontarf in the 1860s envisioned the blending of all of these elements in what they believed would become a maritime suburb and town, which they dubbed the 'New Brighton'. Whatever about the elegant English town, which opened up dramatically to day-trippers from London with the coming of the railway, the management of tourism and leisure in Clontarf was to be very carefully controlled, as attested, for example, by the activities of the commissioners of Clontarf township after 1869. Nevertheless, this body oversaw a coincidence of interests, with many of the suburban developers courting the seaside visitor and the major landlords asserting their patronage of recreational facilities, while attempting to keep a cavalcade of popular excursionism at bay.[20]

As has been mentioned, the area had attracted genteel visitors in the late eighteenth century, but the general decline in coastal facilities at the Sheds appears to have undermined that trend. There were signs in the early Victorian years of the growth of a designated seaside industry, with purveyors of services for visitors, such as lodgings, transport and catering, figuring among the residents of Clontarf in 1839. In 1835 the *Belfast Newsletter* reported that the Hibernian steam locomotive that plied between the city and Clontarf was stationed in John Brierly's Kingscourt Baths near the beginning of the Clontarf road. As was the case with suburban growth in Clontarf in general, however, the tourist business had to grapple with the challenges of poor infrastructure and environmental and visual pollution. The opening of the railway along the eastern boundary of the district did not boost residential or tourist numbers, as is evident from the failure of the first Clontarf railway station in the 1850s, though the advent of the omnibus service from the city centre to Dollymount in 1860 and the tramway in 1874 certainly gave an impetus to day-tripping. The problems on the strand road caused by excessive dustiness in dry weather and flooding after storms persisted beyond 1900. While the dilapidated and unsightly bathing cabins along the front were mostly rased by the mid-1860s, the condition of the sea wall fronting Clontarf and the roughness of the 'mole' or causeway leading to the Bull Island detracted from the seaside experience. Sea-bathing conditions continually gave rise to health concerns owing to the effluent caused by the faulty drainage outlet from the city at the mouth of the Tolka.[21]

More problematic, perhaps, than physical obstacles to the development of the seaside industry at Clontarf were the attitudes of some residents to 'excursionists', especially those from the poorer class of central Dublin. Recreational facilities, including bathing places, were often located in the newly settled suburban resorts, such as Bray, Kingstown, Blackrock and Dalkey on the south side, and Clontarf on the north. The rail company that ran the Dublin–Bray line had its own bathing facilities for the use of day-ticket holders, but working-class patrons were at first deterred by the prices.[22] The remnant of the old Clontarf Island after its dramatic inundation in 1844 was still being used by people from the inner city as a bathing

Fig. 8.11—Alex Williams, 'Old Clontarf Island', 1878 (Irish Naturalist).

place as late as 1870, [8.11] but the lessee, William Collins, was forced to abandon the facilities that he provided owing to the noxious effects of an artificial manure manufactory on the eastern wharf. As was pointed out in an *Irish Times* editorial in 1859, the nearest alternative was now a four- to five-mile walk from the centre to the shelter on the Bull. A correspondent in reply proposed an esplanade along both sides of the railway embankment, with the making of a lake on the west side which could provide early morning bathing facilities for males. The sight of 25 young men bathing in the sea off Warrenpoint in 1870 scandalised another Clontarf correspondent, who feared the engulfing of the area with hundreds of pleasure-seekers. Such prejudices were reflected in the landowners' opposition to a proposed shoreline railway and, later, the resistance of Lord Howth, the

Destructive storm damage on Clontarf Island, 14 October 1844

The most calamitous result of the storm on this coast [yesterday evening] was at the Island of Clontarf, where a man named Christopher Cromwell, and his son, a lad of twelve or thirteen years of age, lost their lives. Cromwell was a very industrious man, and well known to bathers. He rented the island, and kept boats which plied from the opposite wharf, and during the bathing season, he received a good deal of money. He had a small but strongly-built wooden house on the island, in which he, with his son William, usually slept until winter set in. At ten o'clock last evening, the policeman on duty missed the house, and as soon as he could, reported the fact at the station-house. An extra body of men were forthwith dispatched to the scene of the catastrophe, but neither Cromwell nor his son could be seen. The house, with its inmates and furniture, were evidently carried away by the sea, which had swept over nearly the whole surface of the island. At two o'clock today the vicinity of this calamity was thronged with persons. The wife of Cromwell, with two young children, were present, and the poor creature could not be persuaded her husband and son were lost. It was expected that in about an hour afterwards, when the tide fell, the bodies would be found. Several small pleasure boats have been wrecked in the bay of Clontarf. A great deal of the large timber growing on the property of Mr Vernon, Mr Gresham etc. along the northern coast of Clontarf bay, is blown down. The Dodder, the Dargle, and the Tolka rivers rose beyond the level of their banks, and flooded the lower grounds in several districts.

The Belfast Newsletter, 15 October 1844

Disgust at public bathing

Sir,—In the cause of public decency, I shall feel greatly obliged by your giving insertion to the following:- At ten minutes to six this afternoon (Sunday), on returning from the North Bull, I perceived a crowd immediately in front of the remains of what I consider was once a tower facing Warren Point, on the Clontarf road. Arriving at the scene, the cause of the attraction was perfectly perceptible, viz, twenty-five young men bathing in the sea, within thirty yards of the public thoroughfare, and from three hundred to four hundred yards of the Constabulary Barrack. Where were the police? is the question one would naturally inquire, or is it possible that the police have not power to interfere in the cause of public morality? If the Clontarf Township Commissioners do not at once take immediate steps to abolish this evil, the consequences likely to ensue will doubtlessly seriously injure the vicinity, insomuch as hundreds of families who avail themselves of the salubrious air of the locality will patronize some of the other environs convenient to our city, rather than incur the risk of offending their sense of propriety by being compelled to witness such scenes.

I remain, sir, very truly yours,

REFORM

Irish Times, 9 August 1870

owner of the site, to the reopening of a Clontarf rail station on Howth Road: he claimed to have done his duty by 'that class' of excursionists, almost 300,000 of whom had descended annually on Howth since the opening of the railway.[23]

Whatever about these pockets of resistance, it is clear that by the 1870s and 1880s Clontarf was among the Dublin coastal resorts that thousands of excursionists made for on the major bank holidays of the year—those at Easter and Whit, and in August. For a fare of 8d, as it was in 1887, a passenger was brought from the city centre to Dollymount and back on a Sunday and holidays. Day-trippers found more catering facilities as the century neared its end: taverns at the Sheds and in the Dollymount Hotel, confectioners and a restaurant. Longer-stay visitors could avail of summer lettings along the strand in one of the many cottages and villas that were built in the decades from the 1870s to 1900, and these stimulated local services such as groceries, of which there were a number, and even a mobile laundry, which served a number of suburban resorts.

The largest hotel in the area, the Dollymount Hotel, was operating at least as early as the 1850s, under the proprietorship of the Byrne family. Advertisements during the 1860s drew attention to an international exhibition at the hotel. It not only catered for residential guests and day-visitors but was also a venue for social and sporting functions. By 1874 the hotel had pleasure grounds attached, and it hosted orchestral performances on Saturday evenings in the summer season. There were also attached a bowling green and a rifle range. A new wing was added by 1879, as was a 'tastefully laid-out tea-garden'. Trams from town stopped at the door every fifteen minutes during the day. Because of its strategic location near the foot of the Bull Wall and in the heart of Dollymount, the hotel was the location for autopsies when drownings occurred and also for one of the first two emergency telephones in Clontarf in 1894 from which the Dublin fire brigade could be summoned.[24]

As the appeal of the district to tourists and trippers grew in the later Victorian period and new services were installed, there was a commensurate improvement in bathing facilities in Clontarf. As an alternative to open sea-bathing, enclosed baths were available from early in the nineteenth century at Kingscourt House, on the site of the former Charter School at the east of the district, called the Royal Kingscourt Baths. These baths, which continued to function under

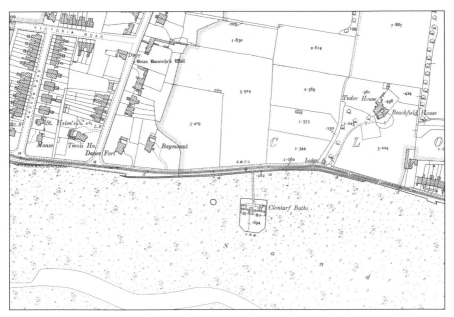

Fig. 8.12 — Extract from Ordnance Survey map of 1907, showing the location of Clontarf Baths, opened in 1864 (courtesy of the National Library of Ireland).

the proprietorship of the Brierly family until at least the 1860s, attracted excursionists by omnibus stationed at Kingscourt. In 1863 hot and shower baths were being provided, as well as suites of apartments for 'first class families' and single ladies and gentlemen. Then in 1881 there was established the Clontarf Baths and Assembly Rooms, located just off the coast between Castle and Vernon Avenues. [8.12] The venture was backed by J.E.V. Vernon and Lord Ardilaun, the former leasing the site and both buying shares in the company. Within a concrete surrounding wall, separate hot and shower baths for male and female swimmers were laid out. A small bridge joined the baths to the seafront, under which there were placed a sea-water tank, a boiler and pump, operated by a steam engine. Within a few years the baths were attracting over 25,000 swimmers during the five-month season, many of them buying inclusive 6d tickets for the baths as well as a return trip from the city. The baths project enjoyed not just the patronage of the major landlords but also the support of major developer-commissioners such as George Tickell and William Graham.[25]

As a focus of much of the bathing and recreational activity in later Victorian Clontarf, the Bull Island provided a beautiful and circumscribed environment for pleasure-seekers. While sports such as horse-racing, athletics and riflery, and aquatic pursuits such as boating and sailing, were common on and around the island by the mid-century, questions of ownership of and public rights to a still-growing land mass persisted until much later. Under the terms of the charter of Charles II to the Vernons, the foreshore was granted to the family, but with the building of the North Bull Wall the Ballast Board (later the Port and Docks Board) had ownership of a strip of land along both sides of the wall. After the 1820s two separate islands grew along the sand bar, the newly formed eastern one in Raheny parish falling to the earl of Howth's possession and Vernon claiming the western one in Clontarf parish, before the tracts merged to form the North Bull Island. A popular opinion expressed in the press was that the island had been formed (accidentally) because of the expenditure of huge sums of public money on the North Bull Wall project and that therefore the area should be regarded as a commons, fully open to the public. J.E.V. Vernon attempted to assert his ownership rights in 1885 by fencing off large sections of the eastern part of the island, but he bowed to recreational interests in leasing a major part of his lands there to the Royal Dublin Golf Club, first in 1889 and then in 1891 for 21 years. Meanwhile, Lord Ardilaun became a stakeholder, first by leasing two acres opposite St Anne's from the earl of Howth in 1890, and then four years later buying out the earl's entire 300-acreage in the eastern part. Finally, the lord of St Anne's became owner of the island, buying the eastern part, amounting to 922 acres, from Edward Vernon in

1902 and stipulating the right of the public to walk the land and bathe from the wall and foreshore.[26]

Of the many sporting clubs and associations that came into being in Clontarf in the Victorian period, the Royal Dublin Golf Club benefited most directly from the availability of the seaside links on the Bull Island. At the time of the Ardilaun purchase in 1902, the club bought 122 acres of the island in Clontarf parish for its exclusive use as a golf-course, and supplemented these lands with a lease of much of the eastern portion in 1904. It was out of the latter terrain that St Anne's Golf Club acquired its course through a lease from Lady Ardilaun in 1921. On the mainland, the 1870s and 1880s were a time for the foundation of sports clubs in Clontarf and their regulation through proper rules and procedures. Within a dozen years the Yacht and Boat Club (1875), the Rugby Club (1876), the Cricket Club (1876) and the Tennis Club (1887) had been established. At first, the premises and grounds used were temporary, rugby being played at Merchamps on Vernon Avenue, cricket on Howth Road and tennis on St Lawrence Road, before permanent club premises were acquired at Castle Avenue (for cricket and rugby) and Oulton Road (for tennis). Patronage of the new clubs and associations was normally extended by Lord Ardilaun and J.E.V. Vernon, and the committee memberships frequently included suburban developers such as George Tickell and Graham Lemon. By the 1890s the clubs and associations had for the most part settled into their new headquarters in the expanding suburb, erecting facilities such as clubhouses and successfully fielding teams in municipal and national competitions.[27]

Clontarf township, 1869–1901

The experience of working together on the part of landed and suburban interests in Clontarf to support the culture of leisure carried over into the political and administrative sphere after the 1860s. Although never becoming a major resort and still lacking adequate facilities until the turn of the century, Clontarf was set on a course of modest expansion in the mid- to later Victorian period, the new developments harmonising well with natural grandeur. The pace of development, which was carefully controlled by the Vernons, Guinnesses and St Lawrences, allowed for a balanced approach when moves towards the setting up of a township gathered pace in the 1860s. This allowed landed estate-owners and leading businessmen-developers such as George Tickell and William Prescott, the laundry magnate, to participate formally in the push for essential utilities, such as lighting, water and drainage, and in supervising the burgeoning tourist sector.[28]

In the summer of 1869 there passed through parliament the Clontarf Township Act, providing for the self-government of the districts of Clontarf, Dollymount and Ballybough (but excluding the Bull Island), an area of 1,400 acres. Under the act, twelve commissioners were given power to raise taxes for the improvement of public services and utilities for the new township. There had been opposition to the bill from two interest groups, the wealthy landowners of Clontarf and Dollymount and the less-affluent ratepayers of Ballybough and Fairview. The fears of the former group that very high rates would prevail were assuaged by the comparisons made with other townships, where taxation was reasonable and property values were said to have risen. From the ratepayers in the west of the district there were strong objections to the make-up of the board of commissioners. With the support of local clergy, they argued that John Edward Venables Vernon and his associates would dominate the board as a 'Tory clique' or an 'Orange Lodge' to the exclusion of Roman Catholics and Liberals. A clause in the proposed bill setting the threshold for qualification as elector in the new township at £8 annual rateable valuation was seen as disenfranchising more reform-minded voters, and a strong, though unsuccessful, case was made for lowering it to £4. There was also a fear, well founded as it turned out, that the acute problem of the discharge of sewage from the city at Ballybough Bridge would not be tackled with urgency by the township.[29]

From 1869 to 1900 Clontarf was governed as a township by its twelve commissioners, groups of four of whom sought re-election in rotation every three years. The name of Vernon was constant as a commissioner throughout, first John Edward Venables and then, on his death in 1890, his son Edward, as was that of Guinness or Lord Ardilaun, the owner of St Anne's estate. Among the other major householders who dominated the board of commissioners for much of the period of the township were Graham Lemon of St Edmund's, George Tickell of Mercamp (Merchamps) and Baymount, John Beggs of Belgrove House, Gibson Black of Blackheath and W.L. Freeman, proprietor of Clontarf Baths. The commissioners met fortnightly at No. 1, The Crescent (until the opening of the Town Hall in 1894), to conduct the business of the township, and the annual meeting took place in the late autumn. Before the end of December the rate was struck for the coming year. Comprising two shillings in the pound for basic services, and lesser charges for Poor Law relief, water, sanitation and public health, the total tax annual burden imposed upon ratepayers was 4s 6d at its peak but settled at about 3s 5d for every pound of rateable valuation on their property. As well as collecting between £3,000 and £4,000 from the ratepayers, the commissioners financed their projects by occasional loans from the Local Government Board and other agencies. Until 1893 meetings of the commissioners were closed to the press, brief summaries of their proceedings being released instead to the newspapers.[30]

By contrast with the previous situation of non-existent or erratic services in Clontarf in areas such as public lighting and the water-supply, the township administration saw the provision of proper and efficient utilities for the neighbourhood. Within a year of its establishment the township had entered into a contract with the Alliance Gas Company for gaslights along the roads and avenues of Clontarf, and the service was successful. Efforts by some commissioners to curtail the lighting season, which ran from September to March, and to confine street-lighting to non-moonlit nights failed, but by the end of the century moves were afoot to investigate the possibility of electric lighting.[31] Before Clontarf got its running water supplies, the populace was dependent on water being carted into the district or on wells on private properties. By the early 1870s Clontarf had been connected up with Dublin Corporation's Vartry water-supply, for which the ratepayers contributed up to a shilling in the pound and the commissioners raised a loan. There were persistent problems with the water pressure in some districts of the suburb, and also with the excessive use of supplies by the inhabitants. By the terms of the contract, Clontarf was allowed a daily supply of twenty gallons per head, but throughout the period levels of consumption were almost double that ration. The use of the supply to water the roads was heavily criticised by the Waterworks Committee of Dublin Corporation, and the supply situation became critical during the severe winter of 1892–3, which was followed by the driest summer in living memory. Various solutions to address shortages were canvassed, including the use of canal water, the pumping of sea water to clean the roads, the metering of the supply to the district and the rationing of water to between the hours of 8am and 12 noon. Eventually, after the threat of draconian measures on the part of the corporation, a compromise was reached whereby corporation inspectors checked the mains in the township, and supply appeared to match demand by the end of the century.[32]

With the establishment of Clontarf township, responsibility for roads in the district passed from the county grand jury to the commissioners. By 1901 developers including Vernon had opened up new avenues, including Haddon, Victoria and Mount Prospect roads, and rows of labourers' cottages had been built at Conquer Hill Road and its intersecting streets. The population of the suburb had almost doubled between the 1860s and 1900, and the number of houses had increased by over 50% during the same period. Apart from lighting and water-supplies for the new thoroughfares, the township bore the cost of keeping all eleven miles of roadway in the district in repair at an annual expenditure of between £600 and £800, though the commissioners had no control over the yearly payment of about £300 to the county grand jury. Many complaints were registered from disgruntled ratepayers about the state of the roads, especially about their inordinate dustiness and their lack of footpaths, but the opening of the tramway along the strand road necessitated significant improvements at least in the condition of that crucial artery. A major issue for the residents was the paving of the footpaths, first with gravel and then with asphalt and concrete. Flagging of the pavements of Clontarf got under way in the late 1880s, and the project, costing over £3,000, was eventually completed after several delays and legal cases.[33]

A key feature of the Clontarf built environment over which the commissioners now had control was the sea wall along the strand road. Repairs after frequent storm damage were very costly, as in 1877, for example, when £465 was expended, and sometimes necessitated donations from leading residents, including J.E.V. Vernon and Sir Arthur Guinness.[34] Echoes of previous battles over the rights to the foreshore were heard during an enquiry into proposals by the Dublin Port and Docks Board (the successors of the Ballast Board) to purchase compulsorily 900 acres in the north inner bay for the improvement of the harbour, the provision of new wharfage facilities at the East Wall and possibly the construction of a drainage pipe for city waste. John Vernon objected to the scheme, adducing his family's charter from the time of Charles II. During the hearing, at which queries were raised about Vernon's dual role as chairman of the commissioners and lord of the manor, it became clear that in 1819 the Vernon family had sold their foreshore rights to the east of the Bull Wall to the corporation but still claimed control over the tidal slob lands to the west, including the oyster-beds, the mine shaft and the island. As a safeguard of these interests, an expanse of shore running 1,000ft to the south of the sea wall had been demarcated as Vernon's property, and the Port and Docks Board declared their lack of intention of intruding upon this.[35] An interesting sidelight on the issue at stake in a controversy in 2011 was the suggestion that a breakwater 4ft in height be constructed, principally to promote the tidal scour along the shoreline but also possibly as a defence against flooding. The latter was a perennial problem throughout this period (as it remains today), with particularly severe inundations occurring in Clontarf in the winter of 1898–9.[36]

An area of public utility that proved to be beyond the capabilities of the Clontarf commissioners to service adequately was the drainage and sewerage system, and this failure opened up deep divisions between the east and the west of the township.[37] The nub of the problem was the outfall from the city sewerage system at the mouth of the Tolka at Annesley Bridge, which created a festering and malodorous cesspool at Ballybough and Fairview. Although Clontarf did not escape the nuisance owing to the current of the river along the foreshore, the effects there were mitigated somewhat by the action of the tides in the bay. Because of opposition on the part of local interests, including Clontarf township, to Dublin city's proposal in the 1860s and 1870s for a main drainage system, Vernon and the substantial property-owners objecting to the possibility of seepage along the coastline,[38] a major municipal scheme of waste disposal was postponed until the late 1890s. Instead, local sewage works in the Fairview district were undertaken at great expense from 1886, mainly concentrated on cleaning up the bed of the Tolka, but the problems persisted, with serious implications for public health. Deputations from the township met with the Public Health Committee of Dublin Corporation amid real fears of the spread of infectious diseases.[39] A partial solution emerged with a plan to reclaim the slob lands between Annesley Bridge and the railway embankment, turning it into a People's Park,[40] but even in respect of the east of the district, with the increase in households using water closets, the commissioners were under pressure to initiate a proper drainage pumping system. Arguments over the cost (upwards of £20,000) and the location (Fairview

Fig. 8.13—Detail from Conquer Hill Road of the architecture of the tram sheds, which later became part of the Bus Garage.

or Dollymount) were finally stilled with absorption of the township within the municipal boundary of Dublin in 1900 and the subsequent completion of the main drainage system at the expense of all of the ratepayers of the enlarged city.[41]

Although the township did not run its own transport company, there is no doubt that its generally supportive policy towards tramways and railway helped the development of Clontarf as a suburb. When the trams came to Clontarf in 1874, they not only brought increased accessibility to the city for the less-affluent residents but also gave a boost to the economy and infrastructure of the area.[42] The cost of widening of the strand road, for example, was contributed to by the Tramway Company, and the establishment of the terminus entailed the building of tramworkers' cottages at Conquer Hill, as well as extensive stables for the horses and sheds for the cars.[43] [8.13] The popularity of the tramway in conveying workers to the city and day-trippers to the seaside was acknowledged by the commissioners, who benefited by the payment of £300 way-leave for the trams' traversing of three miles of township roads.[44] They also negotiated with the company for more frequent services at peak times and lower fares for passengers. When the proposal to electrify the tram system was mooted in the later 1890s there were no major objections, and the new service commenced in 1898. Clontarf became one of the most profitable routes for the Dublin United Tramways Company, and the erection of the new pillars for the overhead wiring

Fig. 8.14—Photograph of one arch of MacNeill's skew bridge, with an approaching tram, early twentieth century (© Irish Historical Picture Company).

was accompanied by the installation of electric lamp standards.[45] [8.14] Less smooth was the proposal by the Clontarf and Hill of Howth Tramway Company for a service between Dollymount and Howth village, objections to which were lodged by the township, but eventually it went ahead, the line being extended from Dollymount along the coast to Howth in 1900. The service was only permitted to begin after several stipulations laid down by Lord Ardilaun were fulfilled: no Howth tramcar could stop between Blackbush Lane (later Mount Prospect Avenue) and Watermill Road, a specially designed fence was to be built along the edge of his property to protect his estate and rifle range (with the service halted on one day per year for an annual shooting competition), and a large gateway was to be built at the coast-road entrance to his domain.[46]

The railway had impinged less on Clontarf, the original station having been closed about 1850 owing to lack of custom. A movement for the reopening of a station at a site on Howth Road gathered pace from the early 1890s. At first the Great Northern Railway Company rejected the township's request for a station, citing the problems of an access road to the embankment, delays to trains to and from Dublin and the expected low volumes of passenger traffic.[47] The plan was revived in 1895 with the support of leading commissioners, including Vernon and

Opening of new train station at Clontarf, 1898

This long-agitated for accommodation to supply the wants of an important northern suburb has now been completed, and today the new station at Clontarf will be opened for traffic. The station is situated at the north side of the railway bridge over the Howth Road, and it is believed that its location will serve the purposes of the people of Clontarf and district. The station is constructed of brick. There are two timber platforms, each 450 feet long. On the east side of the line on the low level there are spacious waiting rooms, a booking hall, offices, lavatories and a compact residence for the station master. Telegraphic facilities are, of course, provided ... Access to the platforms will be obtained by inclined approaches, and the steps have been specially constructed to make access and exit easy. The Clontarf commissioners are making a new route to the station from the shore road on the tramway line, and when this has been completed, the accommodation provided for the inhabitants of the district by the new station will be still more apparent.

Freeman's Journal, 1 April 1898

Ardilaun. It was argued that the township's population of 6,000 increased to 10,000 in the summer and the trams were not able to cope with the passenger traffic.[48] Eventually the station was approved, the roadway was built at a cost of £940, to which some local supporters contributed (but not Lord Howth, it was noted), and the trains began to halt again at Clontarf station in the spring of 1898.[49]

Optimism about a prosperous future for the township of Clontarf was boosted by the construction of a new town hall near the western end of the seafront by 1894. Following the lead of their counterparts in south Dublin, the Clontarf commissioners planned an edifice to reflect local pride, though on a more modest scale than in Pembroke, Blackrock, Kingstown and Rathmines. Having considered Warrenpoint as a possible location, the commissioners eventually decided on the site to the west of St Lawrence Road. The project was financed by means of a loan of £2,000 from the Board of Works, and William Perrott, the township surveyor, drew up the plans. A suite of red-bricked buildings, roofed with pitch pine, was centred on an assembly hall with a capacity of 600 and with a stage at one end, and also incorporated a boardroom and offices. At a formal ceremony in December 1893, the foundation stone of the town hall was laid by Mrs Vernon in the presence of her husband, Lord and Lady Ardilaun, the commissioners and other guests. The ceremony was followed by a luncheon at which several congratulatory speeches were made, emphasising the progress made by the suburb of Clontarf under Vernon patronage. By the following April the building was ready to house the meetings of the commissioners as well as the business of the township officials.[50]

Within six years of its opening, Clontarf Town Hall had lost its *raison d'être*. In 1900 Clontarf was absorbed within the area of the greater Dublin municipality. This major change was effected through the Dublin Boundaries Act of 1900, which extended the city to include the former townships of Clontarf, Drumcondra and Kilmainham. By thus becoming incorporated, the district of Clontarf could now look to the financial power of the metropolis to fund the main drainage scheme and other expensive projects. In a poll of Clontarf ratepayers, a majority voted in favour of the act, despite the determined opposition of Vernon and other leading figures in the east of the township who argued for separation notwithstanding the township's parlous financial state. By 1900 the antagonism of the householders of Ballybough and Fairview to the dominance of the conservative element of large estate-owners on the township commission had become more politically organised. The formation of the Clontarf Improvement and Ratepayers Association in the 1880s, which had focused in the main on the grievances of the Fairview side of the district, led to the election in 1892 of Joseph Bonass as a Clontarf commissioner

A new town hall for Clontarf, 1893

Yesterday the foundation stone of the new Town Hall, Clontarf, was laid by Mrs Vernon of Clontarf Castle in the presence of Lord Ardilaun and the commissioners of the township. The site selected is very central and is on the space of ground known for many years past as Whitehall. The new building will be not only a great advantage to the commissioners in the discharge of their work, but it promises to be a credit to the township as an architectural feature ... The new town hall comprises a public room, suitable for entertainments and meetings. It measures 65 feet by 35 feet. At the rere there is provision for a boardroom, commissioners' offices, lavatories ... and rooms for the caretaker. It is expected that the building will be available for use about 1 March.

Mrs Vernon having laid the foundation stone, Lord Ardilaun said, 'I thank you, Mrs Vernon ... I will only remind all here that the Vernon family have been connected with this district for over 250 years. I will not say more in the presence of the present worthy representative of a long line of ancestors who stands amongst us, and I would say to him in the words of his motto, 'Vernon semper viret', and while I cannot pretend that our ceremony can have as important results as those which flowed from previous great events in Clontarf, still I hope that our proceedings will take a worthy place in the annals of Clontarf'.

Subsequently Lord Ardilaun entertained the commissioners and other friends at luncheon in St Anne's, Dollymount.

Freeman's Journal, 22 December 1893

to represent the interests of lesser ratepayers. Bonass campaigned successfully for the press to be admitted to commission meetings from September 1893. Other non-establishment commissioners were elected, including William Prescott, the owner of the dyeworks, who raised embarrassing issues such as the lack of a proper drainage system in Clontarf and Fairview. Thus, when the question of redrawing the boundaries of the city came up for serious discussion in the late 1890s, a strong movement in favour of the inclusion of Clontarf emerged among the Fairview ratepayers, impelled by the hope of a real improvement in a range of services and utilities under the auspices of Dublin Corporation. After seven centuries, the tradition of stout local independence which Clontarf had enjoyed as village, town and township was at an end.[51]

Perhaps ironically, in view of the impending loss of autonomy, there was a visit to Clontarf in April 1900 by Queen Victoria, under whose monarchy the spirit of technical progress that fostered suburban self-reliance had been elicited. Her afternoon drive took her from the viceregal lodge by the North Circular Road, over the 'romantic' Ballybough Bridge and along the coast road. Unfortunately for the royal visitor, the tide was out and a commentator mentioned 'an unpleasant reminder of the reasons why difficulties have arisen as between the city and the suburb on the question of the boundaries'. The town hall and other buildings were decorated for the occasion, and the queen stopped to meet some of the children of St Vincent de Paul's Orphanage drawn up by the roadside. Continuing on the seafront, the royal carriage turned into St Anne's estate after the Bull Wall at Dollymount and brought the queen to the front of Lord Ardilaun's mansion. There she greeted members of the Guinness and Plunket families before being driven along the avenue of the estate to the Howth Road, the coach then turning down St Lawrence Road and continuing back through Fairview and Drumcondra. Queen Victoria's honouring of Lord Ardilaun by her brief stopover was a fitting tribute to one who had become more and more the leading champion of an independent Clontarf in the previous decade. As regular chairman of the commissioners, his strong support was forthcoming for the Fairview Park reclamation and railway station projects, and he it was who proposed a bill in early 1900 for major improvements in drainage and lighting in Clontarf, as a means of forestalling the looming boundaries extension. In this purpose he failed, but his popularity with the ratepayers of Clontarf was not in doubt.[52] [8.15]

Lord Ardilaun opposes the absorption of Clontarf within the city, 1900

Clontarf could do everything that it wanted with the means at its command. It was a seaside place and ought not to be bound up with the city of Dublin, with an urban population. Lord Ardilaun further said in giving explanations with reference to the finances of Dublin, that the people of Clontarf feared that by annexation they would be saddled with heavy responsibilities, which they ought not in fairness to be called upon to bear, and which would lead to a considerable increase in rates.

Irish Times, 4 July 1900

Fig. 8.15—Statue of Lord Ardilaun, patron of many features of Clontarf's development, in St Stephen's Green, Dublin.

1 Hardy, 'A day's ramble on the north side of the city'; 'Clontarf Castle, County of Dublin', *Irish Penny Journal* 11 (1840), 81–3; Alistair Rowan (ed.), *The architecture of Richard Morrison and William Vitruvius Morrison* (Dublin, 1989), 72–4.

2 For a discussion of the background to suburban development see Seamus Ó Maitiú, *Dublin's suburban towns, 1834–1930* (Dublin, 2003), 19–46.

3 Samuel Lewis, *A topographical dictionary of Ireland* (2 vols, London, 1837), i, 376–7; www.maps. osi.ie/publicviewer/#V1, 720141, 735870, 7, 7 (accessed 4 January 2012); D'Alton, *History of County Dublin*, 51–2; Nicholas Donnelly, *A short history of some Dublin parishes: part xiv: parishes of Clontarf, Fairview, Coolock and Glasnevin* (Dublin, 1900), 31–2; *Dublin Builder*, 1 July 1861, 1 May 1862.

4 Lewis, *Topographical dictionary*, i, 376; D'Alton, *History of County Dublin*, 51; de Courcy, *Liffey in Dublin*, 80.

5 See Jeffrey *et al.* (eds), *North Bull Island*.

6 In *Thom's Directory* for 1839 the following denominations appear under Clontarf: Annsbrook, Back-Strand, Clontarf (later Castle Avenue), Clontarf-Sheds (later Vernon Avenue), Clontarf Strand (later Clontarf Road), Fortview-Avenue, Crab-Lake, Crescent, Diamond (Marino Crescent), Dollymount, Green-Lanes, Dollymount, Rutland-Place (Green Lanes), Seafield-Avenue (Green Lanes): p. 666.

7 Lewis, *Topographical dictionary*, i, 376–7; *Thom's Directory* for 1839 also lists over two dozen named residences, though in some cases the occupiers' names are different: p. 666.

8 Lewis, *Topographical dictionary*, i, 377; D'Alton, *History of County Dublin*, 48; Bernardine Ruddy, 'Baymount Castle, Clontarf', *DHR* 69 (2006), 173; www.maps.osi.ie/publicviewer/#V1, 720141, 735870, 7, 7 (accessed 4 January 2012).

9 Sharkey, *St Anne's*.

10 *House of Commons: Minutes of evidence taken before the committee of the Dublin and Drogheda railway* (London, 1836); Noel Gamble, 'The Dublin and Drogheda railway: parts 1–2', *Journal of the Irish Railway Record Society* 11 (1974), 224–34, 283–93.

11 John D'Alton, *The history of Drogheda, with its environs, and an introductory memoir of the Dublin and Drogheda railway* (2 vols, Dublin, 1844), i, p. lvi; Ó Maitiú, *Dublin's suburban towns*, 43, 147; see William Balch, *Ireland as I saw it* (New York, 1850), 403–5, for an early account of the rail journey from Dublin through Clontarf.

12 For a discussion of the emergence of townships see Ó Maitiú, *Dublin's suburban towns*, 24–46.

13 Phrases taken from *Dublin Builder*, 15 May 1861, 15 August 1861; *IT*, 29 November 1859.

14 Ó Maitiú, *Dublin suburban towns*, 43–6; *Dublin Builder*, 1 October 1859, 1 September 1861; *Thom's Directory* (Dublin, 1850), 837–40; *ibid.* (Dublin, 1852), 908–11.

15 See *Dublin Builder*, 1 July 1859, 1 October 1859, 15 April 1861, 1 May 1861, 15 May 1861, 1 July 1861, 1 August 1861, 1 September 1861, 1 May 1862, 1 August 1862; for J.J. Lyons see www.dia.ie/architects/view/3291/LYONS-JOHNJOSEPH (viewed 28 August 2012).

16 *Dublin Builder*, 15 April 1861, 1 May 1861, 15 May 1861, 1 August 1862.

17 *Thom's Directory* (Dublin, 1874–6); www.dia.ie/architects/view/154/CARSON-EDWARDHENRY (viewed 28 August 2012); *Dublin Builder*, 1 July 1859, 1 May 1862, 1 April 1863, 1 September 1863; *IT*, 21 August 1865, 18 March 1889.

18 *IT*, 28 April 1861, 24 January 1863, 27 November 1871, 9 September 1873, 7 January 1876, 5 April 1877, 29 October 1878, 16 August 1888, 15 April 1890, 25 September 1890, 21 June 1892, 4 October 1892; *Dublin Builder*, 1 June 1862, 15 May 1863; *FJ*, 18 June 1892; Ruddy, 'Baymount Castle', 176–7.

19 *Thom's Directory* (Dublin, 1862–1901).

20 Bray, Co. Wicklow, was being termed 'the Brighton of Ireland' by the 1860s: Mary Davies, *That favourite resort: the story of Bray, Co. Wicklow* (Bray, 2007), 161, 168; for Clontarf and this ascription see Colm Lennon, 'Clontarf in the 1860s: seaside resort or residential suburb?', *Clontarf Annual* (1987), 27–8.

21 *Thom's Directory* (Dublin, 1839); *Belfast Newsletter*, 20 January 1835; *FJ*, 4 September 1889, 25 August 1892, 15 February 1899; *Dublin Builder*, 1 September 1863; *IT*, 25 June 1859.

22 Mary E. Daly, *Dublin, the deposed capital: a social and economic history, 1860–1914* (Cork, 1985), 175; Davies, *That favourite resort*, 169.

23 *IT*, 25 and 28 June 1859, 9 August 1870, 26 April 1873; *FJ*, 21 March 1894.

24 See, for example, *IT*, 16 June 1871, 27 June 1874, 12 March 1879, 17 August 1881, 19 April 1884, 5 August 1890, 25 October 1895.

25 *FJ*, 4 April 1863, 5 February 1884; *IT*, 6 January 1881, 15 November 1886; Bernardine Ruddy, 'Clontarf baths and Assembly Rooms', *DHR* **62** (2009), 27–35.

26 *IT*, 14 August 1868, 6 May 1873, 1 August 1873, 20 May 1875, 7 June 1875, 12 February 1886; *FJ*, 18 September 1885, 10 April 1900; Donal T. Flood, 'Historical evidence for the growth of North Bull Island', in Jeffrey *et al.* (eds), *North Bull Island*, 11–12; Sharkey, *St Anne's*, 59–60, 62, 63, 65.

27 Sharkey, *St Anne's*, 63, 65, 69; *IT*, 14 July 1875, 18 August 1925; www.clontarfrugby.com/about-2/club-history/ (viewed 29 August 2012); www.clontarfcricket.com/clontarfcc/Main/History (viewed 29 August 2012); www.clontarfltc.com/history.php/ (viewed 29 August 2012).

28 Although the records of Clontarf township do not appear to be extant, the activities of the commissioners can be gleaned from the regular reports of meetings in the *Freeman's Journal* and the *Irish Times*.

29 *FJ*, 1 and 5 January 1869, 21 April 1869, 7 and 8 May 1869, 26 and 30 June 1869.

30 *FJ*, 31 July 1872, 6 September 1893.

31 *FJ*, 26 June 1869, 28 March 1870, 21 October 1879, 12 September 1889, 30 December 1896, 7 September 1898.

32 *FJ*, 26 June 1869, 12 and 18 November 1870, 9 June 1871, 24 January 1874, 23 November 1886, 13 January 1891, 16 January 1893, 6 September 1893, 27 October 1893, 21 May 1895, 4 November 1896, 16 December 1896.

33 *Thom's Directory* (Dublin 1896–1901); *FJ*, 3 June 1871, 20 March 1875, 23 October 1877, 21 October 1879, 18 June 1886, 23 November 1886, 6 June 1888, 27 March 1889, 10 June 1891, 23 March 1893, 19 April 1899.

34 *FJ*, 23 October 1877.

35 *FJ*, 1 April 1879.

36 *FJ*, 3 July 1879, 30 November 1898, 15 February 1899; see *IT*, 5 and 17 November 2011, 6 December 2011.

37 For the context see Daly, *Deposed capital*, 251–4.

38 *FJ*, 9 August 1870, 28 February 1871.

39 *FJ*, 29 September 1886, 6 June 1888, 27 March 1891, 18 May 1893.

40 *FJ*, 18 December 1893, 9 January 1900.

41 *FJ*, 7 August 1897, 13 November 1899, 9 January 1900.

42 Ó Maitiú, *Dublin's suburban towns*, 148.

43 *FJ*, 20 March 1875, 12 September 1894, 24 August 1895.

44 *FJ*, 11 January 1899.

45 *FJ*, 23 October 1897, 20 March 1898.

46 *FJ*, 13 October 1897, 22 June 1898; J.M.C. Kilroy, 'Transport', in V.J. McBrierty (ed.), *The Howth peninsula: its history, lore and legend* (Dublin, 1981), 94–7; F.J. Murphy, 'Dublin trams, 1872–1979', *DHR* **28** (1975), 5–6, 8–9.

47 *FJ*, 15 August 1891.

48 *IT*, 10 August 1895; *FJ*, 16 December 1896.

49 *FJ*, 1 April 1898.

50 Ó Maitiú, *Dublin's suburban towns*, 159–64; *Clontarf's Eye* 7 (1991), 5–7; *IT*, 22 December 1893; *FJ*, 19 November 1891, 18 May 1893, 15 August 1894.

51 Ó Maitiú, *Dublin's suburban towns*, 135–44; *FJ*, 23 February 1893, 21 and 23 December 1892, 23 January 1893, 27 October 1893, 18 December 1893, 14 January 1899, 19 April 1899, 16 May 1899, 9, 16 and 22 January 1900, 23 July 1900.

52 *FJ*, 18 December 1893, 9 January 1900, 20 April 1900; *IT*, 31 May 1897, 19 July 1899, 20 April 1900, 4 July 1900, 9 January 1901.

CHAPTER NINE

Parks and avenues: the garden suburb in the twentieth century

WITH ITS FORMAL absorption within the municipality of Dublin in 1901, Clontarf lost its 700-year-long independent status as first a manorial village and then a township. Opponents of the Boundaries Act of 1900, including Lord Ardilaun, had argued strenuously that the area was 'a seaside place' and the population not an urban one.[1] They also feared the cost of increased taxation if municipal rates were applied. By contrast, protagonists of corporation rule, resident mainly in Fairview, put forward a strong case for the extension of the city's boundaries, pointing to the general neglect of their area under the administration of the township, and the specific issue of drainage. The whole district duly came under the aegis of the corporation of Dublin, but in practical terms the dismantling of the township meant the fairly immediate decoupling of the western parts of Fairview and Ballybough from the Clontarf section to the east of the railway embankment. The erection of two separate municipal wards of Clontarf West (for Fairview and Ballybough) and Clontarf East tended to hasten this process.

While it was thanks mainly to the conservatism of Lord Ardilaun and other landowners that eastern Clontarf had preserved much of its *rus in urbe* and seaside character, the district had become distinctly suburban by the early twentieth century, and that trend continued down to the later twentieth century. In this brief sketch of the main developments over these decades it will be seen that, at first, growth carried over from the Victorian period was slow and patchy. Major municipal infrastructural schemes were undertaken, including the installation of main drainage and the reclamation of the land that became Fairview Park between the railway embankment and Annesley Bridge. Civic planning for garden suburbs, including Clontarf, was discussed from about 1912, but a decade of national and international political and social upheaval intervened to discourage development. It was not until well into the 1920s that a new vision for the future of Clontarf emerged through the co-working of Dublin Corporation and the Vernon estate. Its execution took place through the medium of private developers for the most part, but elements of the earlier civic planning were incorporated. Several new roads and hundreds of houses were built by the end of the 1930s as the fields around the neighbourhood were gradually filled in, and existing thoroughfares were extended. Nevertheless, a distinctive architectural style, including maritime villas and domestic bungalows, reflected elements of a seaside resort within the garden suburb. While the pace of growth may have slowed during the years of the Second World War, momentum was resumed thereafter, with significant development taking place to the east of Vernon Avenue in the newly designated suburb of Dollymount.

Although the famed verdure of Clontarf, so prominent in many travellers' accounts, was threatened with encroachment throughout this period of rapid suburbanisation, the role of the municipal corporation in preserving and developing green spaces in the district was important. A new promenade came into being by the middle decades of the twentieth century, as the backfilling of the seafront was undertaken through deposits of municipal waste and dredging operations. Once finally completed in the 1950s, the promenade added greatly to the leisure facilities and aesthetic beauty of the area, as well as to its residential attractions. The corporation also took over the management of St Anne's estate from the Guinness and Plunket families in the 1930s. Apart from some housing schemes on the northern fringes, the landscape was preserved as parkland for the enjoyment of locals and visitors. And in the 1950s the bulk of the Bull Island came under the ownership of Dublin Corporation, which became curator of its wildlife resources and oversaw its status as a special amenity. Despite its huge physical and demographic expansion, therefore, Clontarf managed, in common with other maritime suburbs that formed around village nuclei in the vicinity of Dublin, to retain its identity as a residential and recreational place apart from the city.[2]

Suburban progress, planning and setbacks, 1901–22

Taking into account the internal reconfiguration after the boundary changes in order to draw valid comparisons, the increase in the population of the greater Clontarf area in the two decades from 1891 was significant. From a total of 5,239 in the earlier year, the figure rose to 6,930 in 1901, and to 8,965 in 1911. This represented an overall surge of 70% in a twenty-year period. Contemporaneously, the number of houses rose by roughly the same percentage: from 979 in the greater Clontarf district in 1891, through 1,332 in 1901 to 1,757 in 1911, an overall increase of almost

80%. About 60% of the population was Roman Catholic, 25% episcopalian and the remainder were mostly Protestants of other denominations. Of the population of the district about the turn of the century about a quarter were professionals or public servants, while a fifth were employed in the commercial sector.[3]

For all of the population increase in Clontarf in the first decade or so of the twentieth century the district was not all densely settled; fields still dominated the landscape, dotted with irregular roads, terraces and individual houses. Some of the late Victorian projects such as Haddon, Hollybrook and Victoria roads were advanced, with the substantial houses, built in terraces, eventually being ordered on consecutively numbered avenues. Other larger routes, such as Seafield Road (still referred to for part of its span as Seafield Avenue) and Vernon Avenue, slowly acquired terraces, such as Vernon Terrace and Beachfield Terrace on the latter and Seafield Terrace on the former. Building along the seafront, which was being designated Clontarf Road by 1912, was in irregular terracing west of Castle Avenue, with the length to the east, starting with Victoria Terrace, well filled in as far as the Bull Wall. Some of these terraces were associated with the cluster of habitation at the foot of Vernon Avenue, still referred to as Clontarf Sheds, with Rostrevor and St John's terraces to the west of Vernon Avenue, flanking

Fig. 9.1—View of the seafront of Clontarf, east of Vernon Avenue, early twentieth century, before the construction of the promenade, showing a number of terraces of varying architectural styles (© Irish Historical Picture Company).

the Catholic church of St John, and Hillview, Rutland, Alexandra and Seapoint terraces to the east of Vernon Avenue. The influence of the seaside industry perhaps determined the presence of many small terraces of villas and substantial housing to the east and west of the wooden bridge leading to the Bull Island, including Belview Terrace, Ardilaun Villas and St Anne's Villas to the east, and Pretoria Villas to the west. Apart from the village centre at the Sheds, the other major clustering of population in an estate-style development was in the Dublin United Tramways Company settlement of dozens of cottages at Conquer Hill, Brian Boru Street and Brian Boru Avenue primarily for tramway workers.[4] [9.1]

Major engineering projects which were beyond the financial competence of the township of Clontarf were undertaken by Dublin Corporation for the general health and salubriousness of the district in the first decade of the new century. The long-delayed reclamation of the Fairview slob land was of obvious benefit not just to residents in the immediate locality but also to those who valued a picturesque approach to Clontarf. In 1904 the Dublin Port and Docks Board surrendered to the corporation its rights to 58 acres of the foreshore from the railway embankment to Annesley Bridge in return for compensation of £8,000. The municipal authority undertook the infilling of the expanse with city refuse, engineered through the process of dumping by tramcars at night. Despite objections to the odour and general disruptiveness of the work, the parkland was ready for landscaping by the end of 1910. At the suggestion of Lord Ardilaun, the new amenity was called Fairview Park; it was laid out with tree-lined walks, and a bandstand was erected for outdoor concerts. A nuisance and health hazard thus became a salubrious recreational zone.[5]

'The Promised Land', 1902

As everyone is aware, the Dublin Corporation are filling in that portion of the sea known as the 'Fairview sloblands' and converting it into a pleasure park. Although the work was first thought good many years ago, the reclaimed park is not yet a sufficient size to justify its being dignified by a name. Judge, therefore, the bewilderment of the occupants of an outgoing tramcar the other evening when, as the car slowed up at Fairview corner, the conductor sang out, 'Passengers for the Promised Land alight here'.

Irish Times, 13 September 1902

More complex were the corporation schemes for bringing Clontarf within the main drainage and electric lighting systems of the greater city. The absorption of the district in 1900 under the Boundaries Act was on the understanding that these works would be completed within three and four years respectively. Largely because of the cost, the corporation delayed the extensions of main drainage and lighting to Clontarf, until an action for negligence against the civic body by a substantial local ratepayer, Picton Bradshaw of Mount Temple, was successful. Work on both schemes began in earnest in 1905. The drainage works involved huge excavations from the city centre to Clontarf, and then the main sewer was laid outside the sea wall along the front as far as St Anne's. A system of connecting drains and pumping utilities was also incorporated. By the end of 1911,

Clontarf main drainage scheme, 1907

The history of the scheme is instructive. The Boundaries Act, under which Clontarf became incorporated within the city, was passed in 1900, and while the preliminary commission of inquiry was in progress, it was urged that the Corporation, with its larger resources, would be able to provide Clontarf with a main drainage scheme at a much cheaper price than could the local township body then in existence. The Township Commissioners had, it appears, formulated a drainage scheme which was estimated to have cost about £28,000. The Dublin Corporation asserted that they could carry out the work for £23,300. But now, after seven years, at a time when local rates in Clontarf are about to be assimilated with the very much higher city rates, the Corporation ... are about to fulfil their obligations, with this important difference that the total cost of the scheme be, not £23,300, as was originally stated, but £52,500. The explanation that has been given for this immense increase in the estimate is that the scheme formulated by the Clontarf Commissioners provided only for the construction of a main sewer along the foreshore to connect with the city main drainage system. Instead of dealing with the area along the sea front, the Corporation have drawn up plans for the entire area of the township, [involving] making all the subsidiary drains required. These subsidiary drains will be connected at various points to the main sewer ... When the scheme is carried out, Clontarf will possess a system equal in merit and effectiveness to the City Main Drainage.

Irish Times, 18 March 1907

most of the work of connecting the suburb up with the city sewerage system was complete, at a total cost of £52,000, twice what a local Clontarf township proposal was costed at in 1900. Contemporaneously, the laying down of mains for the installation of electric lighting of the roads in the neighbourhood was undertaken, and the work was mostly complete by the end of the first decade of the century at a cost of £30,000.[6]

While substantial expenditure was being devoted to the reclamation, drainage and lighting schemes for the area, it seems that neglect of routine maintenance was an irritant to residents of Clontarf in the early years of the twentieth century. A self-help group called the Clontarf and Dollymount Improvements Association came into being to call attention to lack of services and amenities and to lobby for their installation. Recalling the reasonably successful efforts on the part of the township to maintain the seafront, the association lamented the poor state of the grass slope along the foreshore, especially in the wake of excavation work. They called for the proper paving and railing in of the pathway to prevent tramcar accidents and the provision of sanitary conveniences for users of the seafront. There were more specific complaints regarding the lack of amenities in parts of the district behind the seafront. Visitors still flocked to the Dollymount resort in great numbers in the Edwardian period, and issues of safety were raised in

Fig. 9.2 — View of the wooden bridge and the Bull Wall (courtesy of the National Library of Ireland).

connection with swimming facilities and traffic. Lord Ardilaun's purchase of the bulk of the Bull Island from the Vernons in 1902 did not restrict access to the strand and the adjoining Bull Wall, which remained under the jurisdiction of the Port and Docks Board. Splintered ownership, however, raised questions about who should pay for the installation of bathing shelters and other facilities, as urged by the Clontarf and Dollymount Bathers' Association, for example. [9.2] The Board did finance the paving of the causeway as far as the Bull Beacon, and also the rebuilding of the wooden bridge, which had been in a decrepit state.[7]

Internal development of Clontarf in an unplanned way had left many hundreds of acres of land available for settlement, and in the context of planning for Dublin's growth and the alleviation of its housing crisis the suburb came in for scrutiny in the 1910s and 1920s. A small amount of local authority accommodation had been provided in Clontarf by 1913, and early additional proposals included the building of more corporation housing in areas of Clontarf, at a density of twenty cottages per acre, with other plantations in large garden settings for rural homesteaders. A major prize-winning plan for the future of Dublin, formulated by Patrick Abercrombie in 1914, incorporated many proposals for the development of the Clontarf neighbourhood. Housing was envisaged as being privately built, though provision for working people was assumed. A major reclamation project in the north inner

Fig. 9.3—Vision for the development of the Clontarf area in Patrick Abercrombie, Sydney Kelly and Arthur Kelly, Dublin of the future: the new town plan (Dublin, 1922).

bay opposite Clontarf would be linked to the suburb through a footbridge over the newly canalised River Tolka, which would flow through a wide parkway. [9.3] This verdant strip or park highway, which would divide Clontarf from the dockland and industrial quarter, was envisioned as running past the Bull Wall and as far as a Howth nature reserve, and serviced by a frequent tramway service.[8]

Plans for the development of marina, 1922

The North Bull ... will be combined with the large lagoon formed by the diverted waters of the Tolka; the water thus collected in the lagoon could be used by a simple arrangement of sluices periodically to flush out the harbour. The Park will be laid out with greater naturalness as it approaches the Howth peninsula, where golf courses might be located. The opportunity to possess a seaboard and Lagoon park at such small cost should not be pretermitted.

Patrick Abercrombie, Sydney Kelly and Arthur Kelly,
Dublin of the future: the new town plan (Dublin, 1922), p. 45

Along the curve of seafront, Abercrombie had the precincts south of Seafield Road and east of Mount Prospect Avenue as a gridded area, settled with housing of a density of sixteen units per acre. An almost totally new development was planned for the areas north of Seafield Road. It was designed in a series of concentric roadways, incorporating gardens and radiating out from a new village centre at the Vernon Avenue/Seafield Road intersection. Here there was scope for new public buildings and a central neighbourhood park, with putting greens, sporting facilities and a playground. The northern lines of this garden suburb were seen as extending to the avenue in St Anne's park. Rich areas of parkland would frame the district, with St Anne's to the north and the promenade of the Tolka parkway to the south. To the west, a newly developed lagoon would separate the seafront from the Bull Island, which would be laid out as a Marine Park. Aside from the south-western golf-course, the central section of the island was to be landscaped in a formal manner, while the north-eastern stretch would be left more or less in its natural state.[9]

Given its ambitious and sweeping proposals, the Abercrombie plan would have proved difficult of accomplishment even in propitious circumstances (though some elements in respect of Clontarf did come to fruition over time). For a decade or so, however, major development at local and municipal levels was adversely affected by the press of political events, both nationally and internationally. Divisions among the populace at large over the general issue of whether or not Home Rule should be granted to Ireland—and, if so, to what extent it should be implemented—were reflected within the community of Clontarf from 1912 onwards. The Volunteers, with their divisions as between Ulster, Irish or National, became the main focus of the tensions down to the 1920s.

Residents of Clontarf experienced these tensions at close quarters for the first time on Sunday 26 July 1914, when a confrontation took place between army and police detachments and a large force of armed Irish Volunteers at the Marino end of the suburb. Earlier that day, a consignment of 900 guns and 26,000 rounds of ammunition had been brought into Howth Harbour on board the yacht *Asgard*, which had transported the weapons from Belgium. This was as a response to the arming of the Ulster Volunteer Force, the opponents of Irish Home Rule, in the Larne gunrunning of two years earlier. Almost 1,000 Volunteers were waiting at Howth to take possession of the rifles, having assembled under the guise of a routine training manoeuvre. Marching back towards the city through Raheny, the Volunteers encountered little obstruction until they came to the Marino end of Howth Road. About 200 soldiers from the Scottish Borderers and 50 policemen were drawn up across the roadway and lining the pavements. The Volunteers attempted to bypass this force by turning into the Crescent, but the army and police regrouped and barred the highway. Assistant Commissioner William Harrel, who was in command though acting on his own initiative, demanded the surrender of the arms and ammunition but was rebuffed by the Volunteer leadership, including Darrell Figgis, Tomás MacDonagh and others. An attempt to seize the weapons at bayonet-point proved ineffective, with only nineteen weapons being recovered, and several shots were fired in the mêlée. Under cover of further negotiations, the bulk of the Volunteers slipped away over the adjoining fields, still in possession of their rifles. In a grim epilogue to the day's events, some returning troops who were pressed by civilian crowds on Bachelor's Walk opened fire, killing three people and injuring over twenty.[10]

Within a few weeks of these events, the outbreak of the Great War in August 1914 caused a total reframing of perspectives on the Irish political question. Although Home Rule for Ireland passed into law, it was postponed indefinitely for the duration of the international conflict. A serious split emerged among the Irish Volunteers between those nationalists who supported Irish participation on the British side and a minority who were antagonistic to such a course. Service in the forces transcended political and religious allegiances, as reflected in the pattern of enlistment in Clontarf and elsewhere, but the 1916 Rising and its aftermath served to deepen divisions between unionists and nationalists, transforming the constitutional arrangements envisaged before the war.

The response to recruitment for the war in Clontarf was positive. Research by Warren Lawless has shown, for instance, that a quarter of the Protestant male population of just over 1,000 enlisted in the military services, with a mortality rate of one in every five soldiers. Enlistment was particularly high among the Catholic and Protestant members of the cricket and rugby clubs, both of which closed down during the period of the war, and across the panoply of clubs and associations a pattern of members joining up in fellowship was apparent. Within the district the suspension of features of normal living and the organisation of special groups and charities were a reminder of the fighting taking place overseas. The Royal Dublin Golf Club on Bull Island was taken over by the War Office for the drilling of troops and their training in musketry. Among civilians, many charitable initiatives were undertaken to support and comfort the troops, including the Church of Ireland ladies' working party which supplied knitted scarves and gloves. Concerts and entertainments were also arranged for the amusement of troops stationed on the Bull Island, many of them under the auspices of the parochial communities. Sporting clubs that continued to operate during the war years, such as Clontarf Golf Club (founded in 1912), put on benefit and charity events. Men and women also joined the medical and nursing organisations working on the home front, such as the St John's Ambulance Brigade and Voluntary Aid Detachment. Forms of self-help in the face of shortages of supplies were popular, including the growing of food on allotments.[11]

Fighting in the national cause came close to Clontarf during the Easter Rising of 1916. An important stage in the planning of the insurrection occurred at a meeting of eleven members of the supreme council of the Irish Republican Brotherhood in Clontarf Town Hall in January 1916. This gathering was facilitated by the caretaker of the building, Michael McGinn, who was sympathetic to the aims of the IRB, which was a secret, oath-bound society. Among those attending were Patrick Pearse, Thomas Clarke and Seán MacDiarmada, three of the signatories of the proclamation of the Irish Republic. A motion proposed by MacDiarmada that a rising should take place at the earliest possible moment was accepted and more detailed planning was thereby launched. Most of the fighting during Easter Week occurred within the perimeter of the two canals of Dublin, but Clontarf was touched either directly, at the Marino end, or indirectly. For the inhabitants the discomforts were fairly minor, engendered by the food shortages and curtailment of lighting and transport owing to failures in the gas

Sandbag defences placed across the road at the Railway Bridge at Clontarf.

Fig. 9.4 — Troops on duty at Clontarf railway bridge, 1916
(© Irish Historical Picture Company).

and electricity supplies. For residents near the railway embankment, however, the dangers of injury or death were real. The railway bridge was a vital artery of communication and was guarded by troops who were being sniped at from rebel bases on the western side, including Croydon Park and its immediate vicinity. There were several casualties in the Fairview district, and a soldier was shot on the embankment. By the end of the week the fighting was dying out and normal life was beginning to resume, with foodstuffs including bread and meat being transported to Clontarf Station by train from Belfast.[12] [9.4]

Among those arrested and interned after the Rising was Arthur Griffith, the founder of Sinn Féin, who was a resident of St Lawrence Road in Clontarf. His organisation had not been directly involved in the planning of Easter Week but its name came to be popularly associated with the insurrection in the public mind in the months and years afterwards. It was during this time that national sentiment began to swing towards the republicans who had staged the rebellion, particularly as a result of the execution of its leaders. Thus, by the end of the Great War in 1918, the Irish participation was being vilified in many nationalist quarters and majority political opinion was supportive of the Sinn Féin party. Its candidate in the Clontarf constituency in the general election of 1918, D. Mulcahy, who had fought in the Rising, defeated the nationalist or Home Rule candidate, Sir P. Shortall, by a margin of almost two to one.[13]

When it came to commemorating the Clontarf dead of the Great War, divided sympathies were evident in Clontarf, as elsewhere. The Protestant churches were to the fore in honouring the troops, as their communities were less ambivalent after 1918 about the efficacy of participation in the struggle than their Catholic, predominantly nationalist, counterparts. Thus the Church of Ireland parish staged a social event in May 1919 to welcome home the demobilised soldiers, attended by the archbishop of Dublin and representatives of the other denominations, and the archbishop was also in attendance when commemorative tablets and panelling were dedicated in the Church of St John the Baptist in 1921. Among those commemorated on a wall plaque in the church was Captain Edward Granville Vernon, son of Colonel Granville and Rosalie Vernon. A large Celtic-style cross was erected in the grounds of the church, inscribed with the names of 33 parishioners who had fallen. It was unveiled in June 1920 by the provost of Trinity College. [9.5] Also in that year there was dedicated in the Presbyterian church at Howth Road a large stained glass window depicting Christ's death and resurrection, commissioned as a tribute to those who had fought and died and created by Harry Clarke. And a marble plaque in the Methodist church at St Lawrence Road contained the names of men and women who had served in the army and the medical services. In the Clontarf cricket and rugby clubs, a roll of honour remembering the members who died comprised soldiers of all faiths, while bench plaques in the Roman Catholic Church of the Visitation, Fairview, commemorated five soldiers who were killed in the war between 1914 and 1918.[14]

Fig. 9.5—Celtic-style cross in the grounds of St John the Baptist Church, Seafield Road, to commemorate parishioners who died in the First World War, unveiled in June 1920. It also bears the names of those who perished in World War II.

Public amenity and private estates: the growth of a garden suburb

Owing to serious political instability and economic uncertainty, there was no further substantial suburban development in Clontarf until the 1920s. What little growth took place before then was mostly in the western part of the district, with the progressing of building schemes already under way. Planning was undertaken in a piecemeal and short-sighted manner, with little regard, for example, for the implications of housing being allowed on ground that would be needed for the extension of major roadways. Connection to the city drainage scheme remained an issue, and the very slow progress of work on the seafront to construct a new sea wall and develop a promenade was a deterrent to potential builders and residents. After its acquisition of the right to almost a 150ft strip along two miles of the foreshore from the Vernon estate, headed by Mr Edward Kingston Vernon, in 1921, Dublin Corporation began infilling the coastal stretch from the railway embankment with refuse and stones, and the construction of the wall continued, costing a total of £90,000. But the project languished at the end of the 1920s because of the objections of residents to the noxious odours and dirt generated by the refuse-dumping, and further progress was not reported until

Clontarf (West), Dublin.

Fig. 9.6—The first phase of the construction of the promenade at the beginning of Clontarf Road, before the 1930s (© Irish Historical Picture Company).

the later 1930s. [9.6] Meanwhile, the nature of suburban development at Clontarf, as discussed in the reports and plans of the 1910s, remained uncertain. While E.A. Aston had advocated the inclusion of semi-rural lands in Clontarf as among those suitable for public authority housing along garden-suburb lines, the Abercrombie plan had appeared to envisage private development to accommodate those whose livelihood would arise from industrial and marine activities in the reclaimed east wall area.[15]

In spite of the difficulties, the shape of the modern suburban village of Clontarf, architecturally integrated and coherently planned, began to emerge by the end of the 1920s. And although Dublin Corporation was directly involved in many initiatives, the pattern of development was through private rather than public housing. Increasingly far-seeing development was evident in the provision for future expansion of the drainage scheme in granting individual permissions for connections, and in the road-widening scheme for Howth Road, north-east of Castle Avenue. The activity of the construction firm of Stewart in 1924 and 1925 in building houses at Vernon Gardens, Vernon Grove and Vernon Avenue was complemented by the corporation's taking charge of the roadways thus created. The bungalows built in this enclave appeared in an advertisement for the Dublin Gas Company's promotion of all-gas-powered housing, including cooking, heating, lighting and hot water. Although the Stewart Company failed, the Vernon estate began to take a proactive role in promoting development, with a view to controlling the type of building and construction in the district. In 1925 the estate advertised building sites for bungalows in Clontarf, ground-rent only being payable, to encourage housing construction with the help of government housing grants. Among the building enterprises attracted were the Public Utility Societies, which facilitated reasonably priced housing through subsidised loans and which were funded by private investors who were motivated by philanthropy as well as modest profit. Elsewhere in the city Dublin Corporation leased land to the Public Utility Societies for building, but in Clontarf the land was in private ownership. So the corporation mediated between builders and landowner there by helping the Vernons to acquire additional lands to complete new road schemes, such as the proposed extension in 1925 of Mount Prospect Avenue, west of Vernon Avenue, intersecting with Castle Avenue near Blackheath and running through to Howth Road.[16]

A more formal arrangement that came into being in 1928 between the corporation and the Vernon estate was to shape the character of the Clontarf district for much of the succeeding period. Essentially, the scheme allowed the Vernons to avail of and control the upsurge in building and development, while

Building sites for bungalows, 1925

The Vernon Estate, Clontarf, Killester, Raheny and Dollymount

No charge for sites   Only small ground rents

BUILDERS GIVEN EVERY FACILITY FOR OBTAINING GOVERNMENT GRANTS

APPLY

Estate Office: FRANKS AND OULTON,

21 LOWER FITZWILLIAM STREET, DUBLIN

Advertisement in *Irish Times*, 29 January 1925

allowing the corporation to let building sites in return for ground-rents and rates payable on new housing. The focus of this partnership was the proposed Kincora Road, with its extended and new connecting links to the seafront, Belgrove Road and Oulton Road respectively. Leasing a large tract of land for 999 years from the estate, the corporation undertook to let out the sites for house-building in a manner to be approved of by architects from both partners. By 1930 many two-storey houses and bungalows had been erected on Kincora Road and Belgrove Road on sites that the corporation made available to builders through its own lease of them from the Vernon estate. As well as individual local builders, there was involvement of Public Utility Societies. In the case of Oulton Road, named after the family which now headed the Vernon estate, the corporation did not become involved in leasing individual sites to builders, but leased back the ground to the Vernon estate in return for rents which provided money for the road-building work. [9.7] The construction of bungalows on reasonably priced sites made housing available at a lower cost to purchasers, and this architectural style was very much a feature of roads newly opened or extended in central Clontarf, as was the extensive garden in low-density developments.[17]

The focus of building in the late 1920s and early 1930s may have been the western part of the suburb most contiguous to the seat of the Vernon estate, and certainly development continued to take place here down to 1939. Hollybrook Park was fully extended during the period, and elaborate shop premises were purpose-

Fig. 9.7—Houses on Oulton Road, which was developed in the 1930s through the cooperation of the owners of the Vernon estate and Dublin Corporation.

Clontarf, Dublin.

Fig. 9.8—Commercial buildings at the intersection of Hollybrook Road and Clontarf Road, early twentieth century, before the construction of the promenade (© Irish Historical Picture Company).

built in the Commercial Buildings at the junction of Hollybrook Road and Clontarf Road. [9.8] The Styles or Stiles road came into being about this time, providing a new link between the sea road and Howth Road. And the Blackheath estate of 22 acres was sold by its proprietor, Mrs Gibson Black, to a new owner who planned a new network of roads and housing. By the end of the 1930s Blackheath Park had been developed, as well as its offshoot cul-de-sac, Blackheath Drive. The corporation also acquired some land here for the widening of Castle Avenue.[18]

For the first time since the late Victorian period, major inland development of Dollymount and the area to the east of Vernon Avenue was undertaken. Some expansion of the Brian Boru/Conquer Hill district took place, but most significant building occurred on new roads as arteries and their offshoots. Avenues and roads on the eastern side of Vernon Avenue now included Vernon Gardens and Vernon Park, while the main avenue itself was properly pavemented and numbered for postal addressing. Bisected by Vernon Avenue now were two important thoroughfares—Kincora Road and Seafield Road—while Mount Prospect Avenue formed a great dog-leg through the eastern district from Vernon Avenue to the sea. [9.9] Along the eastern extension of these roads there were built new houses, many of them bungalows, with intersecting roads, such as Vernon Grove, Seapark Road and Seafield Avenue, and Mount Prospect Park. As they

Fig. 9.9—'International-style' houses built on Kincora Road in 1930–1.

Fig. 9.10 — Bungalows were very much a feature of house-building from the 1930s and 1940s onwards on the roads of central Clontarf, whether newly developed or extended.

were settled, these streets were taken in charge by the corporation. Dollymount Avenue was opened on new lands made available by the Vernon estate between Mount Prospect Avenue and the coast, and it became central to the development of the easternmost part of Clontarf during the 1940s and 1950s.[19] [9.10]

First mooted about 1913 by Alderman Clancy, the promenade along the seafront was to become a vital part of Clontarf's infrastructure, not just to promote recreational activity but also to prevent flooding and to facilitate the widening of the sea road. A slow start was made in the 1920s, as we have seen, with the acquisition by the corporation of the land and the planning of the sea wall to contain the new 150ft strip of promenade. The first stages of reclamation were haphazard and gave rise to objections relating to hygiene and odours, but real progress began to be made from the later 1930s onwards. The sea wall was constructed from the railway embankment to the Bull Wall, and infilling of the space between it and the road was carried on by Dutch dredgers with sand and gravel from the seabed. Gradually the full 2,900 yards of frontage was reclaimed, but the ground was for many years too soft for pedestrians. Extra land was being reclaimed alongside the embankment in the 1950s by the dumping of city refuse behind wooden hoardings erected along the seafront to Hollybrook Grove. By the

Slow progress of Clontarf promenade, 1930

At a meeting of the representative ratepayers of Clontarf, Councillor John Ryan, in outlining how matters stood with regard to the proposed promenade on the sea front, said that the project emanated many years ago from the late Alderman John Clancy. A start was made in a primitive way. A lot of loose stones were laid, and these were backed up by city refuse. The work was stopped by the city commissioners who said that the residents objected on account of the odour from the refuse. It has lain there ever since. A resolution was passed requesting the Lord Mayor, the Corporation and the City Manager to proceed immediately with the construction of the proposed sea wall, and so relieve the residents of the area of the long-standing grievance of the flooding caused by the encroachment of the sea.

Irish Times, 19 December 1930

Completion of Clontarf promenade, 1953

After many years of existence as a not very sightly dump-cum-promenade park, the long strip of reclaimed lands between Fairview and the Bull Wall is at last being transformed into a proper recreation place. Over the years, this land has been walled off from the sea and filled in in successive stages. Now the Dublin Corporation is busily engaged in completing the process of levelling, and is adding a substantial top dressing of soil where it is needed. The top soil and the filling soil are being brought from the housing sites at St Anne's estate nearby by a fleet of lorries, and are being placed and levelled by an excavator and two bulldozers ... When the land has been finally reclaimed and levelled off, grass will be planted, and it is possible that flower beds will be added later on. The grounds will then be completely laid out as a promenade park.

Irish Times, 19 August 1953

mid-1950s the ground of the entire promenade was ready for planting with trees, shrubs and flowers and the erection of the distinctive shelters at intervals along its length. During the construction work the new promenade absorbed some of the old drainage pipes and jetties, as well as the lead-mine shaft that harked back to the Victorian period. The problem of flooding through stormy waters sweeping over the roadway at the sea or through seepage into basements was alleviated but not by any means finally solved.[20]

Closely associated with the work of reclaiming the promenade was a scheme for a marine lake and amusement park, west of the Bull Wall, first mooted about 1930. The lake, popularly dubbed 'the Blue Lagoon', was to be a feature of the area between the island and the shoreline, from Dollymount to Sutton. There were plans for a funfair, open-air theatre, dance hall, restaurant and playground, to be developed at a cost of £100,000. As well as providing an attractive recreational feature, the lagoon was seen as counteracting the swampy waters unscoured by the tides. Damming of the expanse at the Sutton and Dollymount ends of the island would, it was thought, create a standing lake of water. An experimental pool was created in the early 1950s in which marine biologists investigated the possible effects of the sea water on flora and fauna. Owing to delays in the completion of the promenade, as well as difficulties with financing, the project was sidelined, though it was related by some to the plan to build a causeway to the island at Watermill Road.[21]

In 1955 the Royal Dublin Golf Club had bought the fee simple of the Bull Island from Benjamin Plunket, the successor of the Ardilaun proprietors of St Anne's estate, for £8,500. The club then sold all of the lands outside the boundary of the

---

New causeway for Bull Island, 1963

Dublin Corporation has given notice that it has applied to the Minister for Transport and Power for permission to build a causeway to link Bull Island, Dollymount, with the mainland. The causeway is the first stage in a major scheme for the island's development.

The plans of the causeway are available at Clontarf Civic Guard station. They provide for a broad traffic route which will bridge the channel, sweep across the island through one of the greens of St Anne's Golf Club and end in a roundabout on the Dublin Bay side of the island. It will be opened up for bus services with easy access to the beach.

Irish Times, 11 July 1963

---

course to Dublin Corporation for £12,000. The question of the erection of a fence along the boundary of the club by the corporation was contentious owing to public protest, and the municipality compensated the club for the non-fulfilment of this clause.[22] The scheme for a new causeway to the island from the seafront went ahead under corporation auspices and a new roadway was completed by the mid-1960s. While improving access to the island for visitors and vehicles, the new amenity worried conservationists, who were concerned about the future of birds and other wildlife and the stagnation of the existing slob land. Regular calls were subsequently made for the breaching of the causeway to create a tidal scour. In 1986 a new information centre on birds and wildlife, funded by Dublin Corporation, was opened at the heart of the island.[23] [9.11]

To complement its guardianship of the Bull Island, the full conservatory and developmental role of the Guinness family as landlords in Clontarf fell to Dublin Corporation with its acquisition of St Anne's, with the primary aim of providing new housing on the Raheny side. When the estate was put up for sale in the 1930s by the successor as proprietor to Lord Ardilaun, Bishop Benjamin Plunket, the corporation made tentative enquiries, but it was not until the end of the decade that a commitment to buy out the Plunket and other owners by means of a Compulsory Purchase Order was entered into. The sum of £62,000 was paid for the purchase of the estate, but World War II intervened before plans could be implemented for the development of the newly acquired lands and buildings.

Fig. 9.11—View of Dollymount beach, North Bull Island, over which Dublin Corporation extended its conservation role as new owner of the island in the 1950s.

Sale of contents of St Anne's, 1939

The Right Rev. the Hon. Benjamin Plunket has appointed Messrs Jackson Stops and McCabe to sell by auction the entire contents of St Anne's. St Anne's was purchased about 100 years ago by the late Sir Benjamin M. Guinness, Bart., M.P., and practically rebuilt and enlarged in 1880 by the late Lord Ardilaun. Lady Ardilaun lived in it for some years after his death, and, when she died, the estate passed to Lord Ardilaun's nephew, Bishop Plunket. The Corporation of Dublin are acquiring the estate under compulsory powers, and, in consequence of this, the auction of the contents is to take place. Great interest will be shown in this announcement, as it is well known that Lady Ardilaun was an ardent collector of antiques, and also acquired a remarkable collection of literature and relics of Napoleon, Robespierre, etc.

Irish Times, 21 April 1939

During the war years the estate was farmed by tenants, and was also used for crop-growing and allotments for the public. St Anne's mansion, which was being used for, among other things, the storage of Air Raid Precaution materials, was destroyed by fire in 1943. After the war, the corporation pressed ahead with a scheme of tenant purchase housing on the north side of the estate in Raheny, completed in 1954, but the bulk of the estate was preserved as a public park, some tracts being allocated for playing fields and certain social projects such as schools. Sybil Hill House (where Bishop Plunket lived until his death) and its estate were purchased by the Vincentian Order for the purposes of opening a boys' secondary school, which became St Paul's College. Some of the other lodges and estate houses were demolished, including Maryville, but others, such as Bedford Lodge, were preserved. The mansion was deemed dangerous and was rased in 1968, a grassed mound now becoming the focus of the tree-lined avenue. The parklands have been beautifully maintained and, in addition to walks, avenues, ponds, follies and gardens, the rose garden and the red stables have proved very popular with the public.[24] [9.12]

As an adjunct to these major changes in ownership and management, including infrastructure and large expanses of park and coastal land, there came about the definitive settling of the area of greater Clontarf. Framed now by the sward of promenade to the south, the island to the east and the park to the

Fig. 9.12—The rose garden in St Anne's Park, which also came under the ownership of Dublin Corporation after 1940.

north, the district had a coherence that was augmented by better connecting roads and rational house-building. Vernon Avenue became a true artery when its northern extension was added as Sybil Hill Road, as part of the 1950s and early 1960s development of schools and other projects on the fringes of the estate. Apart from the expansive scope given for schools, community halls and institutions and recreational amenities, the St Anne's take-over facilitated private residential building. Around the margins of this estate, which dominated the eastern part of the district, were developed residential roadways that fleshed out the existing suburban housing stock. These included some tracts leased back by the Vernons, on which were built Vernon Drive and some more of Vernon Avenue, Mount Prospect Grove and, near to the Clontarf Road–Mount Prospect junction, Baymount Park, as well as housing on those two major thoroughfares. Other private developers also concentrated on the Dollymount district in the 1950s to open out Dollymount Park and Dollymount Grove. Development at the heart of the neighbourhood was sealed by the building of the Kincora estate on the demesne lands of the castle. The seafront road, already improved during the construction of the promenade, was significantly enhanced with the opening of the James Larkin Road from Dollymount to Watermill Road in 1949. This project included the removal of the now-redundant tram-tracks that were part of the Clontarf to Howth tramway.[25]

The closure of the Clontarf and Hill of Howth Tramway Company (CHHTC) service from Dollymount to Howth village in 1941 brought to an end a transport system through the district that had helped to transform it into a successful suburb. With the advent of the electrified tramway service from the Dublin United Tramways Company (DUTC) from Nelson Pillar to Dollymount in 1898, Clontarf had a highly efficient and speedy service connecting city and township. Then in 1900 there opened the CHHTC's service linking the DUTC's terminus at Dollymount with Howth Harbour. The two companies, which retained their separate identities, shared each other's tracks, with the Howth company's personnel taking over the tramcars that travelled through Heronstown, Kilbarrack and Sutton to Howth. By the end of the 1930s, however, competition for passengers from buses was increasing, and the DUTC tramcar service from the city centre to Dollymount ceased in 1938. The bus service that took over retained the tram's route number (30). Another bus route, the 44A, opened out the hinterland of Clontarf, wending its way up Haddon Road along Victoria Road on to Castle Avenue and thence to Seafield Avenue and Mount Prospect Avenue. The original tram depot at Conquer Hill was to become Clontarf bus garage. Elements of the older transport systems may still be seen at the bus garage in the survival of two lower sheds from the time of the horse-drawn trams and two higher sheds designed for the electric

Fig. 9.13—Serious flooding occurred at Fairview and Clontarf in December 1954, when the railway bridge over the River Tolka was swept away by floods (courtesy of the Irish Times*).*

Sam Mitchell, guard of the Belfast Enterprise Express, waves the train off from Clontarf station, temporary terminus for northbound trains since the collapse of the railway bridge at East Wall.

Fig. 9.14—*Clontarf station gained brief prominence as the terminus of the Dublin–Belfast railway in 1954 after the disruption caused by flooding. The station closed down two years later (courtesy of the* Irish Times*).*

trams. A reminder of the era of tram transport is also to be seen in the tram shelter on the sea side of Clontarf Road at Seafield Road. Meanwhile, the Clontarf rail station near the Howth Road bridge continued to function on the Great Northern Railway service until its closure in 1956. Two years earlier, the station had gained national prominence as the terminus of the Belfast to Dublin rail service in the aftermath of the sweeping away of the Tolka railway bridge by flood-waters. [9.13] A local rail station was not restored to Clontarf—at a location just south of the skew bridge—until 1 September 1997.[26] [9.14]

By the late 1960s the character of modern Clontarf was well established. Within a frame of promenade to the south, the island to the east and parkland to the north, the roads and housing of the district had the appearance and atmosphere of a garden suburb (as envisaged by the Abercrombie plan). The architecture was a harmonious ensemble of terraced red brick and villa-style bungalow, shaped by the maritime location, while the older residential roadways blended with new suburban housing. These features accommodated without too much incongruity the building of townhouses and apartment blocks in the quarter-century or so down to 2000. Over two dozen of these new developments were erected, mostly between existing houses on thoroughfares such as Castle Avenue, Vernon Avenue, St Lawrence Road and Kincora Road, or on the sites of demolished large mansions. By the end of the century the population of Clontarf had reached 30,000, a trebling of the figure of 90 years before. Aspects of the formation of a community within this aesthetically pleasing environment will be examined in the final chapter.

1 *IT*, 3 and 4 July 1900.

2 For an affectionate memoir of life in the early twentieth-century suburb see Knowles, *Old Clontarf*.

3 *Thom's Directory* (Dublin, 1908), 1379; see Warren Lawless, 'Clontarf's Protestant communities in the First World War' (unpublished senior sophister thesis, Trinity College, Dublin, 1995) [http://homepage.eircom.net/~wlawless/ww1/Clontarf.htm, accessed 11 September 2012].

4 *Thom's Directory* (Dublin, 1901–8).

5 *IT*, 31 July 1902, 1 August 1902, 21 July 1904, 6 September 1904, 15 June 1905, 27 November 1906, 12 August 1910, 8 October 1910.

6 *IT*, 20 January 1900, 22 January 1904, 8 November 1904, 15 July 1905, 24 November 1905, 13 and 15 February 1906, 1 August 1906, 4 and 25 September 1906, 1 November 1911.

7 *IT*, 1 May 1900, 21 February 1901, 24 December 1904, 24 February 1905, 16 March 1905, 2 November 1906, 23 March 1909, 9 September 1909, 22 June 1910.

8 Ruth McManus, *Dublin, 1910–1940: shaping the city and suburbs* (Dublin, 2002), 36, 38, 62–3, 282; Patrick Abercrombie, Sydney Kelly and Arthur Kelly, *Dublin of the future: the new town plan* (Dublin, 1922), 26–7, 46.

9 Abercrombie *et al.*, *Dublin of the future*, 43, 'City of Dublin New Town Plan', following p. 48.

10 *Weekly Irish Times*, 1 August 1914; 'The Howth gun-running', *IT*, 25 July 1964.

11 See Lawless, 'Clontarf's Protestant communities in the First World War'; Knowles, *Old Clontarf*, 17–18, 42; *IT*, 11 September 1915, 3 and 13 November 1915, 25 March 1916.

12 Desmond Ryan, *The Rising: the complete story of Easter Week* (Dublin, 1949), 53–4; Dennis McIntyre, 'Clontarf Town Hall and the 1916 Rising', *Clontarf's Eye* 7 (1991), 20–1; D.A. Levistone Cooney (ed.), 'Momentous days: occasional diaries of Frances Taylor', *DHR* 47 (1994), 78–81; Knowles, *Old Clontarf*, 42–3.

13 *Weekly Irish Times*, 4 January 1919.

14 *IT*, 22 May 1919, 28 June 1920, 8 November 1920, 30 May 1921; Lawless, 'Clontarf's Protestant communities'.

15 McManus, *Dublin, 1910–1940*, 36, 38, 62–3, 282; *IT*, 26 July 1921, 26 July 1923, 19 December 1930, 22 September 1931; Abercrombie *et al.*, *Dublin of the future*, 25.

16 McManus, *Dublin, 1910–1940*, 284–6.

17 *Ibid.*, 286–92.

18 *Ibid.*, 292–3; *Thom's Directory* (Dublin, 1936–9).

19 *Thom's Directory* (Dublin, 1939–59).

20 *IT*, 26 July 1921, 9 August 1923, 19 December 1930, 14 and 30 August 1937, 18 October 1941, 4 November 1944, 10 and 30 December 1952, 19 August 1953, 2 November 1956, 23 March 1959.

21 *IT*, 8 January 1931, 24 September 1931, 5 February 1935, 23 April 1937, 2 December 1941, 5 July 1949, 28 December 1951, 25 January 1956, 24 April 1957; see also Eoin MacNeill, 'Our place-names', *JRSAI* (7th ser.) **8** (1938), 193.

22 Sharkey, *St Anne's*, 89; *IT*, 29 October 1955, 28 March 1956.

23 *IT*, 11 July 1963, 13 July 1964, 30 March 1967, 6 November 1969; http://www.dublincity.ie/ RECREATIONANDCULTURE/DUBLINCITYPARKS/VISITAPARK/Pages/NorthBullIsland. aspx (accessed 15 September 2012); V. Lynch, *'No thoroughfare on the tram road': history of Clontarf and its environs* (Dublin, 2007), 101.

24 Sharkey, *St Anne's*, 79–92; *IT*, 3 June 1932, 12 and 16 December 1936, 21 October 1939.

25 *Thom's Directory* (Dublin, 1950–70).

26 Knowles, *Old Clontarf*, 22–31; Kilroy, 'Transport', 94–7; F.J. Murphy, 'Dublin trams', 5–6, 8–9; *IT*, 1 September 1997.

CHAPTER TEN

The formation of a community in Clontarf

A DISTINCTIVE CLONTARF community has been formed through the many forms of social bonding and networking in the locality. Some of these are fairly recent, as has been seen, for example, in the history of the foundation of sporting clubs and associations, and, indeed, in the establishment of a township. The difficulties in the administration of the latter body, however, point up the potential fractiousness of communal relations that are not based on internal forms of social bridging. In the case of the township, serious tensions emerged between the eastern and western parts, which tended to reflect political and social differences, but it could also be argued that the geographical framework of the township did not respect the long-established local identities in Clontarf on the one hand, and Fairview and Ballybough on the other. In exploring the question of what contributes to local identity formation, this chapter will focus on the modes of bonding that arise from associational life and sociability. With the arrival of the Templars at Clontarf, there were laid the foundations of a parish, which provided a framework for social as well as religious integration. Within the late medieval manor, separate avocations of agriculture and fishing appear to have coexisted, if separated into two village centres. Disruption caused by the Reformation resulted in a division of the population into two separate worshipping bodies. Communal tensions that spilled over in the 1640s took a long time to be resolved, as an ascendant Protestant community dominated the Catholic and other denominational groupings during the eighteenth century. Social and civic institutions that emerged in the Clontarf neighbourhood and suburb during the late nineteenth century were integral to the normalisation of relations, as was the rich associational culture that has underpinned society in twentieth-century Clontarf.

Religious identities in Clontarf

Almost every locale in Ireland has its sacred site in the form of an old church, usually adjoining an ancient cemetery and sometimes with a holy well nearby. In seeking such a site in Clontarf, we are drawn to the old churchyard on Castle Avenue, with its graveyard and ruinous seventeenth-century church. Notwithstanding the absence of an older edifice, the feeling of antiquity that suffuses the place is reinforced by a sense of timeless quietude, even at the busy hub of the present-day suburb. Not only has this hallowed spot been marked by worship but its centrality has also helped to give shape and geographical identity to the environs. Church remains, dating in some cases back to the Middle Ages, similarly dominate the centres of other northside Dublin suburban villages, such as Howth, Killester and Raheny. What makes Clontarf somewhat unusual, however, is that there is no documentary or archaeological record of the existence of a church building before the Norman settlement there. Extremely tenuous evidence posits the foundation of a sixth-century monastery by St Comgall of Bangor at Clontarf, linking it to this sacred site. While the tradition of an Early Christian foundation is strong enough in the post-medieval literature not to be summarily dismissed, it is just not possible to speak definitively of the origins of Christianity in the area. What we may venture is that any pre-Norman ecclesiastical building is more than likely to have been erected where now stands the ruined church, itself a successor building to the Norman parish church.[1]

A church or monastery founded in early medieval Clontarf would have served whatever habitation existed, but the only definite evidence of settlement in the immediate district is the weir at Ballybough on the estuary of the Tolka in 1014.[2] That river was important in the ecclesiastical geography of the north Dublin region, monasteries being founded on its banks at Finglas and Glasnevin in the sixth or seventh century. The bishop of Finglas came to exert authority over much of the north of the Dublin region, including Clontarf and other maritime communities before the eleventh century,[3] but it is unknown whether two figures, Aodan and Colman, linked to 'Cluain Tarbh' in Irish manuscripts referring to the pre-eleventh-century period were associated with our Clontarf.[4] An ecclesiastical authority in the region containing Clontarf would have had to come to terms with the secular ruler who came from one of the branches of the kingdom of Brega, centred on Meath, possibly the Uí Cumain. The early Viking raids on the east coast included an assault on Howth and the carrying off of a great number of women into captivity in 819. A Clontarf settlement, secular or ecclesiastical, would have been vulnerable to the marauders, lying along the coast between the peninsula and Dublin. By the tenth century the Scandinavians had developed a kingdom northwards through the plain of Fingal, with Dublin at its hub, and by the eleventh had adopted Christianity. The cathedral of Holy Trinity, or Christ Church, Dublin, built about 1030, attested to their Christian faith. Before the arrival of the Normans in the later twelfth century, the Scandinavian rulers presided over reforms within the Irish church, which included the establishment of a definite diocesan structure, of which the see of Dublin and Glendalough was part. A 'vill' or village at Clontarf before 1170 would have been a Christian settlement.[5]

When the Knights Templar were granted Clontarf in the 1170s, it was they who took on the Anglo-Normans' reforming mission with specific reference to that local church. A religious order as well as a military one, the Knights undertook the organisation of a parish at Clontarf, the clerical members playing a central role. Fully independent of the authority of the archbishop of Dublin, the Templars were holders of the rectory, which meant that they appointed the parish priest or curate with the support of the income from the tithes of the parish. In their exercising of ecclesiastical jurisdiction, they also took charge of the church building which was erected within 150m of the manor-house. It became the hub of devotional and social life for the community, for whom identification with the Christian parish was a bonding force, bridging the divisions of social order and rank. Parishioners shared in the liturgical round of the church's year under the ministry of the order, attending at said or sung Masses and receiving the sacraments. There was also most likely a system of association for male and female supporters to enrol in the confraternity of the order. In return for donations, parishioners were assured of the commemoration of their souls and those of their loved ones after death in the anniversary Masses and prayers of the knightly chaplains. An extra-ecclesial focus of popular piety was the holy well located 200m to the west of the church and dedicated to St Dennis, or alternatively St Philip. It is probable that this hallowed place had a long tradition of devout visitors seeking cures there and carrying out pious rituals on the feast-days of the patron saints.[6]

To what extent the transition in proprietorship of manor and parish from the Templars to the Hospitallers in 1320 impinged upon the lay population of Clontarf is unknown. Yet the essential role performed by the two knightly orders in respect of the locality was similar. The knights represented both social and religious oversight and protection, forming a buffer against episcopal interference in the parish and providing through their chaplaincy functions sacraments and liturgies for the manorial tenants, and probably also the fishing community. No doubt the parish church would have served as a place where members of the agrarian and maritime communities worshipped together and socialised. The Hospitallers' vigilance concerning estuarine rights to fish probably benefited the fishing folk at the coastal haven, perhaps drawing them closer within the manorial nexus. There are suggestions that the inhabitants of the village and its agrarian hinterland were by and large of Norman or English background, while the coastal settlement contained a significant number of Irish-speaking residents. While there is no enumeration of the population until 1659, tentative surname evidence from the fourteenth century onwards as well as indications of Gaelic-speaking among the fishing families may be adduced.[7]

A confraternity, sponsored generally by the Hospitallers for lay men and women, would have helped to bridge such social and ethnic divisions if established in Clontarf. Elsewhere in late medieval Ireland this ubiquitous system of parochial fraternity nurtured a form of devotional expression that included votive altars dedicated to local or international saints, the maintaining of lights before favoured statues and the saying or chanting of Masses commemorating the souls of the faithful departed. There is no reason to believe that Clontarf was any different in the tenor of its devotional practice, though there is no specific evidence of attachment to the confraternity of the Hospitallers among the local

Fig. 10.1—The holy well dedicated to St Anne, which gave its name to St Anne's Park (Patrick Healy collection, South Dublin Libraries).

inhabitants in the form of wills or benefactions. The privilege of burial within the church itself may have rested with the Knights and their aristocratic supporters, though again we lack evidence of chantry foundations or family tombs of pre-eighteenth-century date within the building. Dedication of the parish to St John the Baptist came about with its acquisition by the Hospitallers, who were under the patronage of St John of Jerusalem. The influence of the fashionable cult of St Anne in late medieval Europe is perhaps indicated by the dedication to her patronage of another holy well, this one in the east of Clontarf. [10.1] In the fifteenth and earlier sixteenth centuries, the gentry families, who farmed the parish and manor for the profits to be drawn from both the inland and maritime communities, offered patronage of the local church. These lay families, such as the Dowdalls and Plunkets, took on the responsibility of providing a priest to minister in the parish. They would have regarded their endowment of the local parish as a reflection of their social power, possibly manifesting it in the form of commemorative plaques in the church or the erection of altars or tombs to the memory of their ancestors and for the salvation of their souls.[8]

Despite the absence of senior clerical figures as parish priests of Clontarf, there is no reason why parochial life among the laity may not have been as vibrant there as elsewhere in the Dublin diocese on the eve of the Reformation. Along with their counterpart monastic orders, however, it appears that the Hospitallers had lost much of their spiritual dynamism by the 1530s, when King Henry VIII determined on the dissolution of the religious orders in Ireland, as part of his cutting of the ties between the Irish church and Rome. Only half a dozen religious brethren remained active within the whole of the Irish priory in 1540. The suppression of the Clontarf preceptory of the Hospitallers and the confiscation of its property had far-reaching implications for the order and the parish. The estate at Clontarf, including buildings, lands and resources, was granted to an Englishman, Matthew King, the muster-master of the army in Ireland, and his wife, Elizabeth. The church building now came under his proprietorship as the new lord of the manor, the tithes of the parish were payable to him, and he also had responsibility for selecting a priest to serve the parish cure.[9]

As to the fate of the Christian community of Clontarf, there is little or no evidence that their equanimity as a congregation was much disturbed for many years, as the traditional Catholic service and liturgy continued in use until the later sixteenth century, with perhaps a brief interruption in the time of the Protestant king, Edward VI (1547–53). After Queen Elizabeth's Reformation parliament of 1560, all parish churches were formally vested in the newly established Church of Ireland, which was Protestant in its confession and which took over the medieval Irish ecclesiastical institution. In theory thereafter the parish clergy of Clontarf (and elsewhere) were expected to be ministers of the reformed religion, preaching and teaching according to the norms of the Book of Common Prayer. In practice, however, little was done before 1600 by the state church authorities to evangelise in the Anglican faith, and most clergy continued to minister in the older forms of prayer and worship. The King family, through four generations of which the parish and estate of Clontarf passed down until the 1640s, adhered to the Catholic religion, unlike most of their fellow newly arrived English, who were Protestants. Thus the clerical appointees to the parish cure under their patronage would in all likelihood have been sympathetic to their disposition towards recusancy, or dissent from the state church. Indeed, the proprietor in 1600, George King, was described by his ambitious Protestant rival for the ownership of Clontarf, Geoffrey Fenton, as 'a wicked, malignant papist'.[10]

Eventually the Fenton family did manage to make good their grant, perhaps with the assistance of one of Ireland's richest men, Richard Boyle, the earl of Cork, who married Geoffrey Fenton's daughter. It may have been under Fenton–Boyle patronage that there emerged a Protestant community in the district and that the first seventeenth-century restoration of the church at Clontarf took place after 1609. Boyle had re-edified or built anew other churches in Ireland, such as that at Maynooth. Presumably the Anglican authorities would have wished for the nomination of a university-trained rector to a prominent diocesan parish within a couple of miles of Dublin, but the Church of Ireland community in Clontarf was very small, insufficient perhaps to ensure a competent living for a graduate clergyman. In 1615 one Symon Thelwel was curate in Clontarf, he being a reading minister—that is, a clergyman who did not have a licence to preach but who merely read the service-book to the congregation. By 1630 the Catholic King family had regained the ascendancy over estate and parish, and, perhaps significantly, the church at Clontarf (which did not figure on a list of those visited by the Anglican archbishop of Dublin in that year) appears to have become dilapidated by the mid-seventeenth century. What normally happened in cases of parishes appropriated by gentry families that adhered to the older religion was that the bulk of the income from parochial revenues was withdrawn from the official church building and personnel, and diverted instead to an alternative Catholic system of worship located in domestic residences. In these circumstances, the Church of Ireland minister, Randall Dimmock, who was appointed about 1627, served a union of three parishes, St Doulagh's, Portmarnock and Clontarf, which was necessary in order to maintain his income, and he was still seriously underpaid.[11]

Within the archdiocese of Dublin and elsewhere, with the support of their kinsfolk, Roman Catholic priests returned from their education in Continental seminaries to disseminate the reforms of the Council of Trent. They normally set up an alternative system of pastoral care to the faltering Anglican one, administering the sacraments, tending to the pastoral needs of their congregations and providing catechesis for the young. As the official church buildings were taken over by the state church, Catholics found alternative places for worship and assembly in the houses of the gentry throughout the greater Dublin area. These manor-houses were the unofficial Mass-houses which attracted large congregations of recusants, as they were called, dwarfing the small numbers of Protestant worshippers in most of the parish churches. Thus the foci of Roman Catholic organisation were no longer the older parish churches but the homes of the gentry, located strategically throughout the diocese. Presumably the King family played a decisive role in this respect, and we know for certain that other gentlemen and women in the northern hinterland of Dublin provided patronage for the Catholic seminary priests. These included the Bathe family at Drumcondra, the Plunkets at Killester and the Hollywoods at Artane. The latter family produced one of the most important Counter-Reformation agents in the early seventeenth century in the person of Christopher Hollywood, the head of the first residential mission of the Society of Jesus in Ireland. Contemporaneously, the name of a Father James Drake emerges in the records as the Catholic priest resident at Artane in 1630 and servicing the wider district, including Clontarf. His

Protestant archbishop of Dublin's report on north Dublin parishes, 1630

Santry [nearest to Clontarf]

The church and chancel are uncovered and wants all ornaments. The great tythes are impropriate, belonging to the Sword. There is a vicarage endowed, worth viii libri [£8] per annum. One Randal Dymocke is curate there. All the parishioners, except a very few, are recusants. There is one James Drake, a mass priest, resident at Artane, and commonly sayeth Mass there. There is likewise his brother, Patrick Drake, a popish schoolmaster, to whom the children thereabouts go to school.

Myles V. Ronan (ed.), 'Archbishop Bulkeley's visitation of Dublin, 1630',
Archivium Hibernicum 8 (1941), p. 64

brother, Patrick Drake, who was described as a 'popish schoolmaster', provided education for the children of the area.[12]

Protestants and Catholics in Clontarf formed themselves into separate worshipping communities, one served by the parish church (now part of a larger union of north Dublin parishes), and the other accommodated in the mansions of the gentry. Coexistence between them was shattered by the sectarianism of the early 1640s that affected the Clontarf district particularly grievously. George King, who as proprietor of the estate and parish had already clashed with the Anglican incumbent, Randall Dimmock, over the payment of his stipends worth £20, became committed to the Catholic royalist cause in the uprising of October 1641. Simmering political, social and religious tensions in the north Dublin region boiled over in Clontarf. There is no doubt that Reverend Dimmock felt that his life was in danger when he was forced to flee with his family and seek refuge in Dublin, having been threatened by the rebels, and his son later narrowly escaped hanging. After the plundering of the stranded ship in Clontarf port, one Euer, who attempted to rescue the cargo from rebel hands, saved his life by converting to Catholicism, unlike his companion, a miller, who was killed. When an Englishman, Edward Leech, was forced to flee from Lambay Island by a force led by a soldier-priest, John O'Malony, who boasted of Spanish backing for his Catholic army, he and his party were robbed of their remaining goods near Clontarf. Leech was in no doubt that his Protestantism combined with his Englishness made him a target, women along the shore calling out 'Siggy Sassinagh', meaning 'There come English'. In retaliation for disorder in the village and port, the parliamentarian authorities ordered the burning of Clontarf under Sir Charles Coote on 15 December 1641, the manor-house of George King being a strategic target and the nearby church and Randall Dimmock's house suffering collateral damage. In the assault, nineteen men, women and children were killed.[13]

With the outlawry of George King, his property was confiscated and his family was ousted from Clontarf. The manor and parish were granted in 1649 to John Blackwell, an adventurer and Cromwellian official, who was Calvinist in outlook. He in turn sold it on to Captain John Vernon, the quartermaster of the Cromwellian army, also a dissenter in religion, who, unlike Blackwell, came to reside in Clontarf. With the restoration of the monarchy in 1660 and the acquisition of Clontarf manor by Vernon's cousin, Colonel Edward Vernon, the district came under the jurisdiction of an Anglican landlord. A newly confident Church of Ireland, with its members ascendant in the secular and ecclesiastical spheres, dominated an outlawed Catholic majority who depended on the will of the monarch for the freedom to worship. In Clontarf, as elsewhere, the separateness was reflected in very different models of parochial organisation, but here the memory of the sectarian violence of 1641 would have lived long in the minds of the communities. Of all of the parishes in north County Dublin in 1659, Clontarf had by far the highest proportion of English Protestant residents with 57%, the average elsewhere being about 20%. The nature of the denominational split was to determine communal relations for two centuries to come.[14]

The centrality of the Protestant parish church building, in close proximity to the seat of the new socio-political rulers, the Vernons, was symbolic of Anglican consolidation, whereas the places of worship for Catholics in the district after 1660 were impermanent and peripheral. As well as rebuilding the manor-house or castle, Colonel Edward Vernon re-edified the church building, which had itself been reconstructed in 1609, some time in the 1660s or 1670s. (The ruins of this Vernon church are those now visible in the churchyard of Clontarf.) Thus was restored to the Clontarf area its physical identity as an Anglican parish after a hiatus of several decades. The Vernons as leading lay lords were figureheads of the Protestant community at Clontarf, acting as guarantors of the stability of the parish. Thus, while fending off the threat of the Catholic King family which unsuccessfully claimed its ownership of Clontarf in the 1660s, the new Vernon proprietors also baulked at the affiliation of the rival claimant within the family, John, son of Colonel John Vernon, mainly on the grounds of his not being an Anglican (presumably he was a dissenter or Presbyterian).

While still retaining their social control within the parish, the Vernons relinquished the patronage to the crown, probably on the grounds of the desertion of a previous proprietor, the outlawed George King. Thus in 1670 Henry Brereton, vicar of Santry, was nominated as rector of Clontarf and Raheny by King Charles II. Thereafter, in a remarkable continuity, the rectorship was held by members of the same family until the nineteenth century. Archdeacon Adam Ussher, of the outstanding Dublin family which had produced the great Archbishop James Ussher, was appointed to the rectory of Clontarf in 1680 and retained it until his death in 1713. He was succeeded as rector by his son, Frederick, who held the benefice for 53 years until he died in 1766. Frederick was buried in Clontarf churchyard beside his three sons, who had predeceased him. The next rector was Revd John Ussher, a grandson of Archdeacon Adam through the latter's son, John. Appointed to the parish living of Clontarf in 1766 in succession to his uncle, Frederick, John lived until the age of 93, dying in 1829. He had, however, relinquished the rectorship of Clontarf to Revd Charles Mulloy in 1811. One other Ussher appears in this astonishing 131-year sequence: Revd Adam Ussher, another grandson of Archdeacon Adam, briefly held the curacy of Clontarf for two years until his premature death in 1745.[15]

By contrast with the constancy enjoyed by the Anglican community and parish, the history of the Roman Catholics of Clontarf from the mid-seventeenth century was marked by changeableness. Their religious profession, including worship and education, was outside the law of the state since 1560, and after 1690 their civic rights were seriously curtailed, if not totally abrogated under the Penal Laws. The eclipse of the Catholic gentry class under the Cromwellian regime was a severe blow to the mansion-based pattern of worship and education of the earlier 1630s (though some families, such as the Hollywoods at Artane, survived the confiscations). Despite the unofficial nature of their church, the Catholic bishops embarked on a flexible scheme of parochial reorganisation, forced as they were to deploy their clerical personnel and ecclesiastical resources in innovative ways. Thus Clontarf became part of a grand combination of older medieval parishes that also included Raheny, Drumcondra, Glasnevin, Killester, Artane and Coolock, all under the aegis of Santry. As we have seen, a Father James Drake was the administrator of this large unit in 1630, and he may have continued his ministry down to the 1650s or beyond. Father Richard Cahill came to the district about 1680 as a young man, and availed of the de facto Catholic restoration under King James II to erect a chapel in Coolock about 1689. With the promulgation of the Penal Laws in the 1690s and later, Catholic practice became subject to severe restriction, as evidenced in the examination and prosecution of Mass-attenders from Drumree, Baldoyle, Kilmore, Coolock, Balgriffin, Raheny and Clontarf in 1714, some of whom mentioned the name of Fr Charles or Cormac Cassidy as the celebrant at Coolock and Raheny, though others disavowed such knowledge. The latter was listed as living and working in the parish of Coolock in 1704 in the mandatory registration of priests.[16]

Conditions for Catholic worship in Ireland began to improve from the 1730s onwards. Although there was no chapel listed for Clontarf in a 1731 'Report on the State of Popery', there was mentioned under 'Raheny' a priest and a chapel at Coolock and several itinerant priests. Two years later, in 1733, the Catholic archbishop of Dublin appointed as successor to Father Nicholas Gernon a parish priest to the union of Coolock, Clontarf, Drumcondra, Raheny, Killester, Artane and Glasnevin. The new pastor was Andrew Tuite, who remained in the position until about 1770. Under his ministry there were two chapels to cater for a growing Catholic population, the existing one in Coolock and a new one at Yellow Lane, between Ballymun and Glasnevin. Canon Terence McLoughlin succeeded as parish priest in 1770, with the assistance as curate of William Green, who resided at Black Bull, Drumcondra. Testimony to Catholic worship in the Clontarf area around this time comes from the memoirs of George Anne Bellamy, the noted

Examination of Catholics in north Dublin, 1714

Co. Dublin. The examination of John Mitchell of Drumree in the said county, farmer, taken before the Rt Hon the Lord of Santry, Thomas Stepney, Foliott Sherigley, Laurence Grace, John Jackson and Daniel Wybrandts, six of her majesty's justices of the peace for the said county. Who being duly sworn and examined saith that the last time he heard mass was a Sunday last in the town of Coolock but by whom it was said or celebrated he did not know. Saith that he has a son called James Mitchell and that said James Mitchell teaches the children of Michael O'Hara who lives in Kinsealy in the said county as schoolmaster, and that the said James was beyond the seas for some time and returned into this kingdom about Christmas last past. Saith that he had not known of any popish bishop or regular Romish clergyman in this kingdom (bound to prosecute the same in the sum of £40). James Fottrell of the Grange, Baldoyle, heard mass last Sunday at Coolock. Priest's name was Father Cassidy living at Mrs Hollywood's Artane. Darby Ward of Kilmore and James Walker of Coolock was present. Heard of one Mitchell keeping a school in Kinsealy. Patrick Dodd of Balgriffin confirms the same and adds that his son went to school to Mitchell these eight days. £40. James Cunihan of Raheny, being duly sworn and examined, said that he heard mass said or celebrated on Sunday at Kilmore (house of Darby Ward) in the said county. Said that Darby Ward of the same and John Byrne of the same, Christopher Saver of Clontarf were all present when the mass was said or celebrated. John Wade of Raheny bore testimony for a Sunday later and testified that he heard mass heard or celebrated at Raheny by Father Charles, alias, Cormac Cassidy, and that James Smith and James Erwin of Raheny were present. Bound to prosecute in the sum of £48.

John Kingston, *The parish of Fairview* (Dundalk, 1953), pp 75–6

actress, who resided for some years at the Sheds. In an amusing anecdote she tells how, when visited by her friend, Mrs Madden, on a holy day, the women, who were both Catholics, went to a barn some miles off where service was performed for the convenience of the neighbouring peasants. In fact, most of the congregation in the crowded barn, which was situated at the coast, were fishing folk. Mrs Madden had to leave the place, overcome by uncontrollable laughter at the priest's face being striped with blue dye from his handkerchief, and his sermon about Adam and Eve directed in a 'Hibernian brogue' at the women worshippers.[17]

During the pastorate of Canon John Larkin, who took over as parish priest of the union in 1785, most of the remaining Penal Laws against Catholics were repealed. Before he died in 1797, he had overseen the erection of a new chapel in Balcurris in Ballymun, which was built of rough stone and had a thatched roof, and adjoined a new Catholic school. After the seven-year tenure of Patrick Ryan as parish priest of the union headed by Coolock, Daniel Murray (a future archbishop of Dublin) was very briefly appointed in 1805 to the parish of 'Coolock and Clontarf', the first time the latter name was assigned to the Catholic parish since the early seventeenth century.

With its ecclesiastical identity restored, Clontarf forged ahead as a significant location for Catholic practice in the succeeding decades. A line of able parish priests, administrators and curates, including Dr Paul Long, Father Charles Boyle and Father James Harold, impelled the process of establishing a permanent and elegant place of worship on the coast by the late 1830s. Preceding that first post-Reformation church at Clontarf was a convent of some Dominican nuns, who in 1808 moved from Channel Row in the city to a location on what became Vernon Avenue. The nuns' chaplain, a Father Cruise OP, opened his residence to worshippers prior to the building of a purpose-built chapel. A similar set of circumstances obtained in Fairview, where a chapel had been officially opened to the public on Fairview Strand in 1819 in the premises of a community of

Fig. 10.2—Roman Catholic church of St John the Baptist, Clontarf Road, built by 1838.

Carmelite tertiaries. A map of 1821 shows a chapel at Clontarf located at the south-western end of Vernon Avenue. Dr Long oversaw the building of a new chapel at Summerville beside the Sheds in 1825, with the aid of a £1,000 donation from Michael Keary, a local businessman. An extension comprising a south-eastern wing, 17ft in length, was insufficient to accommodate the congregations drawn from the population of 1,700 Catholics in Clontarf, and the new parish priest, Father James Callanan, set about finding a site for a new church after 1829, the year of Catholic emancipation. This was acquired on the seafront from J.E.V. Vernon, beside Callanan's own residence, where the Holy Faith convent now stands. The foundation stone of the Church of St John the Baptist, which was to accommodate 500–600 people, was laid on 16 June 1835 by Archbishop Murray. Designed by the well-known ecclesiastical architect Patrick Byrne, St John's was 152ft in length and 63ft in width. Once again, major benefaction assisted the project for a church as well as schools in the area, a Mr Michael Keary donating almost £2,000 for these charitable purposes.[18] [10.2]

The impressive dedication ceremony of the Church of St John the Baptist in 1842 represented a coming of age for restored Catholicism in Clontarf. A solemn sung High Mass was celebrated before a large congregation, and Dr Crolly, archbishop of Armagh, preached the sermon. During its course, he exhorted his hearers to extend their charity to all, including Protestants and Dissenters, reminding them that benefactors of all religious persuasions had contributed to their new church, and pointing to the altar as an abiding 'monument to Protestant generosity'. All religious confessions were represented in the church that day. Catholic confidence was further boosted with the opening of the National Schools on Vernon Avenue in 1847, and the arrival of congregations of Loreto and Holy Faith nuns to establish schools in the district. While the sojourn of the former order was brief, the devastating fire at Baymount destroying their plans, the Holy Faith sisters successfully established their schools for girls and junior boys under the patronage of a benefactress, Miss Jane Allingham of Seapoint, Clontarf, who secured the site of Fr Callanan's house for a convent and schools. [10.3] The Allingham family also funded the extension of St John's church and the enhancement of its interior before the end of the century. In 1879 St John's had become a parish church when the archbishop of Dublin decided to divide the vast northside union of parishes at Malahide Road and to designate Clontarf as a parochial unit in its own right (incorporating Killester, Coolock and Raheny).[19]

As a consequence of the burgeoning population of the new suburb of Clontarf from the 1850s, the leaders of the Church of Ireland community determined on the building of a new Anglican parish church. The existing building on the old

Fig. 10.3— Holy Faith convent and school for girls, Clontarf Road, opened in 1890.

Dedication of new Roman Catholic Church of St John the Baptist, Clontarf, 1842

One of the most imposing and magnificent ceremonies of the Catholic church, so frequently witnessed of late years in this country, took place yesterday at Clontarf, on the occasion of the solemn dedication to the Most High of the new parochial church of St John the Baptist. This very beautiful temple, which has been erected within the last few years through the exertions of the Rev. James Callanan, the zealous and excellent pastor of Clontarf, is a plain Gothic structure, 100 feet long by 40 feet broad. The front contains a very fine window, 21 feet in height, with octagon buttresses, terminated by crockets on each side. The interior is very richly furnished, and presents a highly pleasing appearance. The ceiling is groined and supported by corbel columns, and the altar is, in particular, a very chaste and exquisite piece of workmanship. The appearance of the entire speaks highly for the zeal of the rev. founder and the piety and generosity of his flock.

The ceremony of the dedication of the church to the worship and honour of St John the Baptist commenced shortly after ten o'clock. His Grace the Most Rev. Dr Murray, archbishop of Dublin, and primate of Ireland, officiated on the occasion, assisted by His Grace, the Most Rev. Dr Crolly, archbishop of Armagh, and the Right Rev. Dr Denvir, Bishop of Down and Connor, together with a number of the clergymen of the metropolis and of the vicinity. After the ceremonial, which consisted of the usual impressive form prescribed by the Roman Pontifical had terminated, a grand pontifical high mass was celebrated. The Rev. Dr Denvir acted as high priest, assisted by the Rev. Fr Callanan, PP, and by Fr Kennedy as deacon, and the Rev. Mr Harold as sub-deacon. Rev. Mr Laffan acted as Master of Ceremonies. The Very Rev. Dr Doyle, PP, St Michan's, and the Rev. Messrs Boyle, Walsh and McCabe with other clergymen were also in attendance in the sanctuary.

After the gospel, the Most Rev. Dr Crolly ascended the pulpit and delivered a powerful and affecting discourse in his usual eloquent and impressive style ... He referred to the necessity of knowing Christ in grace and love, and of exercising and practising on all occasions that Christian charity which Our Saviour inculcated in the parable of the good Samaritan. That charity should be extended as well to their Protestant and Dissenting brethren as to Catholics, and as the altar which they had that day dedicated was erected through the assistance they had received from their benefactors of all religious persuasions and would for ever remain a monument of Protestant generosity. He trusted sincerely that it would never be stained by any approach to Catholic bigotry or intolerance. He would entreat them to suffer the religious animosity that so long disgraced their country to sink into oblivion, never again to be revived and to let their motto on all occasions be 'Glory to God on high, and peace on earth to men of good will ...'

The choir was under the direction of Mr Haydn Corri, organist to the Metropolitan Cathedral, Marlborough Street. The Mass selected for the occasion was Haydn's No 16 with Zingarelli's Laudate pueri Dominum, which was sung after the offertory by Mrs H. Corri.

The congregation was extremely numerous, and comprised many of the principal gentry of the metropolis and environs, of all religious persuasions.

Freeman's Journal, 30 June 1842

site near the castle was inadequate for the increased congregations, particularly during the summer months. There was some disagreement about its location, many parishioners being happy for the new building to be erected in the Dollymount part of the parish, but the rector in 1860, Revd William Kempston, disagreed and argued for the extension of the old Castle Avenue building at the traditional heart of the district. Eventually a suitable site was donated by J.E.V. Vernon on Seafield Road, within 200m of the existing church. The foundation stone was

Fig. 10.4— The Church of Ireland church of St John the Baptist, Seafield Road, built in 1866 to replace the old church off Castle Avenue.

laid in August 1864, and the new church was dedicated in May 1866. Built at a cost of £7,000 and designed by the firm of William Joseph Welland and William Gillespie, the church, which seated between 600 and 700 people, was beautifully constructed in neo-Gothic style and cruciform shape. [10.4] Thus was bodied forth on a prime location the pride and aspirations of the Church of Ireland community, the association with the historic Christian traditions of Clontarf being assured in its location, and the pre-Reformation position was restored insofar as Clontarf was the nucleus of parish life for north-east Dublin. Like its Catholic counterpart, the Anglican building was also extended to accommodate more worshippers by the end of the nineteenth century. A new chancel was dedicated in March 1899, allowing for 130 additional parishioners.[20]

By the end of the nineteenth century two other Christian communities had become established at Clontarf, formed about new churches. The Gloucester Street Presbyterian congregation got permission from the Dublin Presbytery to transfer to Clontarf in 1888. A tender for a 'neat and substantial building, to seat 300' and to cost £2,000, was put out, and the design of the noted church architect Thomas Drew was accepted. Lease of a site was acquired at the south-west angle of Howth Road from the Vernon estate for 999 years at a rent of £5 per annum. The church was opened for services in May 1890, the building having cost £2,343

Dedication of a new chancel in St John the Baptist Church of Ireland parish, 1899

Mr Fuller, the architect, said that about 130 additional sittings have been added to the church by the extension, a very desirable matter, in consequence of the large increase in the congregation in recent years.

FW Mervyn, the rector of Clontarf, stated that it gave them increased seating space, and also added very much to the appearance of the building. Archbishop Peacocke of Dublin said that the first time he visited the parish was before disestablishment and when the old church which had long closed was still open. Then he came to the new church, and now to the improved church, so that he might look upon that occasion as an illustration of the progress and development of their church life, despite the troubles through which they had to pass.

Irish Times, 11 March 1899

Fig. 10.5—Presbyterian church, built at the bottom of Howth Road in 1890.

to erect. Within a decade, a tower topped the church and an organ was installed, the gift of a member of the congregation, George Gilbert. By 1911 the Presbyterian congregation in Clontarf numbered 458. [10.5]

Although its permanent church was not opened until 1906, the Wesleyan community at Clontarf had had a chapel since 1868. This was a modest building, situated close to where the present edifice stands on the seafront. Prior to the availability of the chapel, the Methodists of Clontarf were accommodated for their service in a room provided gratis by G.O. Lemon. The chapel was extended in 1881, but by the turn of the century it was proving to be inadequate for the worshipping numbers. A new church was built in granite on the seafront site in 1906 to accommodate nearly 500 people. The church organ was donated by Mr George Benson in 1899. By 1911 the Methodist community in Clontarf was 298 strong.[21] [10.6]

Respectful relations between the religions are evident in the munificence of the Vernons towards both Roman Catholic and Presbyterian communities, and also in the benevolent utterances of Archbishop Crolly. Yet much of the benefaction and charity displayed was understandably denominational, as in the cases of donors such as Michael Keary and the Allinghams. While interdenominational charity did operate in cases of neediness, relations between the leading confessional communities could be marked by rancour, as is attested

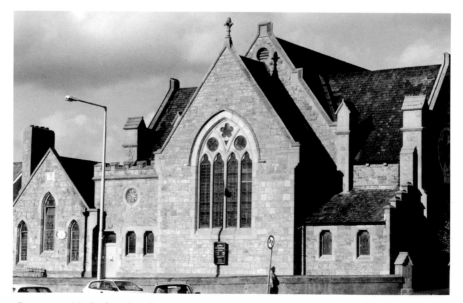

Fig. 10.6—Methodist church, Clontarf Road, built in 1906 to replace a former chapel on St Lawrence Road.

Charitable relief for poor inhabitants

To the inhabitants of Clontarf   14 February 1855

In consequence of the continued inclemency of the weather and the awful distress amongst the labouring Poor of the Clontarf District, it is proposed to Collect a Fund to relieve their temporal wants by a distribution of food and fuel among the most destitute, who are in a starving state.

Subscriptions for the purpose will be received by the Rev. W.A. Kempston, Rector; J.D. Garde, Esq., and W.D. Smith, Esq., Churchwardens; and by Francis Byrne, esq., 11 Castle-avenue, Clontarf.

Subscriptions already received:

B.L. Guinness, Esq.	£5 0 0
E.E. Preston, Esq.	£1 0 0
F. Byrne, Esq.	£5 0 0
J.T. Barlow, Esq.	£1 0 0
Mr John Tamulty	0 5 0
Edward Hogan, Esq. (Sutton)	£1 0 0

Freeman's Journal, 15 February 1855

by the events surrounding the benefit fund for 'Andy', a deceased Catholic bus-conductor, in 1866. Revd John Crawford, rector of Clontarf, had agreed to become treasurer of the fund to support Andy's Protestant widow and his children, who were being educated in Protestant schools. In letters to the press, the rector was attacked as being engaged in 'proselytising', and he was forced to defend his involvement as being 'to better suffering humanity'. Meanwhile, in the face of the great crisis of the Famine of the later 1840s, the sick and destitute in Clontarf turned to the state welfare system of the Poor Law.

This system of relief had been introduced on foot of the Poor Law Inquiry in the 1830s. It had found that, in respect of poor families in the Clontarf area, conditions among those occupying cottages and cabins were wretched. Many of the dwellings had no bedsteads or bedding. It was common for two families to share the same cabin, described in general as being 'miserable and filthy'. Attention was drawn to the particularly dire circumstances of the families of fishermen of Clontarf.[22] The district was covered by the North Dublin Union, with the workhouse for paupers being located in North Brunswick Street. An average of 30 people, mostly old and infirm, were being relieved in Clontarf in the North Dublin Union in the worst years of 1847 to 1849. They were in receipt of outdoor relief, in the form of Indian meal, rather than being admitted to the workhouse, a fact that led to criticism of the relieving officer. On being offered places in the workhouse in 1848, however, the recipients refused, preferring to receive corn as outdoor relief.[23]

Members of the religious communities evolved their own systems of bonding through a variety of cultural and religious associations, which fostered and strengthened group identity. Among the Anglicans of Clontarf there was a profusion of parish associations for men, women and youths in the decades from the 1870s until the 1940s. In part, this was as a response to the uncertainty obtaining after the disestablishment of the Church of Ireland in 1870, which cut the Church of Ireland adrift from the state. Later, the attainment of independence raised questions about the role of a Protestant minority in a new state. Some of the parish associations were inspirational, such as the Missionary Union; others were charitable, including the Social Services Union; but most were sociable outlets for activities such as scouting, unions and brigades of mothers, boys and girls, and clubs for sportsmen and women. These associations were effective in providing a milieu for the preservation of the bonds of Anglican society, especially among younger members when choosing marriage partners. In the case of the Church of Ireland parish of Clontarf, for example, there were almost 40 societies operating in the 1940s, including sporting and games clubs such as lawn tennis, badminton and hockey, youth organisations such as the Girl Guides, the Brownies and the Boys' Brigade, pious associations such as the Young Men's Bible Class, debating societies such as the Clontarf Young Men's Study Circle, and charities such as the Gleaners' Missionary Union. These groups helped the process of identification with the parish. Down to the 1940s the core of the Anglican parish of Clontarf remained stable, with rates of religious intermarriage fairly low. Among the Methodists of Clontarf, social life encompassed the Literary Society and the activity of the Christian Endeavour Society. Clontarf Presbyterians were animated communally through associations such as the Presbyterian Orphan Society, the Ladies' Sewing Party and the Mission Committee, and the various fund-raising activities for church-building and restoration, including the Brian Boru Bazaar held in the Rotunda in 1904, which aimed at collecting £2,000 for the enlargement of the Clontarf Presbyterian church and schools.[24]

On the Catholic side, Sunday schooling for youngsters was being organised mostly by lay people under the banner of the Confraternity of Christian Doctrine by the 1830s. Boys were being taught after Mass between 11.00 and noon by the 'gentlemen of the Clontarf monastery', and girls by the ladies of the parish in 1831. By the 1880s the Sodality of the Sacred Heart had been established among men in the parish of Clontarf and, later, branches of that sodality, as well as the Children of Mary and the Confraternity of the Holy Family, were established for women. By 1905 there was a conference of the Society of St Vincent de Paul in Clontarf, dedicated to the Blessed Virgin. The conference organised a stall at the annual bazaar of the Society in the Rotunda in aid of the relief of the poor. These bodies not only promoted devotion and piety but also offered opportunities for socialising at meetings and on festive occasions and excursions. In common with the other denominations, the Roman Catholic authorities developed a range of pastoral and educational activities in this period. The tradition of charity sermons, established in respect of the Charter School and the widows' almshouse, was carried on in support of the Catholic parochial schools, which grew in pupil enrolment from 500 girls and boys in 1831 to 700 in 1864. Noted preachers, including Nicholas Donnelly, the historian of the Dublin parishes, were enlisted to give the annual sermon at which a collection would be made in St John the Baptist Roman Catholic church until at least 1870.[25]

Social and cultural bonds

Until the mid-twentieth century these denominational communities consolidated their spiritual, educational and social activities within their separate spheres. Each had its own system of primary schooling, for example. Until the foundation of St Paul's College by the Vincentians at Sybil Hill in 1950, the district lacked a Catholic boys' secondary school and pupils travelled to O'Connell's Schools and elsewhere. [10.7] Catholic girls were educated in Holy Faith convent school in the heart of the district. For Protestant pupils at second level, a series of amalgamations of existing schools took place, centred on the mansion of Mount Temple on Malahide Road. The centre-city Mountjoy boys' school, which had its playing fields at Strandville Avenue in Clontarf, moved out to Mount Temple in 1949, merging with the Clontarf-based Hibernian Marine School for boys, which had been founded in 1904. Then in 1972 the combination of educational academies was completed on the site when the Bertrand and Rutland schools for girls, which had come together in the north inner city, joined with Mountjoy and Marine School to form Mount Temple Comprehensive. Meanwhile, Baymount

Fig. 10.7— Sybil Hill House (built by 1760), which was sold to the Congregation of the Mission (Vincentians) for the establishment of a boys' secondary school, St Paul's College.

School, which was opened in 1904 as a preparatory school for public schools, had an ethos that was 'English and Protestant'. It continued to operate until 1946.[26]

Within the majority Roman Catholic population, the organisation of three separate parishes within Clontarf bespoke a growing sense of belonging, especially among the large cohort of newcomer families. In the older, western district, the increased population of worshippers was catered for by the purchase by the Catholic diocese of the town hall as a chapel, its façade being embellished in stone. It became St Anthony's chapel-of-ease in 1927, and later a parish church. [10.8] Dollymount was evolving as a suburb within a suburb, and the building of the large church of St Gabriel, first as a chapel-of-ease and later as a parish centre in its own right, underpinned the new Catholic community. [10.9] Located on a site donated by the local St Vincent de Paul convent, and designed by architects Hugo Duffy and Louis Peppard, the church was consecrated in 1956. In the heart of the district, the Church of St John the Baptist retained its centrality, absorbing much of the increase in settlement along the artery of Vernon Avenue and its radiating roads and avenues. Ultimately, the Clontarf area was divided into three parishes by the Catholic authorities in 1966, which, as Dennis McIntyre has pointed out, correspond to the three distinct areas or villages comprising Clontarf: St Anthony's parish incorporating the centre of the old manor, St John's parish centred on the fishing community and old harbour area, and St Gabriel's representing the later-settled Dollymount and Heronstown district.[27]

Fig. 10.8—Older Roman Catholic church of St Anthony, Clontarf Road, opened in 1925 in the converted Clontarf Town Hall (which had been built in 1895).

Fig. 10.9—Roman Catholic church of St Gabriel, Clontarf, built in 1956.

With their religious identities secure through their activities of church-building and extension, parochial delineation and educational provision, the confessional groups in Clontarf could, by the early to mid-twentieth century, work on building bridges to the wider community. Inter-community relations were, however, scarcely improved as a result of the decade of national and international turmoil down to the 1920s, as evidenced, for example, in the pattern of divisions over commemoration. Gradually, the atmosphere for real dialogue between the religious communities improved, as the protective barriers of denominational clubs and parish associations broke down from the 1960s, and mixing across the confessional boundaries became very much the norm. It was in this changing milieu that, when in June 1971 the existing Church of St Anthony in the remodelled town hall was badly damaged by fire, there were immediate offers of support and accommodation from the neighbouring churches of other denominations. The new Church of St Anthony, built in 1975, was the first in the district to be designed according to the liturgical principles of Vatican II. [10.10] In the past 30 years laity and clergy of all churches have been enthusiastic participants in ecumenical ventures, including commemorative services for the victims of the Omagh bombing in August 1998 and of the attacks in the USA on 11 September 2001, as well as ceremonies of pilgrimage to the site of the old church on Castle Avenue and the annual vigil on the Bull Wall at dawn on Easter morning.

Fig. 10.10—New church of St Anthony, built in 1975 to replace the older church which had been damaged by fire in 1971.

The sphere of local civic culture offered possibilities for the cooperation of those from different religious and socio-political backgrounds in Clontarf. From the 1860s onwards, the campaigns of the *Dublin Builder* and the *Irish Builder* for the environmental improvement of Clontarf adduced the notion of pride in the area as a suburb for the first time. Equally important was the momentum given by the establishment of Clontarf township in 1869, which accustomed the more substantial ratepayers from different social backgrounds to working together successfully for the benefit of the neighbourhood. As has been seen, geographical, religious and political differences were reflected in many of the debates and elections, especially on the issue of the drainage of Fairview, and the absorption of the township into the municipality was in part, at least, a consequence of these divisions. Yet local interest groups such as the Dollymount and Clontarf Improvement Association and the Clontarf and Dollymount Bathers' Association were formed with the object of improving sanitary, lighting and leisure facilities along the seafront, and these included members of the Roman Catholic and Protestant clergy. The work of municipal councillors for the district was supplemented by local representative groups concerned, for example, with the protection of maritime facilities in Clontarf and Dublin Bay in general, culminating in the founding of the Clontarf Residents' Association in 1970. The recent successful mobilisation of thousands of residents over the issue of the plan by the civic authorities for flood defences along the seafront attests the power of local opinion, as expressed through the Clontarf Residents' Association and the more recently founded Clontarf Business Association.[28]

Apart from the networks formed through groups of residents concerned mainly with the environment of Clontarf, a rich tapestry of cultural and sporting associations has been woven in the district throughout the twentieth century. To the networks formed by members and supporters of the rugby, cricket, yachting, tennis and golf clubs from the late nineteenth century were added those developed by enthusiasts for Gaelic games and soccer. For the playing of the former sports, Brian Boru GAA club was founded in 1919, and after its decline Clontarf GAA club began in 1961. Meanwhile, Scoil Uí Chonaill, which had started in 1950, was based in the Clontarf grounds of the secondary school of that name. Organised association football in Clontarf dates back to the foundation of St John Bosco Football Club in the earlier decades of the twentieth century, but the best-known clubs, Belgrove and Oulton, date from 1948 and 1965 respectively. Aquatic activities were catered for since the late nineteenth century by Clontarf Swimming and Water Polo Club, and later by North Dublin Swimming Club, both of which were connected with Clontarf Baths. Sporting success for Clontarf clubs in national competitions has generated closer identification with the area. As the social ties formed by parish associations weakened somewhat from the 1960s onwards, cross-community cultural activities for men and women came to complement or even supplant them. Clontarf Horticultural Society, founded in 1954, enhanced the beauty of gardens in the suburb, and it also played a key role in the development of the renowned rose garden in St Anne's Park. Among the dramatic and choral groups successfully established were the Temple Players and the Castle and Seafield Singers. Recently the area has acquired new cultural amenities in the form of An Clasach for traditional music and the Viking Theatre in the Sheds public house. Irish-language speakers in the neighbourhood have been supported by the annual Éigse Chluain Tarbh festival, among other events.

Along with local histories and memoirs by F.W.R. Knowles, Muriel McIvor, Dennis McIntyre and Val Lynch, the foundation of the Clontarf Historical Society in 1978 has made a significant contribution to the fashioning of local identity. Through its series of lectures and outings the Society has promoted an awareness of the history of Clontarf. It has encouraged the dissemination of research in many fields, including the legacy of the Vernon family, for example, as well as the history of the battle of Clontarf and the role of Brian Boru. While popular acknowledgement of this heritage in the district was evident in the naming of the new estate in the heart of the old Vernon manor 'Kincora' after Brian's palace at Killaloe, the Society has provided a forum for scholarly talks containing revised interpretations of the battle and its hero. As more people from the district and elsewhere have presented the fruits of their research in local history, there is much more openness to the stripping down of legends of the battle in pursuit of historical accuracy, and also to other events and aspects of Clontarf's history over many centuries.

* * *

This consciousness of Clontarf as a place apart owing to its historic heritage and an awareness of its appeal as a residential neighbourhood have generated pride in a local identity. The district's beautiful situation has been celebrated in art and literature since travel writers began lauding its charms from the late eighteenth century onwards, painters of that era focusing on both the castle and the Sheds as social hubs. While the town of Clontarf used to be identified with the settlement in and around the castle and old church, nowadays it is the junction of lower Vernon Avenue with the seafront that has come to represent the village of Clontarf for the local community. In part this has been due to an initiative of the civic corporation for an urban design project in 2000, in conjunction with the Royal Institute of

Architects of Ireland. The refurbishment has included new street lighting and paving on the landward side of Clontarf Road, and the metamorphosis of a pump-house on the promenade into a piece of public sculpture. The scheme also involved raising a grassy bank on the promenade as a measure of flood protection.[29]

The corporation, the latest in a line of ruling authorities over the area, has thus been promoting its notion of a village centre for Clontarf, but in practice social, cultural and economic forces have converged in this space as a core of community during the past couple of centuries. Geographically, the junction is at the centre of the district. The Vernon family promoted careful leasing of the green at the Sheds in the eighteenth century. Most of the signature Victorian houses which face the sea have been restored, making a contrast with the very modern street furniture and urban design. Signs of Vernon lordship are evident not just in the street names of the quarter but also in the adjacent church and school, the building of which was contributed to by the family's patronage. Many of the local businesses are based in premises on the adjoining roads, and there are a large number of eating and drinking places, ranging from the old-established Sheds public house to the several new cafés and restaurants that line the streets in the vicinity. Thus, while the era of the manor and the fishing port may have passed, a village of Clontarf, an entity originally granted to the Knights Templar, still persists in the physical sense of a clustering of roads and houses around a commercial and cultural hub. It also serves as a focus for the identification of an urbanised community with their neighbourhood. *Clontarf semper viret!*

1 Modern authorities do not attribute greater antiquity to the church and parish of Clontarf than the time of the Norman settlement. Myles V. Ronan states that 'nothing is known of the origin of the [early seventeenth-century] church' of Clontarf: Ronan (ed.), 'Royal visitation of Dublin, 1615', 35. In their survey of the medieval churches of County Dublin, Simms and Fagan exclude Clontarf from the number of medieval manorial villages that had an Early Christian site: Fagan and Simms, 'Villages in County Dublin', 86; see also Murphy and Potterton (eds), *The Dublin region in the Middle Ages*, 215.

2 *CGG*, 193; John Kingston, *Parish of Fairview* (Dundalk, 1953), 5.

3 For an overview see Clarke, 'Conversion, church and cathedral', 19–50.

4 Mac Ghiolla Phádraig, 'The Irish form of "Clontarf"'.

5 Bradley, 'Scandinavian settlement in the hinterland of Dublin'.

6 Nicholson, *Knights Templar*, 134; for the tenor of religious life among the Knights at Clontarf see Wood, 'Templars in Ireland', 334, 350–4; Mac Niocaill, 'Suppression of the Templars in Ireland', 215.

7　Pender (ed.), *A census of Ireland circa 1659*, 382–92; Connolly and Martin (eds), *Dublin guild merchant roll*, 8, 29, 80, 104; Wood, 'Templars in Ireland', 337, 350–4; McNeill (ed.), *Registrum de Kilmainham, 1326–39*, 9, 11, 26, 32, 44, 73, 84, 85, 93, 125; Phil Connolly, 'Irish material in the class of ancient petitions in the Public Record Office, London', 12; *Calendar of Christ Church deeds*, no. 304, p. 92; Gillespie (ed.), *Proctor's accounts of Peter Lewis*, 50–1; *Civil Survey, vii, Dublin*, 176; TCD, 1641 Depositions Project, on-line transcript January 1970 [http://1641. tcd.ie/deposition.php?depID<?php echo 810244r274?>, accessed 24 June 2011].

8　See Falkiner, 'Hospital of St John of Jerusalem in Ireland'; O'Malley, *The Knights Hospitaller of the English langue*, 16–17, 94–6; Colm Lennon, 'Confraternities in Ireland: a long view', in *idem* (ed.), *Confraternities and sodalities in Ireland* (Dublin, 2012), 20–2.

9　O'Malley, *The Knights Hospitaller of the English langue*, 252; for the background to the dissolution see Brendan Bradshaw, *Dissolution of the religious orders*; *Cal. exch. inq.*, 90–1.

10　*Cal. S.P. Ireland, 1600–01*, 58.

11　'Royal visitation of Dublin, 1615', 35; M.V. Ronan (ed.), 'Archbishop Bulkeley's visitation of Dublin, 1630', *Archivium Hibernicum* 8 (1941), 64; TCD, 1641 Depositions Project, on-line transcript January 1970 [http://1641.tcd.ie/deposition.php?depID<?php echo 809276r164?>, accessed 24 June 2011].

12　'Archbishop Bulkeley's visitation of Dublin, 1630', 64; for the context see Colm Lennon, 'Mass in the manor-house: the Counter-Reformation in Dublin, 1560–1630', in James Kelly and Dáire Keogh (eds), *History of the Catholic diocese of Dublin* (Dublin, 2000), 112–26.

13　Dublin, Marsh's Library MS, 1637, 'Articles against George King, impropriator of the rectory of Clontarf'; TCD, 1641 Depositions Project, on-line transcript January 1970 [http://1641.tcd.ie/deposition.php?depID<?php echo 809276r164?>, accessed 24 June 2011; http://1641.tcd.ie/deposition.php?depID<?php echo 809214r114?>, accessed 24 June 2011; http://1641.tcd.ie/deposition.php?depID<?php echo 810244r274?>, accessed 24 June 2011].

14　Pender (ed.), *A census of Ireland circa 1659*, 382–92; Ní Mhurchadha, 'Contending neighbours', 284.

15　D'Alton, *History of County Dublin* (1976 edn), 46; for a note on Revd Henry Brereton see www.brereton.org/Brereton%20 Families%20of%Ireland-jan2012%20version.pdf (accessed 23 September 2012); W. Ball Wright (ed.), *The Ussher memoirs*, 147, 155–7, 160, 163, 164, 195, 198–200; Benjamin W. Adams, 'Antiquarian notes, etc. of the parishes of Santry and Cloghran, County Dublin', *Journal of the Royal Historical and Archaeological Association of Ireland* (4th ser.) 5 (1881), 482–98.

16　Donnelly, *Short history of some Dublin parishes*, 10–11, 19–21; Kingston, *Parish of Fairview*, 72, 73–4.

17　Donnelly, *Short history of some Dublin parishes*, 21–7; Kingston, *Parish of Fairview*, 74–8; 'Report on the state of popery in Ireland, 1731: diocese of Dublin', *Archivium Hibernicum* 4 (1915), 134–5; George Bellamy, *An apology for the life of George Anne Bellamy, late of Covent-Garden Theatre* (London, 1785), 24–5.

18 Donnelly, *Short history of some Dublin parishes*, 27–32; Kingston, *Parish of Fairview*, 79–80, 82–3.

19 *FJ*, 30 June 1842; Dennis McIntyre, *The meadow of the bull* (Dublin, 1987), 45; Ruddy, 'Baymount Castle, Clontarf', 174–6; Donnelly, *Short history of some Dublin parishes*, 33–7.

20 McIntyre, *Meadow of the bull*, 56–8; www.dia.ie/works/view/33642building/ CO.+DUBLIN%2C+DUBLIN%2C+ CLONTARF%29%2C+CHURCH+OF+ST+JOHN+THE+BA PTIST (accessed 24 September 2012); *IT*, 11 March 1899.

21 http://clontarfchurch.org/cspc-history/caspc-history.html (accessed 4 October 2012); http://www.dia.ie/works/view/35991/building/CO.+DUBLIN%2C+DUBLIN%2C+HOWTH +ROAD+%28CLONTARF%29%2C+PRESBYTERIAN+CHURCH (accessed 4 October 2012); D.A. Levistone Cooney, 'The Methodist chapels in Dublin', *DHR* 57 (2004), 158; *IT*, 17 May 1890, 8 October 1906.

22 *Reports from Commissioners, Poor Law (Ireland)*, xxxii, session 4 Feb.–Aug. 1836 (London, 1836), supplement, p. 152.

23 *FJ*, 10 and 17 February 1848, 3 and 24 May 1849, 7 and 21 June 1849, 30 August 1849, 10 January 1850, 21 August 1831, 20 August 1864, 16 October 1866, 17 September 1870.

24 Martin Maguire, '"Our people": the Church of Ireland and the culture of community in Dublin since Disestablishment', in Raymond Gillespie and W.G. Neely (eds), *The laity and the Church of Ireland, 1000-2000: all sorts and conditions* (Dublin, 2002), 277–302; *idem*, 'The Church of Ireland parochial associations: a social and cultural analysis', in Lennon (ed.), *Confraternities and sodalities in Ireland*, 97–109; *IT*, 22 May 1896, 27 November 1900, 12 July 1902, 4 November 1904, 18 June 1907, 9 February 1937.

25 Dublin Diocesan archives, 'Visitations of parishes', 1830, 1831, 1834, 1839, 1881, 1960; *FJ*, 21 August 1831, 15 August 1863, 20 September 1864, 17 September 1870; *IT*, 18 January 1905, 5 June 1926.

26 Ruddy, 'Baymount Castle, Clontarf'; *idem*, 'Mount Temple, Clontarf', *DHR* 61 (2008), 183–93.

27 *IT*, 11 August 1925, 5 June 1926; *Souvenir brochure of official opening of Church of St Gabriel, Clontarf, Dublin* (Dublin, 1956); McIntyre, *Meadow of the bull*, 47.

28 *FJ*, 4 April 1864, 23 January 1893, 11 May 1893, 30 September 1893; *IT*, 26 February 1861, 30 December 1904, 26 May 1906, 2 November 1906.

29 *IT*, 28 July 2000.

APPENDIX

Gazetteer of places

This gazetteer lists the roads and terraces in Clontarf, with the date of the earliest reference found.

ABBREVIATIONS

Ancient Records:	*Calendar of ancient records of Dublin*, ed. J.T. Gilbert (7 vols, Dublin, 1889–92).
Census:	www.census.nationalarchives.ie/.
Commons journal:	*Journal of the House of Commons of Ireland* (1789) (Dublin, 1789).
Cosgrave:	D. Cosgrave, *North Dublin: city and environs* (Dublin, 1909; 2005 edn).
FJ:	*Freeman's Journal.*
II:	*Irish Independent.*
IT:	*Irish Times.*
McManus:	R. McManus, *Dublin, 1910-1940: shaping the city and suburbs* (Dublin, 2002).
OS:	Ordnance Survey of Ireland.
Phillips:	T. Phillips, 'Maps of the bay and harbour of Dublin, 1685', RIA, RR, MC 3/1–12.
Rocque:	J. Rocque, *An actual survey of the county of Dublin, 1760* (Dublin, 1760).
TD:	*Thom's Directory* (Dublin, 1844–).

1. NAMES OF ROADS AND AVENUES

Annsbrook	Off Clontarf Road. Annsbrook 1837 (OS).
Ardilaun Villas	Ardilaun Villas, Clontarf East 1911 (Census).

Bayview Avenue	Bayview Avenue, Clontarf 1838 (*FJ*)
Belgrove Road	Rutland Avenue extended 1928 (*IT*).
Beverly Court	Off Vernon Avenue West. Beverley Court 1984 (*IT*).
Blackbush	Clontarf Road North. Blackbush/Heronstown 1837 (OS).
Blackbush Lane	Blackbush Lane 1837 (OS).
Blackheath Avenue	Blackheath Avenue 1958 (*TD*).
Blackheath Court	Blackheath Court 1986 (*IT*).
Blackheath Drive	Blackheath Drive 1939 (McManus, 293).
Blackheath Gardens	Blackheath Gardens 1939 (*TD*).
Blackheath Grove	Blackheath Grove 1949 (*TD*).
Blackheath Park	Blackheath Park 1939 (*TD*).
Black Quarry Lane	Black Quarry Lane 1789 (Commons journal)
Brewery Lane	Brewery Lane 1893 (*FJ*).
Brian Boru Street	Brian Boru Street 1907 (OS).
Brian Boru Avenue	Brian Boru Avenue, Clontarf 1907 (OS).
Brooklawn	Brooklawn apartments 1982 (*IT*).
Byrne's Lane	Byrne's Lane 1863 (*TD*).
Carlton Court	St Lawrence Road East 1983 (*IT*).
Castilla Park	Castilla Park 1969 (*TD*).
Castle Avenue	Unnamed lower part 1685 (Phillips). Castle Avenue 1848 (*FJ*).
Castle Court	Off Castle Avenue East 1984 (*IT*).
Castle Grove	Castle Grove 1949 (*TD*).
Castle Road	Castle Road 1949 (*TD*).
Chapel-house Square	Ruins 1861 (*Dublin Builder*).
Chapel Lane	Chapel Lane, Clontarf East 1911 (Census).
Chelsea Gardens	Chelsea Gardens 1975 (*IT*).
Churchgate Avenue	Off Vernon Avenue West 1972 (*IT*).
Clontarf Park	Clontarf Park 1958 (*TD*).
Clontarf Road	Unnamed 1685 (Phillips).
Clontarf Sheds	The Shades of Clontarf 1718 (*Ancient Records*, vii, 66–7).
Conquer Hill Avenue	Tramway Cottages Clontarf 1901 (Census).
Conquer Hill Road	Conquer Hill 1901 (Census).
Crescent, Marino	Marino Crescent 1792 (Cosgrave, 93).
Dollymount Avenue	Dollymount Avenue 1933 (McManus, 292).
Dollymount Grove	Dollymount Grove 1958 (*TD*).
Dollymount Park	Dollymount Park 1949 (*TD*).

Dollymount Rise	Dollymount Rise 1981 (*TD*).
Dunluce Road	Dunluce Road 1939 (*TD*).
Dunseverick Road	Dunseverick Road. Newly built houses 1947 (*IT*).
Dyehouse Lane	See Strandville Avenue 1846 (*FJ*).
Fingal Avenue	Fingal Avenue 1863 (*TD*).
Fortview Avenue	Fortview Avenue 1850 (*TD*).
Green Lanes	Green Lane (Mount Prospect Avenue West) 1837 (*OS*).
Grosvenor Court	Off Vernon Avenue Extension South 1987 (*IT*).
Haddon Court	Off Haddon Road East. Built by 1980 (*IT*).
Haddon Park	Haddon Park 1929 (*TD*).
Haddon Road	Haddon Road 1899 (*TD*).
Hampton Court	Off Vernon Avenue Extension South 1972 (*IT*).
Hazel Lane	Off Kincora Road 2000 (*TD*).
Hollybrook Grove	Hollybrook Grove, Clontarf 1958 (*TD*).
Hollybrook Park	Hollybrook Park 1883 (*TD*).
Hollybrook Road	Hollybrook Road, Clontarf 1899 (*TD*).
Howth Road	Unnamed 1685 (Phillips).
Kilronan Court	Off St Lawrence Road West 1977 (*IT*).
Kincora Avenue	Kincora Avenue, Clontarf 1958 (*TD*).
Kincora Court	Kincora Court, Kincora Road, Clontarf 1982 (*IT*).
Kincora Drive	Kincora Drive 1963 (*IT*).
Kincora Grove	Kincora Grove, Clontarf 1961 (*IT*).
Kincora Park	Off Oulton Road East. Kincora Park 1949 (*TD*).
Kincora Road	Opened 1928 (*IT*).
Kincora Walk	Off Kincora Road NE [see Hazel Lane].
Knightsbridge	Knightsbridge, Castle Avenue, Clontarf 1991 (*IT*).
Lambourne Village	Off Kincora Grove 1985 (*IT*).
Mooney's Lane	Mooney's Row, Clontarf 1881 (*FJ*).
Moore's Place	Moore's Place, Clontarf Road 1875 (*TD*).
Mount Prospect Avenue	Unnamed 1837 (*OS*).
Mount Prospect Drive	Mount Prospect Drive 1949 (*TD*).
Mount Prospect Grove	Mount Prospect Grove 1949 (*TD*).
Mount Prospect Lawn	Off Mount Prospect Avenue 2002 (*IT*).
Mount Prospect Park	Mount Prospect Park 1939 (*TD*).
Oakley Park	Off Vernon Avenue West 1960 (*IT*).
Oulton Road	Oulton Road, Clontarf 1932 (*IT*).
Paddocks, The	Off Stiles Road 1993 (*IT*).

Park Lawn	Off Mount Prospect Avenue East 1978 (*IT*).
Redcourt Oaks	Off Seafield Road East 2004 (*IT*).
Rutland Place/Lane	Rutland Place 1862 (*TD*).
St David's Court	Off Castle Avenue East 1975 (*IT*).
St Edmund's	St Edmund's, Sea Road, Clontarf East 1911 (Census).
St Gabriel's Road	St Gabriel's Road, Clontarf 1964 (*II*).
St John's Wood	Off Castle Avenue West 1978 (*IT*).
St Joseph's Square	Off Vernon Avenue, Clontarf 1911 (Census).
St Lawrence Road	St Lawrence Road 1892 (*TD*).
St Lawrence's Grove	Off Howth Road West 1987 (*IT*).
Sandon Cove	Off Castle Avenue East 1984 (*IT*).
Sea Court	Off St Gabriel's Road 1974 (*IT*).
Seafield Avenue	Seafield Avenue 1949 (*TD*).
Seafield Close	Off Kincora Road 1989 (*TD*).
Seafield Downs	Off Kincora Road/Seapark Drive 1989 (*TD*).
Seafield Grove	Off St Gabriel's Road 1989 (*TD*).
Seafield Road	Unnamed 1760 (Rocque).
Seapark Drive	Seapark Drive, Clontarf 1949 (*TD*).
Seapark Road	Seapark Road, Clontarf 1939 (*TD*).
Sea Road	Sea Road, Clontarf East 1911 (Census).
Seaview Avenue	Seaview Avenue, Clontarf 1850 (*TD*).
Snugborough	Off Vernon Avenue. Snugboro 1861 (*Dublin Builder*).
Stiles Court	Off Stiles Road. Stiles Court 1993 (*IT*).
Stiles Road, The	Styles Road, Clontarf 1939 (*TD*).
Strandville Avenue East	Strandville Avenue, Clontarf 1841 (*FJ*).
Sybil Hill Road	Sybil Hill Road, Clontarf 1968 (*IT*).
Summerville	Summerville, Clontarf 1993 (*IT*).
Telleden Cottages	Telleden 1869 (OS).
Tutor's Avenue	Tutor's Avenue, Clontarf 1904 (*TD*).
Vernon Avenue	Unnamed 1760 (Rocque).
Vernon Avenue Extension	Unnamed 1760 (Rocque).
Vernon Court	Vernon Court, Clontarf Road 1979 (*IT*).
Vernon Drive	Vernon Drive, Clontarf 1958 (*TD*).
Vernon Gardens	Vernon Gardens, Clontarf 1929 (*TD*).
Vernon Grove	Vernon Grove, Clontarf 1929 (*TD*).
Vernon Heath	Off Vernon Avenue 1993 (*IT*).
Vernon Park	Vernon Park, Clontarf 1939 (*TD*).

Vernon Rise	Vernon Rise, Furry Park, Clontarf 1975 (*IT*).
Vernon Wood	Off Vernon Avenue 1990 (*IT*).
Victoria Place	Off Vernon Avenue East. Victoria Place 1860 (OS).
Victoria Road	Victoria Road, Clontarf 1903 (*TD*).
Warrenpoint	Clontarf Road 1852 (*TD*).
Woodside	Woodside, Vernon Avenue, Clontarf East 1911 (Census).

2. NAMES OF TERRACES AND ROWS

Albert Terrace	Clontarf Road 1897 (*TD*). Subsumed within Clontarf Road.
Alexandra Terrace	Clontarf Road 1864 (*TD*). Subsumed within Clontarf Road.
Annesbrook Terrace	Clontarf West 1911 (Census).
Beechfield Terrace	Beechfield Terrace, Vernon Avenue 1907 (OS).
Belgrove Villas	Belgrove Villas, Sea Road, Clontarf East 1911 (Census).
Belview Terrace	Belview Terrace, Clontarf East 1911 (Census).
Cabra Villas	Cabra Villas, Sea Road, Clontarf 1911 (Census).
Castle Terrace	Castle Avenue 1873 (*TD*). Subsumed within Castle Avenue.
Crablake	Crab-lake 1850 (*TD*). Subsumed within Clontarf Road.
Daemar Villas	Daemar Villas, Vernon Avenue, Clontarf East 1911 (Census).
Esplanade Villas	Esplanade Villas, Dollymount (three premises) 1883 (*TD*).
Ellesmere	St Lawrence Rd 1894 (*TD*). Subsumed within St Lawrence Road.
Fortview Terrace	Fortview 1837 (OS). Subsumed within Clontarf Road.
Gresham's Buildings	Dollymount 1850 (*TD*).
Haddon Terrace	Haddon Road 1901 (*TD*). Incorporated in Haddon Road.
Hillview Terrace	Clontarf Road 1856 (*FJ*). Subsumed within Clontarf Road.
Hollybrook Terrace	Hollybrook Terrace 1870 (*TD*). Subsumed within Howth Road.
Hunter's Row	Seapark Road West, Clontarf 2000 (*II*).
Mount Vernon	Mount Vernon, Clontarf East 1911 (Census).

Ormond Terrace	Vernon Avenue. Ormond Terrace 1857 (*FJ*).
Pretoria Villas	Pretoria Villas 1903 (*TD*).
Redhall Terrace	Redhall Terrace, Clontarf East 1911 (Census).
Rossborough Terrace	Vernon Avenue 1852 (*TD*).
Rostrevor Terrace	Clontarf Road, Clontarf East 1911 (Census).
Rutland Terrace	Rutland Terrace 1850 (*TD*).
St Anne's Terrace	St Anne's Terrace, Clontarf East 1911 (Census).
St George's Terrace	St Lawrence Road 1896 (*TD*). Subsumed within St Lawrence Road.
St John's Terrace	Clontarf Road 1850 (*FJ*). Subsumed within Clontarf Road.
Seabank Terrace	Clontarf Road 1863 (*TD*). Subsumed within Clontarf Road.
Seafield Terrace	Seafield Avenue 1907 (OS). Subsumed within Seafield Road.
Seapoint Terrace	Seapoint Terrace 1908 (*TD*). Subsumed within Clontarf Road.
Seaview Terrace	Clontarf Road 1850 (*TD*). Subsumed within Clontarf Road.
Tristram Villas	St Lawrence Road 1904 (*TD*). Subsumed within St Lawrence Road.
Vernon Parade	Clontarf Road 1850 (*TD*). Subsumed within Clontarf Road.
Vernon's Buildings	Castle Avenue 1850 (*TD*). Subsumed within Castle Avenue.
Victoria Terrace	Clontarf Road 1865 (*IT*). Subsumed within Clontarf Road.
Walpole Terrace	Castle Avenue 1861 (*TD*). Subsumed within Castle Avenue.
Whitehall Terrace	Clontarf Road 1904 (*TD*). Subsumed within Clontarf Road.
Zetland Terrace	St Lawrence Rd 1904 (*TD*). Subsumed within St Lawrence Road.

Bibliography

A. GUIDES, DIRECTORIES AND WORKS OF REFERENCE

Annual Register (London, 1758–).

Burke's Landed Gentry of Ireland (London, 1912).

Dictionary of Irish Biography (9 vols, Cambridge, 2009).

Oxford Dictionary of National Biography (60 vols, Oxford, 2004).

Thom's Directory (Dublin, 1844–).

B. PRIMARY SOURCES

1. Manuscripts

Dublin City Library and Archive, Pearse Street, Wide Street Commissioners maps, WSC, C1/S1/130, 'Map of Donnycarney district', 1704.

Dublin Diocesan Archives, 'Visitations of parishes, 1830–1960'.

Dublin, Genealogical Office MS 48, 'Genealogy of family of King', 1569–1620.

Dublin, Marsh's Library, MS Z I 1 13, 'Cases of John Vernon and of Mary Vernon', seventeenth and eighteenth centuries.

Dublin, Marsh's Library, MS, 'Articles against George King, impropriator of the rectory of Clontarf', 1637.

Dublin, National Library of Ireland, MS 4839, 'Notes from the archives of the Order of St John of Jerusalem at Valetta, 1350–1560'.

Dublin, National Library of Ireland, MS 8068, 'Petition to the privy council of Capt. George King', 1599.

Dublin, Trinity College, MSS 809–10, 840, '1641 depositions' [www.1641.tcd.ie/deposition.php?depID<?php echo].

2. Printed records

'Act for ... the roads leading to Dublin through Raheny and Clontarf, 1788' and 'Petition of landholders and inhabitants of Clontarf, 1789', *Journal of the House of Commons of Ireland* (Dublin, 1788–9).

Acts of the Privy Council in Ireland, 1556–71: manuscripts of Charles Haliday of Dublin (Historical Manuscripts Commission, Report xv, appendix iii) (London, 1897).

Annals of Innisfallen, ed. S. MacAirt (Dublin, 1951).

Annals of Loch Cé. A chronicle of Irish affairs from AD 1014 to AD 1590, ed. W. Hennessy (2 vols, Dublin, 1939).

Annals of Ulster (to AD 1131), part 1, text and translation, ed. S. MacAirt and G. MacNiocaill (Dublin, 1983).

'The book of Howth', in J.S. Brewer and W. Bullen (eds), *Calendar of Carew Manuscripts* (6 vols, London, 1867–73), vol. vi (1873).

Calendar of ancient records of Dublin, vols i–viii, ed. J.T. Gilbert (Dublin, 1889–1892).

Calendar of Christ Church deeds, ed. M.J. McEnery and R. Refaussé (Dublin, 2001).

Calendar of documents relating to Ireland, 1171-1284 (London, 1875–81).

Calendar of exchequer inquisitions, 1455-1699, ed. M.C. Griffith (Dublin, 1991).

Calendar of fine rolls, vol. ii (1307-19) (London, 1912).

Calendar of the justiciar rolls, Edward I (Dublin, 1905).

Calendar of the manuscripts of the marquess of Ormond, vol. ii (London, 1903).

Calendar of material relating to Ireland from the high court of Admiralty examinations, 1536-1641, ed. J.C. Appleby (Dublin, 1992).

Calendar of patent rolls, Ireland, i–ii (1514–1603) (Dublin, 1861–3).

Calendar of state papers, domestic, 1689-1702 (London, 1927–37).

Calendar of state papers, Ireland, 1509-1670, 24 vols (London, 1860–1912).

Calendar of state papers, Ireland, Tudor period, 1566-7, ed. B. Cunningham (Dublin, 2009).

'Cath Cluana Tarbh', ed. J. O'Donovan, *Dublin Penny Journal* 1 (1832), 133–6.

Cath Cluana Tarbh: 'The battle of Clontarf', ed. M. Ní Úrdail (Dublin, 2011).

A census of Ireland circa 1659 with supplementary material from the poll money ordinances 1660-1661, ed. S. Pender (Dublin, 1939).

Chartularies of St Mary's Abbey, Dublin, 2 vols, ed. J.T. Gilbert (London, 1884).

Chronicon Scotorum: a chronicle of Irish affairs, from earliest times to AD 1135, ed. W. Hennessy (London, 1866).

Civil Survey, vol. vii: County of Dublin, ed. R.C. Simington (Dublin, 1945).

Cogadh Gáedhel re Gallaibh: the war of the Gaedhil with the Gaill, or the invasions of Ireland by the Danes and other Norsemen, ed. J.H. Todd (Dublin, 1867).

The Dublin guild merchant roll, c. 1190-1265, ed. P. Connolly and G. Martin (Dublin, 1992).

Extents of Irish monastic possessions, 1540-1541, from manuscripts in the Public Record Office, London, ed. N.B. White (Dublin, 1943).

A general history of Ireland in its antient and modern state (Dublin, 1781).

'Hearth money roll for County Dublin, 1664' (second part), *Journal of the County Kildare Archaeological Society* 11 (1930-3), 386–466.

Historical Manuscripts Commission, ninth report (London, 1883-4).

House of Commons: Minutes of evidence taken before the committee of the Dublin and Drogheda railway (London, 1836).

Irish fiants of the Tudor sovereigns, ed. (with new introduction) K.W. Nicholls (Dublin, 1994).

Journal of the House of Commons of Ireland (1789) (Dublin, 1789).

Letters and papers, foreign and domestic, of Henry VIII, 1509-47 (London, 1862–1932).

The Lismore papers of Richard Boyle, earl of Cork, vols i–ii, ed. A.B. Grosart (1886).

Njal's Saga, or The story of Burnt Njal (Njal's Saga): The Online Medieval and Classical Library, no. 11, produced, edited and prepared by D.B. Killings [see website below].

The post-chaise companion: or traveller's directory through Ireland (Dublin, 1786).

The proctor's accounts of Peter Lewis, 1564-1565, ed. R. Gillespie (Dublin, 1996).

Reports from Commissioners, Poor Law (Ireland), xxxii, session 4 Feb.–Aug. 1836 (London, 1836).

Reports of cases upon appeals and writs of error in the high court of parliament, 1701-1779, ed. J. Browne, vol. iv (London, 1781).

'Report on the state of popery in Ireland, 1731: diocese of Dublin', *Archivium Hibernicum* 4 (1915), 131–77.

Registrum de Kilmainham, 1326-39, ed. C. McNeill (Dublin, 1932).

Registrum Octaviani: the register of Octavian de Palatio, archbishop of Armagh, 1478–1513, ed. Mario Sughi (Dublin, 1999).

Resolution by inhabitants on depredations committed in Clontarf (Dublin, 1775).

Rotulorum patentium et clausorum cancellariae Hiberniae calendarium, Hen. II–Hen. VII (London, 1828).

A sermon preached at Christ Church, Dublin, on 20th day of March 1747 by Michael Cox, bishop of Ossory, before the Incorporated Society for Promoting English Protestant Working Schools in Ireland (Dublin, 1748).

Speech of John Vernon opposing the lord mayor on the riding of the franchises of Dublin at their attempting to enter his manor of Clontarf, 6 August 1731 (Dublin, 1731).

Statutes and ordinances and acts of parliament of Ireland: King John to Henry V, ed. H.F. Berry (Dublin, 1907).

The Ussher memoirs, ed. W. Ball Wright (Dublin and London, 1889).

John Vernon, Esq., appellant; William Maple, merchant, respondent. The appellant's case (London, 1730).

3. Newspapers and journals

Belfast Newsletter

Clontarf's Eye

Daily Courant

Dublin Builder (later *Irish Builder*)

Faulkner's Dublin Journal

Freeman's Journal

Irish Independent

Journal for the Preservation of Irish Memorials of the Dead

Irish Times

Preston Chronicle

Sydney Morning Herald

Weekly Irish Times

4. Maps

Thomas Bolton's map, 1717.

J. Bowles, *A new and correct map of the bay and harbour of Dublin* (London, 1728).

Bernard de Gomme, 'The city and suburbs of Dublin, from Kilmainham to Rings-end wherein the rivers, streets, lanes, alleys, churches & c. are exactly described 1673', scale 1,760 yards to one English mile. National Maritime Museum, Greenwich, P/49 (11).

Ordnance Survey of Ireland maps.

Thomas Phillips, 'Observations explanatory of a plan for a citadel at Dublin' (RIA, Haliday MS Map no. 1: survey of the city of Dublin and part of the harbour, 1685).

Thomas Phillips, 'Maps of the bay and harbour of Dublin, 1685', RIA, RR, MC 3/112.

John Rocque, *An actual survey of the county of Dublin, 1760* (Dublin, 1760).

The A to Z of Georgian Dublin: John Rocque's maps of the city in 1756 and the County in 1760, ed. Paul Ferguson (Lympne Castle, 1998).

C. SECONDARY SOURCES

Aalen, F.H.A. and Whelan, K. (eds), *Dublin city and county: from prehistory to the present. Studies in honour of J.H. Andrews* (Dublin, 1992).

Abercrombie, P., Kelly, S. and Kelly, A., *Dublin of the future: the new town plan* (Dublin, 1922).

Adams, B.W., 'Antiquarian notes, etc. of the parishes of Santry and Cloghran, County Dublin', *Journal of the Royal Historical and Archaeological Association of Ireland* (4th ser.) 5 (1881), 482–98.

Anon., 'Clontarf Castle, County of Dublin', *Irish Penny Journal* 11 (1840), 81–3.

Anon., *Souvenir brochure of official opening of Church of St Gabriel, Clontarf, Dublin* (Dublin, 1956).

Arnold, L.J., *The restoration land settlement in County Dublin, 1660–1688: a history of the administration of the acts of settlement and explanation* (Dublin, 1993).

Aylmer, G.E., 'Blackwell, John (1624–1701)', in H.C.G. Matthew and B.H. Harrison (eds), *Oxford Dictionary of National Biography* (Oxford, 2004).

Balch, W., *Ireland as I saw it* (New York, 1850).

Ball, F.E., *Howth and its owners* (Dublin, 1917).

Barrett, C., 'Irish nationalism and art, 1800–1921', *Studies* **64** (1975), 393–409.

Barrow, G.L., 'The franchises of Dublin', *Dublin Historical Record* **36** (1983), 79–80.

Bateson, J.D., 'Roman material from Ireland: a re-consideration', in *Proceedings of the Royal Irish Academy* **73**C (1973), 21–97.

Bellamy, G., *An apology for the life of George Anne Bellamy, late of Covent-Garden Theatre* (London, 1785).

Boate, G., *Ireland's naturall history* (London, 1652).

Borchardt, K., Jaspert, N. and Nicholson, H. (eds), *The Hospitallers, the Mediterranean and Europe: festschrift for Anthony Luttrell* (Aldershot, 2007).

Bowden, C.T., *A tour through Ireland* (Dublin, 1791).

Boydell, B., 'Venues for music in eighteenth-century Dublin', *Dublin Historical Record* **29** (1975), 28–34.

Bradley, J., 'Some reflections on the problem of Scandinavian settlement in the hinterland of Dublin during the ninth century', in J. Bradley, A.J. Fletcher and A. Simms (eds), *Dublin in the medieval world: studies in honour of Howard B. Clarke* (Dublin, 2009), 39–62.

Bradley, J., Fletcher, A.J. and Simms, A. (eds), *Dublin in the medieval world: studies in honour of Howard B. Clarke* (Dublin, 2009).

Bradshaw, B., *The dissolution of the religious orders in Ireland under Henry VIII* (Cambridge, 1974).

Butler, S., *Irish tales* (ed. I. Campbell Ross, A. Douglas and A. Markey) (Dublin, 2010).

Canny, N., *The upstart earl: a study of the mental and social world of Richard Boyle, first earl of Cork, 1566-1643* (Cambridge, 1982).

Childs, W.R., 'Irish merchants and seamen in later medieval England', *Irish Historical Studies* **32** (2000), 22–43.

Clarke, H.B., 'Conversion, church and cathedral: the diocese of Dublin to 1152', in J. Kelly and D. Keogh (eds), *History of the Catholic diocese of Dublin* (Dublin, 2000), 19–50.

Cole, G., *Memoir of localities of minerals of economic importance and metalliferous mines in Ireland* (Dublin, 1922).

Collins, G., *Great Britain's coasting-pilot ... A new and exact survey of the sea-coast of England* (London, 1693).

Connolly, P. (ed.), 'Irish material in the class of ancient petitions in the Public

Record Office, London', *Analecta Hibernica* **34** (1987), 1–106.

Cooney, D.A.L. (ed.), 'Momentous days: occasional diaries of Frances Taylor', *Dublin Historical Record* **47** (1994), 78–81.

Cooney, D.A.L., 'The Methodist chapels in Dublin', *Dublin Historical Record* **57** (2004), 152–63.

Cosgrave, D., *North Dublin: city and environs* (Dublin, 1909; 2005 edn).

Cosgrove, A., *Late medieval Ireland, 1370-1541* (Dublin, 1981).

Cudmore, P., *The battle of Clontarf and other poems* (New York, 1895).

Cunningham, B., *The world of Geoffrey Keating: history, myth and religion in seventeenth-century Ireland* (Dublin, 2000).

D'Alton, J., *History of County Dublin* (Dublin, 1838).

D'Alton, J., *The history of Drogheda, with its environs, and an introductory memoir of the Dublin and Drogheda railway* (2 vols, Dublin, 1844).

Daly, G.J., 'Captain William Bligh in Dublin, 1800–1801', *Dublin Historical Record* **44** (1991), 30–3.

Daly, M.E., *Dublin, the deposed capital: a social and economic history, 1860-1914* (Cork, 1985).

Davies, M., *That favourite resort: the story of Bray, Co. Wicklow* (Bray, 2007).

Davis, T., 'Hints for Irish historical paintings', in T.W. Rolleston, *Thomas Davis: selections from his prose and poetry* (London, 1890).

de Courcy, J.W., *The Liffey in Dublin* (Dublin, 1996).

de Latocnaye, J.-L., *Promenade d'un français dans l'Irlande* (Dublin, 1797).

Dollard, J.B., *Clontarf: an Irish national drama in four acts* (Dublin, 1920).

Donnelly, N., *A short history of some Dublin parishes: part xiv: parishes of Clontarf, Fairview, Coolock and Glasnevin* (Dublin, 1900).

Dowling, N. and O'Reilly, A. (eds), *Mud Island: a history of Ballybough* (Dublin, no date).

Downham, C., 'The Battle of Clontarf in Irish history and legend', *History Ireland* **13** (5) (2005), 19–23.

Drummond, W.H., *Clontarf, a poem* (Dublin, 1822).

Duffy, S. (ed.), *Medieval Dublin I* (Dublin, 2000).

Duffy, S., 'Brian Bóruma [Brian Boru] (*c.* 941–1014)', in H.C.G. Matthew and B.H. Harrison (eds), *Oxford Dictionary of National Biography* (Oxford, 2004).

Duffy, S., *Brian Boru and the battle of Clontarf* (Dublin, 2013).

Dunton, J., 'Letter No. 5', in E. MacLysaght, *Irish life in the seventeenth century* (2nd edn, Cork, 1950), 366.

Dunton, J., *The Dublin scuffle* (Dublin, 2000).

Empey, A., 'The layperson in the parish, 1169–1536', in R. Gillespie and W.G. Neely (eds), *The laity and the Church of Ireland, 1000–2000: all sorts and conditions* (Dublin, 2002), 7–48.

Etchingham, C., 'North Wales, Ireland and the Isles: the Insular Viking zone', *Peritia* 15 (2001), 145–87.

Fagan, P. and Simms, A., 'Villages in County Dublin: their origin and inheritance', in F.H.A. Aalen and K. Whelan (eds), *Dublin city and county: from prehistory to the present. Studies in honour of J.H. Andrews* (Dublin, 1992), 79–119.

Falkiner, C.L., 'The Hospital of St John of Jerusalem in Ireland', *Proceedings of the Royal Irish Academy* 26C (1906–7), 275–317.

Fletcher, A.J. (ed.), 'The earliest extant recension of the Dublin Chronicle', in J. Bradley, A.J. Fletcher and A. Simms (eds), *Dublin in the medieval world: studies in honour of Howard B. Clarke* (Dublin, 2009), 390–409.

Flood, D.T., 'Letter to the Editor', *Dublin Historical Record* 27 (1974), 72.

Flood, D.T., 'The birth of the Bull Island', *Dublin Historical Record* 28 (1975), 142–53.

Flood, D.T., 'Historical evidence for the growth of North Bull Island', in D.W. Jeffrey, R.N. Goodwillie, B. Healy, C.H. Holland, J.S. Jackson and J.J. Moore (eds), *North Bull Island, Dublin Bay: a modern coastal natural history* (Dublin, 1977), 9–12.

Flood, W.H.G., 'Fishamble Street Music Hall, Dublin, from 1741 to 1777', *Sammelbände der Internationale Musicgesellschaft* 14 (1912), 51–7.

Fraser, R., *Review of the domestic fisheries of Great Britain and Ireland* (Edinburgh, 1818).

Gamble, N., 'The Dublin and Drogheda railway: parts 1–2', *Journal of the Irish Railway Record Society* 11 (1974), 224–34, 283–93.

Gilbert, J.T. (ed.), *A contemporary history of affairs in Ireland* (Dublin, 1879), vol. i.

Gilbert, J.T. (ed.), *A history of the Irish confederation* (7 vols, Dublin, 1882–91).

Gillespie, R. and Neely, W.G. (eds), *The laity and the Church of Ireland, 1000–2000: all sorts and conditions* (Dublin, 2002).

Giraldus Cambrensis, *Topographia Hibernica*, in J.F. Mimock (ed.), *Giraldi Cambrensis opera* (London, 1867), vol. v, 186–8.

Goedheer, A.J., *Irish and Norse traditions about the battle of Clontarf* (Haarlem, 1938).

Gogarty, C., *From village to suburb: the building of Clontarf since 1760* (Dublin, 2013).

Gray, T., *The fatal sisters* (1769) [http://www.thomas.gray.org/].

Haliday, C., *The Scandinavian kingdom of Dublin* (Dublin, 1881).

Harbison, P., *Beranger's rambles in Ireland* (Dublin, 2004).

Harbison, P., 'Note on Thomas Snagg (1746–1812), *View of Clontarf Castle, 1805*', in *Whyte's catalogue of Irish and British art*, 12 March 2012 (Dublin, 2012), 35.

Hardy, P.D., 'A day's ramble on the north side of the city', *Dublin Penny Journal* **2** (1834), 273–5.

Harris, A.L., 'The funerary monuments of Richard Boyle, earl of Cork', *Church Monuments* **13** (1998), 70–86.

Haughton, S., 'On the time of high water in Dublin Bay on Good Friday the 23rd April 1014 the day of the battle of Clontarf', *Proceedings of the Royal Irish Academy* **7** (1857–61), 495–8.

Hime, R.H., *Brian Boru and the battle of Clontarf* (London, 1889).

Holinshed, R., *Chronicles of England, Scotland, and Ireland* (London, 1577).

Hughes, J.L.H., 'The Dublin Fishery Company, 1818–1830', in *Dublin Historical Record* **12** (1951), 34–46.

Jackson, J.S., 'The future of the Island', in D.W. Jeffrey, R.N. Goodwillie, B. Healy, C.H. Holland, J.S. Jackson and J.J. Moore (eds), *North Bull Island, Dublin Bay: a modern coastal natural history* (Dublin, 1977), 116–24.

Jeffrey, D.W., Goodwillie, R.N., Healy, B., Holland, C.H., Jackson, J.S. and Moore, J.J. (eds), *North Bull Island, Dublin Bay: a modern coastal natural history* (Dublin, 1977).

Kearney, H., 'The Irish wine trade', *Irish Historical Studies* **9** (1954–5), 400–42.

Keating, G., *Foras feasa ar Éirinn: the history of Ireland* (ed. D. Comyn and P.S. Dineen) (4 vols, London, 1902–14).

Kelly, J. and Keogh, D. (eds), *History of the Catholic diocese of Dublin* (Dublin, 2000).

Kilroy, J.M.C., 'Transport', in V.J. McBrierty (ed.), *The Howth peninsula: its history, lore and legend* (Dublin, 1981), 92–106.

Kingston, J., *Parish of Fairview* (Dundalk, 1953).

Knowles, F.W.R., *Old Clontarf* (Dublin, c. 1970).

Lawless, W., 'Clontarf's Protestant communities in the First World War' (unpublished senior sophister thesis, Trinity College, Dublin, 1995) [http://

homepage.eircom.net/~wlawless/ww1/Clontarf.htm].

Lennon, C., 'Clontarf in the 1860s: seaside resort or residential suburb?', *Clontarf Annual* (1987), 27–8.

Lennon, C., *The lords of Dublin in the age of Reformation* (Dublin, 1989).

Lennon, C., 'Mass in the manor-house: the Counter-Reformation in Dublin, 1560–1630', in J. Kelly and D. Keogh (eds), *History of the Catholic diocese of Dublin* (Dublin, 2000), 112–26.

Lennon, C. (ed.), *Confraternities and sodalities in Ireland: charity, devotion and sociability* (Dublin, 2012).

Lennon, C., 'Confraternities in Ireland: a long view', in C. Lennon (ed.), *Confraternities and sodalities in Ireland: charity, devotion and sociability* (Dublin, 2012), 15–34.

Lennon, C. and Montague, J. (eds), *John Rocque's Dublin: a guide to the Georgian city* (Dublin, 2010).

Lewis, R., *The Dublin guide, or a description of the city of Dublin and the most remarkable places within fifteen miles* (Dublin, 1787).

Lewis, S., *A topographical dictionary of Ireland* (2 vols, London, 1837).

Longfield, A.K., *Anglo-Irish trade in the sixteenth century* (London, 1929).

Lord, E., *The Knights Templar in Britain* (London, 2002).

Lynch, V., 'No thoroughfare on the tram road': history of Clontarf and its environs* (Dublin, 2007).

Lyons, M., 'John Rawson', in H.C.G. Matthew and B.H. Harrison (eds), *Oxford Dictionary of National Biography* (Oxford, 2004).

McBrierty, V.J. (ed.), *The Howth peninsula: its history, lore and legend* (Dublin, 1981).

McCarthy Morrogh, M., *The Munster plantation: English migration to southern Ireland, 1583-1641* (Oxford, 1986).

MacCorristine, L., *The revolt of Silken Thomas: a challenge to Henry VIII* (Dublin, 1987).

McCullough, N., *Dublin, an urban city: the plan of the city* (Dublin, 2007).

McCurtin, H., *Brief discourse in vindication of the antiquity of Ireland* (1717).

McEvansoneya, P., 'History, politics and decorative painting: James Ward's murals in Dublin City Hall', *Irish Arts Review Yearbook* 15 (1999), 142–7.

McGettigan, D., *The battle of Clontarf, Good Friday 1014* (Dublin, 2013).

MacGeoghegan, J., *History of Ireland* (1758–62).

Mac Ghiolla Phádraig, B., 'The Irish form of "Clontarf"', *Dublin Historical Record* 11 (1950), 127–8.

McGowan-Doyle, V., *The book of Howth: Elizabethan conquest and the Old English* (Dublin, 2011).

McGurk, J.J.N., 'Lambart, Charles, first earl of Cavan (*c*. 1600–1660)', in H.C.G. Matthew and B.H. Harrison (eds), *Oxford Dictionary of National Biography* (Oxford, 2004).

McIntyre, D., *The meadow of the bull* (Dublin, 1987).

McIntyre, D., 'Clontarf Town Hall and the 1916 Rising', *Clontarf's Eye* 7 (1991), 20–1.

McIvor, M., *Clontarf past and present* (Dublin, no date).

MacLysaght, E., *Irish life in the seventeenth century* (2nd edn, Cork, 1950).

McManus, R., *Dublin, 1910–1940: shaping the city and suburbs* (Dublin, 2002).

McNeill, C., 'The Hospitallers at Kilmainham and their guests', *Journal of the Royal Society of Antiquaries of Ireland* 24 (1924), 15–30.

MacNeill, E., 'Our place-names', *Journal of the Royal Society of Antiquaries of Ireland* (7th ser.) 8 (1938), 189–95.

Mac Niocaill, G. (ed.), 'Documents relating to the suppression of the Templars in Ireland', *Analecta Hibernica* 24 (1967), 181–226.

Maguire, M., '"Our people": the Church of Ireland and the culture of community in Dublin since Disestablishment', in R. Gillespie and W.G. Neely (eds), *The laity and the Church of Ireland, 1000–2000: all sorts and conditions* (Dublin, 2002), 277–302.

Maguire, M., 'The Church of Ireland parochial associations: a social and cultural analysis', in C. Lennon (ed.), *Confraternities and sodalities in Ireland: charity, devotion and sociability* (Dublin, 2012), 97–109.

Massey, E., *Prior Roger Outlaw of Kilmainham, 1314-41* (Dublin, 2000).

Milne, K., *The Irish Charter Schools, 1730-1830* (Dublin, 1997).

Moore, N., *Dublin docklands reinvented: the post-industrial regeneration of a European city quarter* (Dublin, 2008).

Mount, C., 'The collection of early and middle Bronze Age material culture in south-east Ireland', *Proceedings of the Royal Irish Academy* 101C (2001), 1–35.

Murphy, F.J., 'Dublin trams, 1872–1979', *Dublin Historical Record* 28 (1979), 2–9.

Murphy, M. and Potterton, M. (eds), *The Dublin region in the Middle Ages: settlement, land-use and economy* (Dublin, 2010).

Murray, D., *Romanticism, nationalism and Irish antiquarian societies, 1840–80* (Maynooth, 2000).

Nex, J. and Whitehead, L. (eds), 'A copy of Ferdinand Weber's account book', *Royal Musical Association Research Chronicle* 35 (2000), 89–150.

Nicholson, H., *The Knights Templar: a new history* (Stroud, 2001).

Ní Mhaonaigh, M., *Brian Boru: Ireland's greatest king?* (Stroud, 2007).

Ní Mhurchadha, M., 'Contending neighbours: society in Fingal, 1603–1660' (unpublished Ph.D thesis, NUI Maynooth, 2002).

Ní Mhurchadha, M., 'Clontarf' (unpublished paper, no date).

Ní Úrdail, M., '*Annala Inse Faithleann* an ochtú céad déag agus Cath Chluain Tarbh', *Eighteenth-century Ireland* 20 (2005), 104–19.

O'Conor, C., *Dissertations on the history of Ireland* (1753; 2nd edn 1766).

Ó Corráin, D., *Ireland before the Normans* (Dublin, 1972).

O'Doherty, T., *A history of Glasnevin* (Dublin, 2011).

O'Gorman, T., 'On the site of the battle of Clontarf', *Journal of the Royal Historical and Archaeological Society of Ireland* (4th ser.) 5 (1879), 169–82.

O'Halloran, C., 'The triumph of "virtuous liberty": representations of the Vikings and Brian Boru in eighteenth-century histories', *Eighteenth-century Ireland* 27 (2007), 151–63.

O'Halloran, S., *General history of Ireland* (1778).

Ó Maitiú, S., *Dublin's suburban towns, 1834–1930* (Dublin, 2003).

O'Malley, G., *The Knights Hospitaller of the English langue, 1460–1565* (Oxford, 2005).

Perry, J., *The description of a method humbly proposed for the making of a better depth coming over the barr of Dublin, and also for making a bason within the harbour* (Dublin, 1721).

Perry, J., *An answer to objections against the making of a bason, with reasons for the bettering of the harbour of Dublin* (Dublin, 1721).

Petty, W., *Hibernia delineatio* (1685).

Quinn, D.B. (ed.), 'Calendar of Irish council book for 1581–86', *Analecta Hibernica* 24 (1967), 93–180.

Rogers, T., *Observations on a road or safe anchorage at Ireland's Eye* (Dublin, 1800).

Ronan, M.V. (ed.), 'Royal visitation of Dublin, 1615', *Archivium Hibernicum* 8 (1941), 1–55.

Ronan, M.V. (ed.), 'Archbishop Bulkeley's visitation of Dublin, 1630', *Archivium Hibernicum* **8** (1941), 56–98.

Rowan, A. (ed.), *The architecture of Richard Morrison and William Vitruvius Morrison* (Dublin, 1989).

R.S., *A collection of some of the murthers and massacres committed on the Irish in Ireland since 23rd of October 1641* (London, 1662).

Ruddy, B., 'The Royal Charter School, Clontarf', *Dublin Historical Record* **57** (2004), 64–80.

Ruddy, B., 'Baymount Castle, Clontarf', *Dublin Historical Record* **59** (2006), 171–81.

Ruddy, B., 'Mount Temple, Clontarf', *Dublin Historical Record* **61** (2008), 183–93.

Ruddy, B., 'Clontarf baths and Assembly Rooms', *Dublin Historical Record* **62** (2009), 27–35.

Rutty, J., *An essay towards a natural history of the County of Dublin* (Dublin, 1771).

Ryan, D., *The Rising: the complete story of Easter Week* (Dublin, 1949).

Ryan, J., 'The battle of Clontarf', *Journal of the Royal Society of Antiquaries of Ireland* **68** (1938), 1–50.

Ryan, J., *Remembering how we stood: bohemian Dublin at the mid-century* (Dublin, 1987).

Seller, J., *The English pilot, first book, describing the coasts of Ireland* (London, 1690).

Sharkey, J.U., *St Anne's: the story of a Guinness estate* (Dublin, 2002).

Shea, J.A., *Clontarf, or the field of the green banner: a historical romance* (New York, 1843).

Simington, R.C. (ed.), *The transplantation to Connacht 1654–1658* (Dublin, 1970).

Sleater, M., *Introductory essay to a new system of civil and ecclesiastical topography and itinerary of counties of Ireland* (Dublin, 1806).

Smith, C.V., *Dalkey: society and economy in a small medieval town* (Dublin, 1996).

Stanihurst, R., 'Description of Ireland', in L. Miller and E. Power (eds), *Holinshed's Irish Chronicle 1577* (Dublin, 1979).

Stanihurst, R., 'History of Henry VIII's reign', in L. Miller and E. Power (eds), *Holinshed's Irish Chronicle 1577* (Dublin, 1979).

Steele, R. (ed.), *A bibliography of royal proclamations of the Tudor and Stuart sovereigns, 1485–1714* (Oxford, 1910), vols 5–6.

Tait, C., 'Colonising memory: manipulations of death, burial and commemoration in the career of Richard Boyle, first earl of Cork (1566–1643)', *Proceedings of the*

Royal Irish Academy **101**C (2001), 126–32.

Temple, J., *The Irish rebellion* (Dublin, 1713).

Tipton, C., 'The Irish Hospitallers during the Great Schism', *Proceedings of the Royal Irish Academy* **69**C (1970), 33–43.

Todd, J.H., 'On the history of the battle of Clontarf', *Proceedings of the Royal Irish Academy* **7** (1857–61), 498–511.

Valante, M., 'Dublin's economic relations with hinterland and periphery in the later Viking age', in S. Duffy (ed.), *Medieval Dublin I* (Dublin, 2000), 69–83.

Valante, M., *The Vikings in Ireland: settlement, trade and urbanisation* (Dublin, 2008).

Vossen, A.F. (ed.), *Two bokes of the histories of Ireland compiled by Edmund Campion* (Assen, 1963).

Warburton, J., Whitelaw, J. and Walsh, R., *History of the city of Dublin* (2 vols, London, 1818).

Ware, J. (ed.), *The historie of Ireland, collected by three learned authors, viz. Meredith Hanmer, Edmund Campion and Edmund Spenser* (Dublin, 1633).

Went, A.E.J., 'Fisheries of the River Liffey: notes on the corporation fishery up to the dissolution of the monasteries', *Journal of the Royal Society of Antiquaries of Ireland* **83** (1953), 163–73.

Westropp, T.J., 'The hero of Clontarf', *Irish Monthly* **42** (1914), 133–41, 177–89, 246–59.

Wood, H., 'The Templars in Ireland', *Proceedings of the Royal Irish Academy* **26**C (1906–7), 327–77.

D. WEBSITES

Clontarf Online: www.clontarfonline.com

'Clontarf Castle, Dublin', in Database of Irish Excavation Reports: www.excavations.ie/Pages/Details.php/Dublin 1715

Clontarf Church of Ireland parish: http://clontarfchurch.org/cspc-history/

Clontarf Cricket Club: www.clontarfcricket.com/clontarfcc/Main/History

Clontarf Lawn Tennis Club: www.clontarfltc.com/history.php/

Clontarf Rugby Club: www.clontarfrugby.com/about-2/club-history/

Dictionary of Irish Architects: www.dia.ie/architects/view/

Dublin City Council: http://www.dublincity.ie/RECREATIONANDCULTURE/

Ordnance Survey of Ireland: www.maps.osi.ie/publicviewer/

Royal Dublin Society (membership): www.rds.ie/cat_historic_member_detail.
jsp?itemID=1097586

Thomas Gray works: http://www.thomas.gray.org/

Trinity College, 1641 Depositions Project on-line: www.1641.tcd.ie/deposition.
php?depID<?php echo

Index

Scoil Uí Chonaill Gaelic Athletic
  Association club, 261
Scott, Sir Walter, 51
Scurlock, Katherine (née King), 131
Scurlock, Martin, 118, 130
Scurlock, Patrick, 130, 131
Seabank, 12
Seacourt, 12
Seafield Avenue, 225
Seafield Road, 12, 139, 153, 168, 176, 178,
  186, 211, 216, 225, 232, 233
Seafield Singers, 262
Seafield Terrace, 211
Seapark, 177
Seapark Road, 12, 25
Seapoint, 12
Seapoint Terrace, 212
Seaview Avenue, 12
Sedgrave, James, 116, 117
Senan, Saint, 25
Shannon, River, 11
Shea, John Augustus, 55
Sheds of Clontarf, 1, 12, 52, 53, 54, 107,
  116, 118, 139, 144–5, 146, 148, 152,
  154–5, 159, 162–6, 175, 180, 185, 187,
  192, 211, 212, 247, 249, 262, 263
Shetland Islands, 30
Shortall, Sir P., 219
Sigurd, earl of Orkney, 17, 23, 31, 34,
  35, 37, 60
Simnel, Lambert, 94
Sinn Féin, 219
Sitric Silkenbeard, 21, 29, 30, 34, 35,
  37, 60
Skeffington, William, lord deputy of
  Ireland, 101, 102
Skerries, 90, 91

Sláine, daughter of Brian Boru, 29
Snagg, Thomas, artist, 10, 51, 157, 161
Snugborough Cottages, 175–6, 189
South Bull, 141, 146
South Wall, 141, 151, 157, 167
Southwell, Thomas, 144, 158
Spanish Armada, 106
Staffordshire, 129
Stanihurst, Richard, 45, 46
Stewart Company, 222
Stiles Road, 225
Strand, the, 155, 159, 161
Strandville Avenue East, 178, 257
Stuart monarchy, 14, 47, 51, 102
Sulcóit, battle of, 28
Summerville, 249
Sutton, 7, 155, 228, 232
Sutton Creek, 142, 169
Svínafell, 37
Swords, 32, 120, 122
Sybil Hill, 154, 158, 179, 230, 257
Sybil Hill Road, 231, 258
Sydney, New South Wales, 5–6
Syria, 85

Tadc, son of Brian Boru, 37, 39
Tadc (Tady) ua Cellaig, king of Uí
  Máine, 45
Tairdelbach, son of Murchad,
  grandson of Brian Boru, 17, 23, 34
Tairdelbach, son of Tadc, grandson of
  Brian Boru, 22
Talbot, Adam, 107
Talbot, John, lord lieutenant of Ireland,
  91
Talbot, Mary, 118
Talbot family, 93

Tara, 4, 21, 29

Taylor, John, 158–9

Teeling, John, 101

Temple Players, 262

'The fatal sisters', poem, 51

Thelwel, Symon, 242

Thomas Palfreyman, 87, 92

Thomond, 21

Thom's Directory, 178–9

Thornhill House (later site of St Anne's mansion), 155, 179

Thorsteinn's Saga, 34

Tickell, Adelaide, 187

Tickell, George, 186–7, 194, 195, 196

Tickell, John, 187

Tivoli, 187

Tobertown, 118

Todd, J.H., 50, 56–7

Tolka River, 7, 8, 10, 18, 57, 58, 89, 92, 101, 107, 116, 117, 135, 140, 141, 144, 145, 155, 180, 190, 216, 233, 238

tolled or turnpike roads, 158–9, 180

Tomar's Wood, 18, 58

Tour through Ireland, A, 51

Tower of London, 102

transplantation to Connacht, 123

Trent, Council of, 243

Trinity College, Dublin, 57, 220

Tudor administration of Ireland, 5, 13, 14, 166

Tuite, Andrew, 246

Turner, J.M.T., artist, 10, 51, 157, 161

Tyrell, Patrick, 106, 110

Tyrell, William, 106

Ua Conchobair, Ruaidhrí, 43

Ua hArtacháin, Dúnlaing (Dolyne Ahertegan), 31, 34, 45

Uí Brian, 19, 22, 44, 50

Uí Conchobair, 44

Uí Cumain, 9, 238

Uí Fáilghe, 23

Uí Fhiachrach Aidne, 23

Uí Máine, 23

Uí Néill, 22

Ullester, John, 92

Ulster, 21, 22, 80, 119, 123

United States of America, 55

urban townships, 182

Ussher, Archdeacon Adam, 245

Ussher, Revd Adam, 245

Ussher, Revd Frederick, 245

Ussher, James, archbishop, 245

Ussher, John, 245

Ussher family, 162

Vallancey, Charles, 53

Vatican Council II, 260

Vernon, Dorothy (née Grahn), 148, 161

Vernon, Edward (Colonel), 129–34, 166, 244, 245

Vernon, Edward (nephew of Colonel Edward), 133, 144

Vernon, Edward (son of John Edward Venables), 194–5, 196, 201–2

Vernon, Edward Granville, 220

Vernon, Edward Kingston, 221

Vernon, Elizabeth (daughter of Colonel Edward), 133

Vernon, George (d. 1787), 134, 148, 158

Vernon, George (d. 1822), 147, 166, 170

Vernon, Granville, 220

Vernon, Jane (née Brinkley), 202

Vernon, John (Captain), 123–4, 129–30, 131–2, 136, 244, 245

Vernon, John (grand-nephew of